1821274

Propositions, Functions, and Analysis

Propositions, Functions, and Analysis

Selected Essays on Russell's Philosophy

PETER HYLTON

CLARENDON PRESS · OXFORD

OXFORD
UNIVERSITY PRESS

Great Clarendon Street, Oxford OX2 6DP

Oxford University Press is a department of the University of Oxford.
It furthers the University's objective of excellence in research, scholarship,
and education by publishing worldwide in

Oxford New York

Auckland Cape Town Dar es Salaam Hong Kong Karachi
Kuala Lumpur Madrid Melbourne Mexico City Nairobi
New Delhi Shanghai Taipei Toronto

With offices in

Argentina Austria Brazil Chile Czech Republic France Greece
Guatemala Hungary Italy Japan Poland Portugal Singapore
South Korea Switzerland Thailand Turkey Ukraine Vietnam

Oxford is a registered trade mark of Oxford University Press
in the UK and in certain other countries

Published in the United States
by Oxford University Press Inc., New York

British Library Cataloguing in Publication Data

Data available

Library of Congress Cataloging in Publication Data

Data available

Typeset by Newgen Imaging Systems (P) Ltd., Chennai, India
Printed in Great Britain
on acid-free paper by
Biddles Ltd., King's Lynn, Norfolk

ISBN 0–19–928635–3   978–0–19–928635–5

1 3 5 7 9 10 8 6 4 2

To the memory of Burton S. Dreben, 1927–1999

ACKNOWLEDGEMENTS

The intellectual debts incurred in writing each of these essays are acknowledged in a note written when I wrote the essay; I shall not reiterate those acknowledgements here. I do, however, want to thank those who have helped in one way or another with this volume and with its Introduction. The original idea for such a volume came from André Carus, almost exactly six years ago. As my work on the volume proceeded, by fits and starts, I also received advice and encouragement from Warren Goldfarb, Bill Hart, Gary Kemp, Andrew Lugg, Tom Ricketts, and Sally Sedgwick. (In compiling this list I have the sense that I may well have omitted one or more crucial contributors; I can only ask the forgiveness of anyone who falls into that category.)

I should like to thank my Department, and in particular its Chair, Bill Hart, for providing an unusually supportive and collegial environment in which to work.

Those I worked with at Oxford University Press, primarily Rebecca Bryant and Peter Momtchiloff, were invariably understanding and helpful. Jacqueline Pritchard was my copy-editor for the second time and was again both meticulous and tactful.

The book is dedicated to the memory of Burt Dreben. My understanding of Russell, and indeed of philosophy quite generally, owes more to him than is suggested by the acknowledgements attached to the several essays. I greatly miss his friendship, his wise advice, and his unsparing criticism.

SOURCES OF THE ESSAYS

With one exception, all of these essays have been previously published; the exception was commissioned for a volume which has yet to appear. I should like to thank the publishers and editors mentioned below for permission to reprint the essays.

1. 'The Nature of the Proposition and the Revolt Against Idealism,' *Philosophy in Context*, eds. R. Rorty, J. Schneewind and Q. R. D. Skinner, (Cambridge: Cambridge University Press, 1984), pp. 375–97; reproduced here with permission from the publishers.

2. 'Beginning With Analysis,' *Bertrand Russell and the Origins of Analytical Philosophy*, eds. R. Monk and A. Palmer, (Bristol: Thoemmes Press, 1996), pp. 183–216; reproduced here with permission from the publishers.

3. 'Logic in Russell's Logicism,' *The Analytic Tradition*, eds. D. Bell and N. Cooper, (Oxford: Basil Blackwell, 1990), pp. 137–72. Reprinted in *Bertrand Russell: Critical Assessments*, ed. A. Irvine, (London: Routledge, 1998); reproduced here with permission from the publishers.

4. 'The Vicious Circle Principle: Comments on Philippe de Rouilhan,' *Philosophical Studies*, 65 (1992), pp. 183–91; reproduced here with permission from the publishers, the Taylor and Francis Group, plc (http://www.tandf.co.uk).

5. 'Russell's Substitutional Theory', *Synthese* 45 (1980) pp. 1–31; reproduced here with permission from the publishers, Springer SBM.

6. 'Review of Dummett, *Origins of Analytical Philosophy*,' in *The Journal of Philosophy*, vol. XCII, n. 10 (October 1995), pp. 556–63; reproduced here with permission from the *Journal*.

7. 'Frege and Russell', to appear in *The Cambridge Companion to Frege*, ed. T. Ricketts, forthcoming; reproduced here with permission from the publishers.

8. 'Functions and Propositional Functions in *Principia Mathematica*,' *Russell and Analytic Philosophy*, ed. A. Irvine and G. Wedeking, (Toronto: University of Toronto Press, 1994), pp. 342–60; reproduced here with permission from the editors.

9. 'Functions, Operations, and Sense in Wittgenstein's *Tractatus*', *Early Analytic Philosophy: Essays in Honor of Leonard Linsky*, ed. W. W. Tait, (LaSalle, III.: Open Court Press, 1997), pp. 91–105; reproduced here with permission from the publishers.

10. 'Russell on Denoting', *Cambridge Companion to Russell*, ed. N. Griffin, (Cambridge: Cambridge University Press, 2004), pp. 202–40; reproduced here with permission from the publishers.

CONTENTS

Introduction

The work of Bertrand Russell had a decisive influence on the emergence of analytic philosophy, and on its subsequent development. More than any other single figure, Russell set the tone and the agenda for anglophone analytic philosophy in at least the first half of the twentieth century. Frege takes precedence in the development of something resembling a modern system of logic, and in the use of that logic to resolve philosophical problems. Russell's version of logic, however, was far more influential than Frege's. More important, Russell completely rejected the views of Kant and of the post-Kantian idealists, deploying his logic to bolster this opposition. In particular, he completely rejected the idea of necessary structures of thought which impose an *a priori* form upon our knowledge. Russell came to see mathematics as the crucial test-case. Like Frege, he argued that mathematics is reducible to logic; in Russell's hands, however, this claim was part of a general argument against Kant and the idealists.

In other ways, too, Russell's ambitions for the use of logic in philosophy were greater than Frege's. Two related points are particularly worth stressing. First, it is in Russell's work that one can first clearly see the application of modern logic to empirical knowledge. According to Russell's view, the foundation of all knowledge is a kind of direct and unmediated contact between the mind and the known entity, which may be either abstract or given in sensation. This direct contact is what Russell himself calls *acquaintance*. He claims that logic is the means by which something like the rich and far-ranging knowledge that we take ourselves to have can be assembled out of the simple constituents given to us in acquaintance. Showing how this could happen is then an extremely ambitious and far-reaching philosophical programme. Many philosophers, of course, have rejected this programme. Many have also rejected the underlying idea that our knowledge is based on a fundamental kind of direct sensory knowledge. But Russell's influence is manifest in the extraordinary tenacity of his ideas—the frequency with which they were, and are, disputed and rejected—as well as in their occasional revivals.

The second point I wish to stress is that Russell articulates the idea of a *logically perfect language*. (The idea is, again, foreshadowed in Frege, but in Russell it is full-blown.) The syntax or structure of such a language would be given by logic; its vocabulary would be terms which have a meaning in virtue of the speaker's being acquainted with the corresponding entities (which may be abstract). The logically perfect language would thus fully reveal the structure of our thought and our knowledge. It would give us the solutions to metaphysical problems: we could read the nature of the world off from the language, so to speak. More modestly, the idea of a logically perfect language goes along with a view which, in one form or another, has run through much twentieth-century analytic philosophy: that in philosophy we are misled by the apparent structure of our language. (So-called ordinary language philosophy is an ironic reversal of this, with its insistence that it is only the philosopher's misunderstanding of ordinary language, or his distortion of it, that leads to philosophical problems.)

The essays reprinted here concern Russell's work in what I take to be its most influential and important period, namely the two decades following his break with Idealism in 1899. All of them to some extent relate it to the work of other philosophers, but in most it is Russell's thought that is at the focus of attention. (Exceptions are Chapters 8 and 9, where important themes are the work of Frege and of Wittgenstein, respectively, and Chapter 6, which ranges somewhat more widely.)

In 1990 I published a book on this period of Russell's work and on its background.[1] Like the book, the essays chiefly aim at recapturing and articulating Russell's philosophical vision. (Partial exceptions are noted in the previous paragraph.) This is clearly a historical task. It requires that one strive for interpretations which are soundly based on Russell's texts, and which take account of the intellectual background against which they were written; it also requires a sensitivity to ways in which Russell's aims and assumptions differ from ours, even when they are articulated in an idiom which seems familiar. But my reasons for undertaking this work are by no means disinterestedly historical. I think of my motivation, rather, as philosophical. The idea of philosophy, however, is not one to be taken for granted here. The challenge is to explain how the striving after historical accuracy can be in service of something that can plausibly be thought of as philosophical understanding. To do so would be to explain how there can be history of philosophy in which the goals of being historically responsible and of being philosophically enlightening work together, rather than in opposition; it would be to explain how the history of philosophy can be truly part of philosophy, in a way in which the history of biology, say, is clearly not part of biology.

I have spoken of the essays as concerned to recapture and articulate Russell's philosophical vision. In doing this, one sees something of what it is to have a philosophical vision, as opposed merely to expressing opinions about this or that topic. One sees how ideas can interact to support each other. One idea lends credibility to others which in turn lend credibility to others, and so on; the whole forms a system which is more powerful and perhaps more plausible than any of its parts. But it is not just credibility which is at stake here. It is also the meaning

---

[1] *Russell, Idealism, and the Emergence of Analytic Philosophy* (Oxford: Oxford University Press, 1990).

and the significance of the claims which are under consideration. The assertions of philosophers are, for the most part, so abstract that their meaning—even their meaningfulness—is always in question. Understanding such an assertion is, very largely, a matter of seeing how it functions in context—seeing what the philosopher concerned takes to tell for or against the claim and, again, seeing how various claims interact to form a system. One result which may be achieved by serious historical engagement with a philosopher such as Russell is thus that one sees what a serious system of philosophical thought amounts to, and what gives it power and coherence. (And this may form a yardstick against which to measure one's own attempts.) One also sees the crucial role of the context of philosophical thought, including aspects which are often unarticulated. In seeking to understand Russell's thought it is often crucial to appreciate not only which doctrines he tacitly assumed but also which problems he found minor and which he found pressing, how he conceived of those problems, what he counted as possible answers, and so on—what we might think of as the substructure of his thought. (This might also lead one to ask what presuppositions are taken for granted in one's own thought.)

In the case of Russell, in particular, there is something else to be said. His thought is recognizably continuous with that of later analytic philosophy. In seeking to understand his thought, and what gives it its coherence, we—at least those of us who are analytic philosophers, or their intellectual descendants—are not seeking to understand something alien to us. The continuity means, for one thing, that anything that we come to understand about the nature of the philosophical enterprise by studying Russell is likely to be applicable also to our own attempts at philosophical understanding. However different his thought may be from ours, he is, for the most part, clearly engaged in the same general sort of enterprise. More important, perhaps, is the role that Russell played in the formation of analytic philosophy. In thinking about his philosophy we are thinking about one of the major formative influences on analytic philosophy; seeking to understand his philosophical thought is thus one way of seeking an understanding of the context in which our own philosophical thinking takes place, and so of understanding our own philosophical position.[2]

Three of the essays in this collection were written before the completion of the book mentioned above. Two of the three, Chapters 1 and 3, articulate very general themes of the book in relatively concise fashion. Another, Chapter 4, goes into a more or less technical aspect of Russell's work which I decided to omit from the book. The others all represent work that is new since the book appeared.

---

[2] I revert to these ideas in the last few pages of the first essay in the collection; see also the introduction to *Russell, Idealism, and the Emergence of Analytic Philosophy*.

Apart from the last of them, the essays fall into three groups, and I have arranged them accordingly (rather than chronologically). I shall say a little more about each of them, and about the order in which they appear.

The first group, made up of the first two chapters, focuses on the notion of a proposition. This notion played a central role in Russell's thought in the period with which I am concerned. The first essay seeks to explain this fact; in particular, it seeks to explain why the issue of the *unity* of the proposition loomed so large for him; it thus traverses some of the same ground that is covered in the book mentioned above but from a somewhat different direction and far more rapidly. The explanation proceeds partly in terms of the background to Russell's thought, his wish to combat the views of Leibniz and, more especially, of Kant and the post-Kantian idealists. (Russell tended to interpret Kant as an idealist, and to make little distinction between him and his idealist successors.) I conclude by drawing a more general moral: the significance of Russell's thought depends upon its historical context. The same is, presumably, true of our own philosophical thought; and, Russell's work plays an important role in forming that context.

The second essay critically discusses the idea, explicit in Russell but by no means confined to him, that philosophical thinking can and should *begin* with an analysis of propositions. Russell sometimes presents the idea of a proposition, and of the analysis of propositions, as fundamental, as starting points for philosophy. I argue, to the contrary, that they cannot be taken for granted in that way. My claim here is a general one: supposedly fundamental philosophical ideas have presuppositions, and one way to reveal those presuppositions is to see how the ideas develop and change over time. The essay argues for this claim, and tracks some of the relevant changes, in the particular case of Russell's conceptions of a proposition and of the analysis of propositions.

The second group of essays all relate to Russell's logic. Chapter 3, like Chapter 1, articulates a major theme in Russell's thought: his conception of logic and of the philosophy of logic. It begins by raising the question of the philosophical significance that logicism, the reduction of mathematics to logic, had for Russell when he first developed that doctrine. The answer is that it was part of a complex argument against Kant and post-Kantian Idealism. For this argument to work, logic must be thought of as made up of absolute and unconditioned truths. A certain conception of logic is thus implicit in the philosophical use that Russell makes of logicism. The essay articulates this conception and contrasts it with a widely held modern conception according to which the central notion is truth in an interpretation, rather than truth *tout court*; the notion of an interpretation is alien to Russell's thought. Given his general conception of logic, I argue, it is natural, perhaps inevitable, that logic will be higher-order logic, equivalent to set theory. Russell's use of logicism, however, is cast in doubt by the need to accommodate the paradox that bears his name. The theory of types undermines his conception of logic as consisting of universal and unconditioned truths. The infinitude of objects can no longer be proved, but is taken as an explicit assumption when needed; this threatens the idea that it is indeed *mathematics* which is being reduced to logic. The magnificent intellectual achievement of *Principia Mathematica* is thus, I argue, cut off from the philosophical motivations that lay behind Russell's initial formulation of logicism.

Chapter 4, the second essay in this group, deals with an approach to logic that Russell worked out between 1905 and 1907 in the attempt to avoid some of the problems of the theory of types. Rather than assuming the existence either of classes or of propositional functions (in terms of which classes may be defined), Russell attempted to achieve the same effects by means of what he called the substitutional theory: he assumed only propositions, and the idea of substituting one entity for another within a proposition. But in the end, I argue, the new approach raises difficulties precisely analogous to those raised for Russell by the assumption of propositional functions. To avoid paradox he has to make distinctions of type among propositions, just as the other approach requires him to make distinctions of type among propositional functions; the former are no less damaging than the latter. Hence the added complications of the substitutional theory are not worthwhile, and Russell abandons that approach.

Chapter 5 takes up the subject of the vicious-circle principle. Russell frequently invokes this principle as part of his justification of his version of the theory of types (i.e. what has become known as 'ramified type theory'). But exactly what the principle is, how it is meant to justify type theory, and whether it can succeed, are issues which have been the subject of much controversy; the essay is an attempt to resolve these issues. I argue that much of the controversy over the vicious-circle principle has been misdirected. The principle itself is a relatively straightforward claim about what follows when one entity presupposes another—a principle that might, indeed, be taken as partially definitive of the vexed notion of presupposition. What requires discussion, I argue, is not so much the principle itself as Russell's use of it, which is based on claims about relations of presupposition among propositional functions and between propositional functions and propositions. It is to these claims that we should look for an understanding of the basis of his type theory.

Chapter 6 is perhaps something of an anomaly in this group. It is an extended review of Michael Dummett's book *The Origins of Analytical Philosophy*. I include it in a group of essays relating to Russell's logic because the chief ground on which I criticize Dummett is that his account of the formation of analytic philosophy neglects the role of logic (and, largely in consequence, it also neglects the contribution of Russell).

Each of the essays in the third group emphasizes the significance of the distinction between Russellian propositional functions and functions in the ordinary mathematical sense. As Chapter 7 points out, propositional functions are fundamental to Russell's mature theory of types, the theory set out in the early portions of *Principia Mathematica*. But what are propositional functions? And what is their relation to the more general notion of function (more or less the ordinary mathematical notion)? It would perhaps be natural to assume that propositional functions are simply a kind of function—that is, that Russell takes for granted the more general notion of function and then distinguishes propositional functions as a special case. But in fact this is not what he does in *Principia Mathematica*. Rather, he takes propositional functions for granted and then introduces ordinary functions (descriptive functions, he calls them) as and when needed. Technically this procedure is unproblematic; the interesting question is why Russell proceeds in this fashion. The essay argues that ordinary functions inevitably give rise to complex referring expressions, and that an explanation of how such expressions function requires some analogue of Fregean *Sinn*—some intermediary between the person who understands the expression and the object which the expression is about. But Russell has an overwhelming reason, of a quite general philosophical kind, to want to avoid invoking such intermediary entities; they would violate the direct realism implicit in his idea of acquaintance. Hence he has every reason not to assume (ordinary) functions. Propositional functions, however, are not vulnerable to the same sorts of objections, from Russell's point of view. The crucial consideration here is that propositional functions are complex structured entities, and that the result of applying such a function to an object is a proposition which contains that object, and shares the structure of the propositional function. It is because propositional functions are complex structured entities that Russell's theory of types (ramified type theory) makes sense. And it is for this reason that Russell's logic has something of the appearance of intensional logic—not because he has an interest in formulating a logic for dealing with intensional notions such as belief.

Chapter 8, the second essay in the group, takes up an important and disputed issue in the interpretation of Wittgenstein's *Tractatus Logico-Philosophicus*, and uses ideas articulated in the previous essay to shed light on it. What we call truth-functions are central to Wittgenstein's thought; they play the crucial role not only in accounting for logic but also in explaining the possibility of any language or thought beyond the most elementary. Yet his account of the truth functions is by no means easy to understand. In particular, Wittgenstein calls them *operations,* and insists that they must be sharply distinguished from functions; yet most of what he says about them seems to apply equally to functions. I suggest that when Wittgenstein uses the word 'function' he is following Russell, and speaking of Russellian *propositional* functions. Reading him in this way can make sense of the contrasts he draws between functions and operations. This enables us to achieve a better understanding of his notion of an operation. On the basis of this understanding, I argue that operations in his sense cannot be identified with ordinary mathematical functions or with Fregean functions. The account that Wittgenstein gives of them cannot be separated from his general project of reconceiving the way in which language and thought represent the world; we cannot understand it in other terms.

Chapter 9 compares and, more especially, contrasts Frege with Russell. Again, a crucial role is played by the distinction between Russellian propositional functions and ordinary functions, and by the fact that Russell takes the former as fundamental. Frege takes the function-argument method of analysis as fundamental, and the conception of a function which he employs is an extended and clarified version of the ordinary mathematical notion. Russell, however, denies that there are functions in this sense. Expressions which appear to refer to such functions can be defined, in terms of propositional functions, as needed. In the course of a general comparison of the two thinkers I attempt to show that this apparently rather minor difference is directly connected with differences between their philosophical views on quite general issues, including their understandings of philosophical analysis, their ontological views, and their conceptions of logic.

The tenth and final chapter of the volume does not fit neatly into any of the groups that I have distinguished. It deals with one of the most frequently discussed topics in Russell's philosophy, namely his theory of definite descriptions, first set forth in one of the most celebrated essays of twentieth-century anglophone philosophy, the celebrated 1905 essay 'On Denoting'. In the first and the last sections I discuss the theory of definite descriptions, and objections to it, more or less independently of Russell. The bulk of the essay, however, deals with the way in which the theory fits into Russell's philosophy. His thought in the period before he wrote 'On Denoting' gave rise to a certain problem which he attempted to solve by means of what I call the theory of denoting concepts. This theory, and its solution, were, however, unsatisfactory to him in various ways. So, when he had the central idea of the theory of descriptions, he discarded his earlier view. This change had far-reaching effects on his philosophy in general, and I discuss these at some length.

The essays are reprinted here almost without changes from their original form. (Chapter 5 is the sole exception, for reasons explained in a footnote to that chapter. Even here the changes only amount to the excision of a few lines.) I have corrected typographical errors, and have in a few cases removed infelicities of style. I have not made substantive changes, or added notes to indicate points at which I would now put things differently. I could find no sharp line between points I now think are mistaken and those which merely emphasize matters differently from the way I now would. In the absence of such a sharp line, it seemed best to leave the essays unchanged. In a few places it would have been possible to cut some material and replace it with a reference to one of the other essays, but here again I decided to leave them unchanged. There is no place at which more than half a page or so could be cut in this fashion, and for so small a saving it did not seem worth interrupting the reader, or the flow of the essay.

1

The Nature of the Proposition and the Revolt against Idealism

Writing in 1900, soon after his rejection of neo-Hegelianism, Russell made the following striking statement: 'That all sound philosophy should begin with an analysis of propositions is a truth too evident, perhaps, to demand a proof' (*Leibniz*, 8). What is remarkable about this statement is not just that Russell thinks the analysis of propositions to be of crucial philosophical importance, but that he thinks this fact is *obvious*. G. E. Moore was very closely associated with Russell at this time, and the first work that he published after rejecting idealism shows a similar concern with the nature of the proposition. It is called 'The Nature of Judgment'. In that article, and in the longer work from which it is drawn, Moore uses the notion of judgment as a point of attack against Bradley and Kant, and goes on to begin to articulate a metaphysics fundamentally opposed to that of Kant or Bradley or any other idealist.[1] So, at the moment when Russell and Moore rejected idealism the problem of the nature of the proposition was a central concern of theirs. In spite of what Russell says, it is I think not obvious why this should be so. What I want to do in the first part of this paper, then, is to sketch an explanation, in historical terms, of why this problem might have seemed to them, at that moment, a central and inescapable concern. In the second part of the paper I shall indicate how this explanation may shed some light on Russell's early views. Finally I shall talk very briefly about the point of the sort of historical enterprise that I have undertaken in this paper.

I begin with Russell's conception of the nature of the proposition in 1900 and immediately thereafter. This conception gives rise to a problem for which Russell has no solution, and it is this unsolved problem that forms the chief theme of this paper. Russell took propositions to be abstract, non-linguistic entities. These entities are complex, i.e. made up of simpler entities which Russell calls *terms*. Because propositions are made up of simpler entities they must, according to Russell, be decomposable into those entities. (The validity of this process of

---

[1] Moore, 'The Nature of Judgment'. By 'the longer work from which it is drawn' I mean the 1898 version of Moore's Research Fellowship dissertation, 'The Metaphysical Basis of Ethics'. Most of chapter 2 of the dissertation is missing, but the internal evidence strongly suggests that the missing material was used in 'The Nature of Judgment'. I should like to thank the Librarian of Trinity College, Cambridge for allowing me access to Moore's two dissertations.

decomposition, or analysis, as a philosophical method is a central claim of the new philosophy of Moore and Russell, and a point of sharp disagreement with their idealist precursors. It is important to note that Moore and Russell, at this period, thought of analysis as almost analogous to physical decomposition. It is not a matter of the definition of words, but of finding the parts of which things are in fact made up.[2]) Thus the proposition that Socrates is wise is seen as made up of two elements, one, corresponding to 'Socrates' and one to 'wisdom'. (Russell sometimes suggests that there is a third element in a proposition of this form, corresponding to the copula 'is'; but his position on this seems to remain vague or agnostic—see *Principles*, section 53.) Now granting all of this—and it is granting a lot—Russell still faces a difficulty about the nature of the proposition. In section 54 of *Principles* he says:

Consider, for example, the proposition 'A differs from B'. The constituents of this proposition, if we analyze it, appear to be only A, difference, B. Yet these constituents, thus placed side by side, do not reconstitute the proposition. The difference which occurs in the proposition actually relates A and B, whereas the difference after analysis is a notion which has no connection with A and B. It may be said that we ought, in the analysis, to mention the relations which difference has to A and B, relations expressed by *is* and *from* when we say 'A is different from B'. These relations consist in the fact that A is referent and B relatum with respect to difference. But 'A, referent, difference, relatum, B' is still merely a list of terms, not a proposition. A proposition, in fact, is essentially a unity, and when analysis has destroyed the unity, no enumeration of constituents will restore the proposition. The verb, when used as a verb, embodies the unity of the proposition, and is thus distinguishable from the verb considered as a term, though I do not know how to give a clear account of the precise nature of the distinction.

Without our accepting this as a definitive formulation, it will provide us with a useful way of getting at the unsolved problem which is posed by Russell's conception of the proposition, and which I shall sometimes refer to as the problem of the unity of the proposition.

I turn now to the task of sketching an explanation, in historical terms, of why this problem should have impressed Russell as a central one. Perhaps the first

---

[2] This conception of analysis is manifest in Moore's discussion of the notion of definition, and of the sense in which good is indefinable (*Principia Ethica*, section 8). After distinguishing two kinds of verbal definition, using the definition of 'horse' as an example, and saying of each that it is not what he means, Moore goes on to say: 'But (3) we may, when we define horse, mean something much more important. We may mean that a certain object, which we all of us know, is composed in a certain manner: that it has four legs, a head, a heart, a liver, etc., etc., all of them arranged in definite relations to one another. It is in this sense that I deny good to be definable. I say that it is not composed of any parts, which we can substitute for it in our minds when we are thinking of it. We might think just as clearly and correctly about a horse, if we thought of all its parts and their arrangement instead of thinking of the whole . . . but there is nothing whatsoever which we could so substitute for good; and that is what I mean, when I say that good is indefinable.'

thing to do is simply to stress that the problem, or something recognizable as continuous with it, *has* a history; it did not spring fully formed from Moore's forehead in 1898. T. H. Green, in his Introduction to Hume's *Works*,[3] says that after Hume the nature of the proposition 'becomes the central question of philosophy, the answer to which must determine our theory of real existence just as much as of the mind' (Green, *Works*, p. 185, section 224). So to a philosopher of the idealist tradition the question of the nature of the proposition was as central a question as it later was for Russell. How can we explain this?

I begin the attempt to answer this question by looking very briefly at a claim of Leibniz's. It is well known that Leibniz held that in every true proposition the subject-concept *includes* the predicate-concept. In his correspondence with Arnauld, for example, Leibniz says: 'I have given a decisive reason, which I take to have the force of a demonstration. It is that always, in every true affirmative proposition, whether necessary or contingent, universal or particular, the notion of the predicate is in some way included in that of the subject. *Praedicatum inest subjecto*; otherwise I do not know what truth is.'[4] It is, I think, correct to see this view as arising from what is in some sense the same concern as that which we have seen in Russell: how do the components of a proposition come together, what unifies them? In Leibnizian terminology, what is the relation between substance and attribute which makes it intelligible that a substance can *have* an attribute? Leibniz's answer has the form of a rejection of the question: nothing is required to unify the components of a proposition. They are already unified—the subject-concept contains the predicate-concept. The attribute is not something separate from the substance, whose relation to it may be problematic; it is already included in the substance. This answer connects with some of the most fundamental features of Leibniz's metaphysics. Since every substance contains its attributes, genuine relations are ruled out, as Russell emphasized in his book on Leibniz. According to Leibniz, then, the world is made up of completely self-contained substance—monads—among which there are no genuine interactions. Thus although Leibniz in some sense rejects the question, it is certainly not a rejection that denies all force to the question. On the contrary, Leibniz seems to acknowledge that a central metaphysical issue is at stake: '*Praedicatum inest subjecto*; otherwise I do not know what truth is.'

Not surprisingly, we can see Kant as responding to these views of Leibniz's. And again, the response can be phrased in terms of the problem of the unity of the proposition. As against Leibniz's view that the problem of the unity of a proposition does not arise, Kant emphasizes the need for what he calls 'logical functions of unity in judgment'. These logical functions of unity are, so to speak,

[3] Green's Introductions are reprinted in Green, *Works*.
[4] Letter to Arnauld 4/14 July, 1686, translated in Leibniz, *Philosophical Papers*, i. 517.

ways in which a judgment can be unified. For reasons which need not delay us here, Kant holds that there are exactly twelve such ways, twelve logical functions of unity in judgment. Now if we consider judgment not wholly abstractly, but rather as applied to sensible intuition, these twelve logical forms of unity in judgment become the twelve Kantian categories, as Kant makes clear in section 20 of the B Deduction (B. 143).[5]

The categories, Kant claims, are the only ways in which what he calls *synthesis* of the diverse elements given in sensible intuition can take place. This synthesis is the source of the unity and relatedness of these diverse elements. As Kant says at B.130, the combination or unity of diverse representations is not something that can be 'given through objects'; the unity of representations cannot be just a further representation on a level with the others. This unity is rather the product of synthesis, which is our own *act* of combining the various representations. This act of combination is the source of the unity of the manifold elements given in sensible intuition and this unity is necessary if the sensory manifold is even to be an object of awareness. Since, to repeat, this act of combination must take place in accordance with the categories, and the categories are derived directly from the functions of unity in judgment, it follows that 'The same function which gives unity to the various representations *in a judgment* also gives unity to the mere synthesis of representations *in an intuition*' (B.104–5). Experience for Kant is thus judgmental through and through. Even the simplest kind of experience, on Kant's account, involves bringing intuitions under concepts, and is therefore subject to categories.

I am not, of course, trying to summarize the Transcendental Deduction, but rather to extract from it a line of thought which is crucial for my purposes. We can see this line of thought as made up of two claims, and a conclusion from those claims. The first claim is that there are *conditions* on the unity of judgment, or synthesis: that it comes about only in certain definite ways, subject to certain constraints. The second claim is that experience is judgmental in character, and is therefore subject to the same conditions or constraints. The conclusion from these two claims is that the conditions of judgment are the conditions of possible experience, and thus also the conditions of any possibly experienceable world— conditions that must be satisfied by any world that we could possibly have experience of.

This Kantian conclusion is not the same as the claim which one might take as central to post-Kantian idealism, that there are necessary conditions of judgment, or a necessary structure to thought, which are also the necessary conditions or structure of reality as a whole. But the two are sufficiently close to make it

---

[5] I follow the usual practice of citing the second edition of Kant's *Kritik der reinen Vernunft* (1787) simply as 'B', followed by the page number of that edition. The translation used is by Kemp Smith (1929).

comprehensible that Russell should have largely ignored the differences between them, and taken Kant to be an idealist. One point is worth making very briefly here about the differences between Kant and later idealists in this respect. The Kantian formulation refers to 'possible experience', or to 'a world that we could possibly have experience of', not simply to 'reality'. This is of course because of the Kantian distinction between phenomena and noumena, and the accompanying doctrine that the noumenal world, the world as it is in itself, is not an object of possible experience for finite beings. Kant's idealist successors, almost without exception, rejected the Kantian distinction and its accompanying doctrine that the noumenal world is beyond possible experience. They found the idea of a world beyond all possible experience to be incoherent. Reality, on this view, is not transcendent; it is not wholly beyond experience but is somehow immanent within it.

All of this has taken us a long way from Russell's worry about the unity of a proposition. Yet there is, I hope, enough continuity here to make it unsurprising that Russell and Moore should have taken the issue of the nature of judgment as a central metaphysical problem. The Kantian notion of synthesis can be thought of as providing a solution to a problem which structurally, at least, is very close to the Russellian problem. And given this Kantian move, the way is open, as I have tried to indicate, for an idealist metaphysics. If the necessary conditions of judgment are also necessary conditions of reality, or at least of the knowable world; and if judgment is in some sense our own act; then it is hard not to see the world as at least partially constituted by this act. Crucial to this account is the idea that the nature of the proposition is formed by what is in some sense a mental *act*—Kant emphasizes that synthesis is 'an act of spontaneity', which does something that could not be done by any representation which we received from objects (B.130). In the early stages of his reaction against idealism Russell opposes the view that sees propositions as in any sense formed by an act of the mind. The basic intuition behind this opposition can, I think, be expressed quite simply. The intuition is that what is true is true; it is true absolutely and objectively, and true regardless of any mental states or of the acts of any mind— it would be true even if there were no minds at all. But if a truth is to be true quite independently of any mind, then we must, it seems, oppose the view that says that propositions are constituted by acts of the mind, for this view makes the entities which are the bearers of truth or falsehood mind-dependent.

What I am taking as Russell's basic intuition here is one which, in some forms, is hard to deny. Hardly any philosopher, I think, would want to say that I can take some arbitrary proposition and make it true or false by my acts or beliefs, or other mental acts; in some sense, almost any philosopher will agree that whether or not a proposition is true is independent of whether I happen to believe it. (I assume that we are not talking about propositions which are about me or my beliefs.) What is striking is not that Russell too wants to make these assertions, but that he interprets Kantianism in a way that makes it incompatible with them. In the Leibniz book he describes a view which he says 'constitutes a large part of Kant's Copernican Revolution' as the view 'that propositions may acquire truth by being believed' (*Leibniz*, 14); and in the *Principles* he describes Kantianism, in a similar vein, as 'the belief that propositions which are believed solely because the mind is so made that we cannot help but believe them may yet be true in virtue of our belief' (*Principles*, 450).

Now as interpretations of Kant such passages are quite misleading. Kant would of course deny that I can make something true by believing it; or that something which I cannot help believing must for that reason be true. Kant is not talking about mind in any sense of 'mind' in which you have one mind and I have another, perhaps quite different, mind; again, Kant is at pains to distinguish the empirical from the transcendental sense of such expressions as 'outside us' or 'independent of us'. Russell rides roughshod over such crucial Kantian distinctions. But this should not be seen as mere error on Russell's part; it is more interestingly the expression of a certain philosophical attitude. If asked, is this truth independent of the mind? a Kantian will presumably reply: in the ordinary sense, yes of course it is; but there is another sense of 'independent' and another sense of 'mind' in which . . . and so on. Russell, if I read him aright on this point, writes from a philosophical mood which is perhaps familiar, in which carefully drawn distinctions seem to be just equivocations, and all of one's opponent's subtlety looks like sophistry. The Kantian must say that terms such as 'objective' or 'independent of us' call for careful interpretation, and are perhaps ambiguous; Russell's position is that they have a perfectly clear sense to those unencumbered by a false theory. For Russell, the question: are there propositions which are true wholly independently of us and our beliefs? is not a subtle or ambiguous question, not a question which calls for a yes-in-one-sense-but-no-in-another-sense answer; the only possible answer is *yes*—full-voice, flat-out, no ifs, no buts. Anything less is tantamount to saying no. Russell, we may say, insists that there are naive senses of 'objective', 'independent of us' and 'true', and that these naive senses are all we need.

Russell's attack on Kantianism must, I think, be understood along these lines. But now, to avoid the Kantian position, Russell insists that the source of the unity of the proposition is in *no* sense a mental act or synthesis. A proposition, to put it another way, has to be something which we do not in any sense *make*; it has to be something objective in the most simple-minded sense, something *out there*. The tone of Russell's extreme naive realism about abstract objects can be seen in this passage from *Principles*: 'all knowledge must be recognition, on pain of being mere delusion. Arithmetic must be discovered in just the same sense in which Columbus discovered the West Indies, and we no more create numbers than he created the Indians' (*Principles*, 451). This realism is hardly less marked in the case of propositions. Not only the entities which make up the propositions, but also, crucially, the propositions themselves, are out there, in Russell's version of some platonic heaven. Our relation to them is simply one of apprehension or recognition; the human mind, on this picture, is purely passive in judgment.

The most obvious problem raised by this way of thinking about propositions is the one with which we began the discussion: the problem of the unity of the proposition. Russell takes an extreme realist view both of the things which can be constituents of propositions—Socrates, wisdom, etc.—and of the propositions themselves—Socrates is wise, for example. Now in a case of this sort, the proposition is clearly made up from the entities in some way; but in *what* way? How do the entities combine to form the proposition? Russell admits that he has no answer to this question; but in fact the situation is worse than he suggests. The problem is in principle unsolvable within the metaphysical framework which he establishes.

It would require more space than I have at my disposal to argue this point with any care. Very roughly, the point is that according to Russell's early metaphysics everything—'Whatever may be an object of thought, or may occur in a true or false proposition, or can be counted as *one*', as he says (*Principles*, section 47)— is a *term*, i.e. is independent and object-like. At bottom, we may say, he has only one ontological category, and it is that category which is most obviously exemplified by the subjects of subject-predicate propositions. It is this metaphysical vision that Russell relies upon to support the idea that philosophical analysis, as he understands it at this period, is a valid philosophical method (see pp. 9–10 and n.2 above). An obvious contrast to the view that everything is object-like is Frege's distinction of concepts from objects; Russell's argument against this distinction is instructive. If the distinction were correct, Russell points out, concepts could not be logical subjects. In that case, he claims, we could not say anything about concepts, and nothing could be true or false of them. But the distinction cannot be drawn if we can say nothing about concepts, and if the distinction held, then there would be something true of concepts, namely that they are different from objects. So the distinction cannot be correct (see *Principles*, sections 49 and 481).[6] If everything is, so to speak, object-like, what *could* be the source of the unity of

---

[6] For Frege's distinction between concepts and objects, see 'Über Begriff und Gegenstand'. It might be thought that Frege's notion of a concept embodies a solution to the problem of the unity of the proposition, but this opinion is mistaken both philosophically and textually. Concepts and objects can unite because concepts are, as Frege says, 'unsaturated' (*ungesattigt*); but this cannot be an explanation, for we have no understanding of this notion of unsaturatedness except in terms of the ability of concepts to unite with objects. It is, moreover, clear from Frege's writing that he did not hold that the idea of unsaturatedness has any explanatory power, for he intended that the notion of unsaturatedness, and thus also of a concept (and also, I believe, of an object), was to be understood in terms of the prior notion of a complete thought. As well as 'Concept and Object', see Frege, *Begriffsschrift*, section 9, and Frege, *Nachgelassene Schriften*, i. 17–19, 273.

the proposition? Anything one might put forward as an answer would turn out to be just one more item in need of unification. One way to think of this is in the terms that Russell used in the passage I quoted from section 54 of *Principles* about the proposition 'A is different from B'. Russell's attitude there was that any component of the proposition would be—well, just one more component with the same status as the others. Only something with quite a different status, Russell implied, could play the role of unifying the components into a proposition. But Russell's metaphysics rules out the possibility of there being anything with this kind of different status. Russell's anti-Kantianism forbids an appeal to what is in any sense an *act* of unification or synthesis; and his metaphysics forbids any other kind of answer. The constraints within which Russell was working in the years immediately following his rejection of idealism make the problem of the unity of the proposition in principle unsolvable for him at that time.

Given the role which the issue of the nature of judgment plays in the idealist tradition, this fact ought to be a very serious embarrassment for Russell. We can see this more clearly if we talk about the issue of relations. Russell placed great weight on the reality and objectivity of relations. In *Principles*, for example, he argues that a refusal to accept the reality and externality of relations was responsible for many of the contradictions that philosophers had claimed to find both in mathematics and in space and time. Russell emphasizes relations in this way in large measure because the British idealists, much more than their German counterparts, had made essential and explicit use of the notion—Bradley, I suppose, is notorious for having denied the reality of relations.[7] Bradley's metaphysics, however, is highly eccentric and atypical, so I shall talk instead about T. H. Green— much more nearly a nice normal British neo-Hegelian. Green, unlike Bradley, did not argue for the unreality of relations, but he did argue that they are mind-dependent. And since it is clear that it is not your mind or my mind that they depend upon, Green argued that there must be a single eternal mind, in which you and I partake, but which is independent of us.[8] (Nice normal British neo-Hegelianism tends to have a theological twist to it.) Now this is just the sort of view that Russell wants to reject by insisting upon the objectivity and independence of relations. But if one examines Green's arguments, it is clear that what is really moving him when he talks about relations is the problem of *unity*—in particular the problem of the unity of judgment and of fact. The issue is always how the *relatedness* of two things comes about. But this issue cannot be dealt with by Russell's tactic of just assuming that relations are among the things which there are in the world. For, as we saw in the case of 'A is different

---

[7] See especially Bradley, *Appearance and Reality*, ch. 3.
[8] See, for example, Green, *Prolegomena to Ethics*, section 51.

from B′, assuming the abstract relation of *difference* is not a means of accounting for the relatedness of A and B. It would not, I think, have occurred to Green to distinguish the relation as such from the relation as actually relating, as the source of relatedness. But if one makes this distinction, as Russell did, it is clear that Green's concern is with the latter, with the possibility of relatedness, the way in which a relation actually *relates* its objects. And on this issue, as we have seen, no plausible line of reply is open to Russell in the early years of his anti-idealism. I think it is correct to say of the British idealists quite generally, as I said of Green, that their concern with relations is always a concern with the unity of the diverse and, in particular, with the unity of judgment. The fact that Russell has no coherent account of the unity of the proposition therefore seriously undermines his claim to have a refutation of the idealist view of relations.

Thus far I have been talking about Russell's views from the period 1900 to 1906. Sometime between 1906 and 1910, however, he comes to hold quite different views about the issues that I have been discussing. It is these new views, and Russell's reasons for preferring them to the old, that I shall now consider. My emphasis, once again, will be on the role played by the problem of the unity of the proposition.

The chief reason why Russell abandons his earlier view of the proposition has to do with the need to give an account of truth. We have seen that Russell unequivocally insists upon a straightforward view of truth: what is true is true absolutely and completely independently of us. Russell argues vehemently against the idea that truth could be a matter of degree, and against the view that it could depend upon the coherence of a number of beliefs with one another. Now the most natural view of truth, for someone with this sort of strong realist and objectivist attitude, is that it is based on some sort of correspondence between our judgments on the one hand and the reality that we judge about on the other hand. This sort of view of truth, however, is not available to one who holds the view of propositions which Russell held in the early years of this century. One way of seeing why this should be so is to emphasize the fact that Russell, in those early years, has no account of the unity of the proposition. Although he takes propositions as complex, i.e. as made up of other entities, he has no account of the way in which those entities unite to form the proposition. He treats judgment, therefore, as a relation between a person and a proposition, and in his account of this relation the composite character of the proposition plays no role. This fact is enough to rule out the view of truth as correspondence to reality as an option for Russell at this period. We cannot say that judgment is a relation between a person and a *fact*, because this threatens to make a false judgment into a relation between a person and nothing at all—whereas the same reality which makes our true judgments true also makes our false judgments false. The correspondence view of truth, in any form, thus requires that we see judgments as essentially composite or articulated. Judgments must be seen as having parts which correspond to parts of reality; only in this way can they be guaranteed a connection with reality which is independent of their truth. The correspondence view of truth is unavailable to Russell because he cannot, in this way, treat judgment as composite.

With the correspondence view of truth ruled out, it is no surprise to find Russell, in the early years of the century, treating truth and falsehood as simple properties—much as Moore had treated *good* in *Principia Ethica*, except that truth and falsehood are properties of propositions. According to this view, a true proposition is a complex that stands in a certain relation to the concept of *truth*; a false proposition is a complex which stands in that same relation to the concept of *falsehood*; and the concepts *truth* and *falsehood* are simple and indefinable. To say that truth is simple and indefinable, however, is to say that it is inexplicable, that we have no account of what it is for a proposition to be true, or of the way in which a true proposition differs from a false one. Russell's insistence on the objectivity and absoluteness of truth is at the heart of his opposition to idealism; but this insistence appears hollow in the face of his inability to tell us in what this truth which he so emphasizes consists. Since we have no account of *truth*, or of *falsehood*, or of the difference between them—they are simple and indefinable—we have no understanding of the difference between true propositions and false propositions. We can dramatize the difficulty that this created for Russell by showing that his inability to give an account of truth or of falsehood led him to two consequences which are very hard to accept. First, the fact that each proposition is either true or false, and that none is both, must be accepted as completely inexplicable, as a brute contingency. Second, and perhaps worse, if truth is indefinable and inexplicable then no connection is made between the truth of a proposition, on the one hand, and reality or fact on the other hand. If we cannot make this connection, and cannot say how truth differs from falsehood, then we cannot explain why our beliefs aim at truth rather than at falsehood. At one stage Russell realized, and accepted both of these consequences. In his article on Meinong (1904),[9] he says:

It may be said—and this is, I believe, the correct view—that there is no problem at all in truth and falsehood; that some propositions are true and some false, just as some roses are red and some white . . . But this view *seems* to leave our preference for truth a mere unaccountable prejudice, and in no way to answer to the feeling of truth and falsehood.[10]

---

[9] Russell, 'Meinong', reprinted in Russell, *Essays in Analysis*, The passages quoted in the text are from *Essays in Analysis*, 75–6.

[10] Compare Wittgenstein, *Tractatus*, 6.111: 'All theories that make a proposition of logic appear to have content are false. One might think, for example, that the words "true" and "false" signified two properties among other properties, and then it would seem to be a remarkable fact that every proposition possessed one of these properties. On this theory it seems to be anything but obvious, just as, for instance, the proposition "All roses are either yellow or red", would not sound obvious even if it were true.'

Then a page or so later:

the analogy with red and white roses seems, in the end, to express the matter as nearly as possible. What is truth and what falsehood, we must merely apprehend, for both seem incapable of analysis. And as for the preference which most people—so long as they are not annoyed by instances—feel in favour of true propositions, this must be based, apparently, upon an ultimate ethical proposition: 'It is good to believe true propositions and bad to believe false ones.' This proposition, it is to be hoped, is true; but if not, there is no reason to think that we do ill in believing it.

Such a position is, I take it, evidently absurd. Even Russell, who had a White Queen-like talent for believing the impossible, came to find it so. In an article on the nature of truth written in 1906[11] he professes doubt about his view of propositions. When this article was reprinted in 1910 (in *Philosophical Essays*) the last section was replaced by a separate piece in which the doubt of the 1906 article is replaced by the firm opinion that his former views were wrong. Russell gives up the idea that there are propositions which are independent of our acts of judgment. Rather than conceiving of an act of judgment as the apprehension of a single entity entirely distinct from the act—a proposition—Russell now says that there are no such entities. He now takes judgment to be a relation between a person and various non-propositional entities which the person judging somehow unites so that a judgment is formed. This is the view which is known as the 'multiple-relation' view of judgment, because judgment no longer appears as a two-place relation (between a person and a proposition) but as a three-or-more-place relation (among the person and the various entities which, to use the language of the old theory, make up the proposition that is judged). It is important to note that the multiple-relation theory of judgment is not merely a theory about propositional attitudes, but also a theory about propositions. More accurately, a theory about propositional attitudes now has to carry much of the weight which was formerly carried by the theory of propositions. According to Russell's new view there are no propositions, and all apparent references to propositions have to be understood as being in fact references to mental acts of judgment or of understanding.

Now the most striking thing about this view, from the present perspective, is that it seems to accept just that feature of Kantianism which we saw Russell reject so vehemently: propositions become dependent for their existence (or pseudo-existence) upon mental acts. Russell's willingness to take this step must be seen in part as a result of a shift in his concerns. By 1910 the battle with

---

[11] The original article was titled 'The Nature of Truth', and published in the *Proceedings of the Aristotelian Society*, 1906–7. In Russell, *Philosophical Essays*, the first two sections of that article are reprinted under the title 'The Monistic Theory of Truth'. The third and last section of the original article is discarded, its place being taken by a separate essay entitled, 'On the Nature of Truth and Falsehood'.

idealism is, to his mind, long since over; Kantianism no longer poses the threat to him that it did in 1900. But this is only part of the explanation. More important is the fact that the step which Russell takes is not as large as it might appear. The crucial point here is that the mental act of unification which is involved in judgment imposes no constraints on what can be judged or, therefore, on what can be true. Unlike the Kantian notion of synthesis, Russell's appeal to a mental act of judgment imposes no limits or conditions upon what can be judged; so no general metaphysical consequences follow.

This un-Kantian feature of Russell's multiple-relation theory of judgment can be seen as leading to the downfall of that theory. In the case of the crude 1910 version of that theory which I outlined above, this point is relatively straightforward. Because the mental act which the theory of judgment involves remains purely formal and without the power to impose constraints on what is judged, that theory has the consequence that anything whatsoever can be judged. As far as Russell's theory is concerned, there is no reason why I cannot form a judgment from any selection of objects with which I am acquainted, and so judge, for example, that this table penholders the book.[12] Russell cannot say that what is judged must be a proposition, for his theory of judgment is not subservient to an independent theory of the proposition. The theory of judgment is, rather, intended to play the role of a theory of the proposition. Nor can Russell happily claim that the mental act of judgment itself imposes constraints upon what can be judged, for such a claim is a significant step towards a Kantian view of judgment. Russell's 1910 theory of judgment, therefore, does not explain why it is impossible to judge nonsense; it is thus quite inadequate to play the role that Russell intended it to play.

Given the inadequacy of the 1910 version of the multiple-relation theory of judgment, it is no surprise to find that Russell produced a more sophisticated version of that theory in 1913.[13] Central to the 1913 theory is the notion of logical form. It is still a mental act of judgment which unites objects so that a proposition is formed, but it is logical form which explains *how* these objects are united in the proposition. Logical form is, Russell says, 'the way in which the constituents are put together' ('Theory of Knowledge', 98). To make a judgment, therefore, one must be acquainted not only with certain objects but

---

[12] See Wittgenstein, *Notebooks*, 95, 103; and *Tractatus*, 5.5422. This criticism of Wittgenstein's seems to have been made not of Russell's 1910 theory but of his 1913 theory, which I discuss below.

[13] In a manuscript entitled 'Theory of Knowledge' which is the draft of portions of a book which Russell never completed. Some parts of that manuscript were published in the *Monist* between January 1914 and April 1915. My references are all to material that was not published in Russell's lifetime. (At the time I wrote the essay it was still unpublished; I am grateful to the Russell Archives at McMaster University for allowing me access to it, and for permission to quote from it.) All the material that Russell wrote of the book is now published under the title *Theory of Knowledge*, and my references are to the published edition. (November 2004: I have rewritten this footnote to take account of the fact that the material has been published since the essay was written.)

also with the logical form which is the way in which those objects are united in the proposition formed by the judgment. If there is no such logical form for a given group of objects, then that group of objects cannot be united to form a proposition—the act of judgment, in such a case, cannot be carried out. Logical form is thus the source of the constraints on what can be judged. Russell identifies the logical form of a given proposition with a certain wholly abstract fact: that fact which is obtained if we replace all of the constituents of the proposition with existentially quantified variables. Thus the logical form of 'The book is on the table' is 'Something has some relation to something' $((\exists x)(\exists y)(\exists \Phi)\ \Phi xy)$. (Although we can best think of logical form by beginning with a proposition and replacing its constituents with variables, this process reflects only the order of our knowledge. The wholly abstract fact is prior to, and simpler than, the propositions of which it is the logical form; acquaintance with the abstract fact is a prerequisite of the act of judgment from which the less abstract propositions are formed. Relying upon the distinction between the logical and the psychological, Russell says that 'we need not be alarmed by this inversion of the psychological order'—'Theory of Knowledge', 130.) The obvious objection to make at this point is that our understanding of the proposition 'The book is on the table' is explained in terms of our understanding of the proposition 'Something has some relation to something', but that this latter understanding is left completely unexplained. Thus we seem to be left with a problem of exactly the same kind as that with which we began. In Russell's theory, however, the problems are not of the same kind. The understanding of wholly abstract propositions—those with no constituents other than variables—is different in kind from the understanding of all other propositions. In the case of wholly abstract propositions, understanding the proposition is identified with being acquainted with the corresponding fact. Understanding propositions cannot in general be explained in this way, for this would imply that every proposition which we can understand corresponds to a fact and is therefore true. For the special case of wholly abstract propositions, however, Russell is willing to accept this consequence: for propositions of this sort there is no duality of truth and falsehood; any such proposition must be true. Russell suggests that this fact is connected with the self-evidence of logical truth, but the part of the manuscript that was completed does not explore this connection.

Even from this brief sketch, it is clear that the 1913 version of the multiple-relation theory of judgment is much more complex than the 1910 version. The added complexity, however, is to no avail. The later theory succeeds no better than the earlier in reconciling Russell's atomistic and object-based metaphysics with an explanation of the unity of the proposition. The failure of the theory can be brought out in two ways. The first, which seems to me the more straightforward, is to focus on the notion of logical form, and to show that Russell can offer no coherent account of logical forms. The second is to show that the 1913 theory is vulnerable to the same objection as the 1910 theory, i.e. that it cannot show why it is impossible to judge nonsense. This objection, although less clear-cut, is of greater historical interest because it seems to have played a large part in Wittgenstein's rejection of Russell's attempts to come up with a theory of judgment.[14] I shall briefly discuss both objections.

According to Russell's multiple-relation theory, a judgment is formed by a mental act of combination. This act is of course subjective—it is the act of the mind which judges. This view is, however, as far as Russell can go towards the idea that propositions are constituted by the mind; he holds that not only the constituents of propositions but also the ways in which they are combined are objective. Russellian logical forms—unlike Kantian logical functions of unity in judgment—are thus objective and entirely independent of the mind. For Russell (and not for Russell alone), to conceive of something as objective in this strong sense is to conceive of it as an object. Russellian logical forms are objects ('Theory of Knowledge', 97). This immediately suggests a difficulty. Logical forms must, in virtue of the role assigned to them, be wholly different in kind from other sorts of objects; what account can be given of this difference? Russell says that logical forms, although they are objects, 'cannot be regarded as "entities" ' (ibid. 97), but nowhere says how we are to think of them, or what the distinction between object and entity amounts to. This is not simply a matter of an unexplained notion, however: worse is to come. Russell argues that the logical form of a proposition is not itself a constituent of that proposition:

[The logical form] cannot be a new constituent, for if it were, there would have to be a new way in which it and the two other constituents are put together, and if we take this way as again a constituent, we find ourselves embarked on an endless regress.

It is obvious, in fact, that when *all* the constituents of a complex have been enumerated, there remains something which may be called the 'form' of the complex, which is the way in which the constituents are combined in the complex. (ibid.: 98)

Yet in some propositions logical forms presumably *do* occur as constituents—in those propositions of the 'theory of knowledge' that discuss particular logical forms, for example. How this is possible—how we are able to talk about logical forms—is an issue that Russell never faces. The point, however, is very similar to that which he used as a reason for rejecting Fregean *Begriffe* (see p. 15 above). Whatever we can talk about, whatever there can be truths about, must presumably be capable of occurring in propositions. It is therefore absurd to suppose that

---

[14] See note 12. I do not mean to imply that this is Wittgenstein's only criticism of Russell's theory. In particular, Wittgenstein also attacks the view that one sentence's making sense can depend upon the truth of another sentence—the one which expresses the fact which is the logical form of the first sentence. See Pears, 'The Relation between Wittgenstein's Picture Theory of Propositions and Russell's Theories of Judgment'.

there are objects which cannot occur in propositions.[15] Yet Russell's logical forms appear, at least, to be objects of just this kind.

The second objection to the 1913 theory of judgment is that it, like the 1910 theory, does not show that it is impossible to judge nonsense. If the theory were to show this, it would have to show that some groups of objects can, while other groups cannot, be combined in the way indicated by a given logical form. Because the logical form here is an object, distinct from the group of objects which can or cannot be combined, the issue is one of the relation between the logical form on the one hand and the group of objects on the other. There must be a relation which a logical form has to those groups of objects which can be combined in the way represented by that logical form, and which it fails to have to groups of objects which cannot be combined in this way. If we are to have an explanation of the fact that certain groups of objects can be combined into propositions, while others cannot, we must have an explanation of the fact that this relation holds in certain cases and not in others. But it is quite mysterious what such an explanation might look like, and what facts it might appeal to. The point can be put like this. Given Russell's conception of an object, the potentiality, or lack of potentiality, which two objects have for combining into a proposition cannot be explained simply in terms of features of those objects: we have to invoke the notion of logical form. But if the potential for combination which the objects have cannot be explained in terms of features of those objects, then neither can the fact that the pair of objects stands in the appropriate relation to a logical form. The introduction of logical forms, or of further objects, is simply irrelevant to the task of explaining why certain groups of objects can be combined to form propositions, while other groups cannot. The 1913 theory is thus no better able to explain this than was the 1910 theory.

The objection of the previous paragraph is, as I have said, Wittgenstein's—although the method of explaining and arguing for it is not. Wittgenstein's criticisms had a devastating effect on Russell. Writing to Lady Ottoline Morrell in May 1913 he said:

I showed him [Wittgenstein] a crucial part of what I have been writing. He said it was all wrong, not realizing the difficulties—that he had tried my view and knew it wouldn't work. I couldn't understand his objection—in fact he was very inarticulate—but I feel in my bones that he must be right, and that he has seen something I missed.[16]

---

[15] This issue is more complicated than appears from the text. It would be more nearly accurate to say that the supposition that there are objects which cannot appear in propositions is one that is absurd unless some kind of explanation of this fact is given for the particular kind of objects in question. In particular, this explanation would have to show that it is nevertheless possible for us to talk about such objects. Russell attempts no such explanation for logical forms, and it is not apparent that any such explanation is possible in that case.

[16] Russell to Lady Ottoline Morrell, 28 May 1913. Quoted in Clark, *The Life of Bertrand Russell*, 204.

By the end of the summer Russell had abandoned 'The theory of knowledge', and the book was never completed. Three years later, writing to Lady Ottoline Morrell about that period, he wrote: 'His [Wittgenstein's] criticism . . . was an event of first-rate importance in my life, and affected everything I have done since. I saw he was right, and I saw that I could not hope ever again to do fundamental work in philosophy.'[17] There is, I think, a sense of 'fundamental' on which this assessment is correct. For further insight into the issues that I have been discussing we must look not to any work of Russell's but to Wittgenstein's *Tractatus*. There we see the issue of the nature of the proposition resolved, and with it questions about the nature of truth and of the status of logic. The metaphysical price for this resolution, however, is no lower for Wittgenstein than it was for the idealists. And indeed, one might well be struck by the way in which the *Tractatus* not only contains ideas which are familiar from our discussion of Russell's work, but also resurrects certain idealist themes. The idea of logical form, and more particularly, the idea that the logical form of a proposition is a *fact*, are clearly Russellian ideas which Wittgenstein transforms; again, the idea that logical form is something about which we cannot speak is an idea strongly suggested by Russell's work, although Russell himself would not have accepted it. Doctrines familiar to idealism are interwoven with these Russellian ideas. The unspeakability of logical form goes along with a distinction between the transcendental and the empirical standpoints: the transcendental standpoint is that of the unspeakable truths and the superlative facts which make possible the ordinary facts and truths of the empirical standpoint. Again, there is a sense in which the logical form of which the *Tractatus* speaks is one, a single and indivisible whole. While still atomistic on the empirical level, the *Tractatus* revives a kind of monism at the transcendental level. Most obvious of all, perhaps, is the idea of a necessary structure to thought or language which is also the necessary structure of the world. That it is language, rather than thought, which bears the metaphysical weight in the *Tractatus* is a fact which, from a sufficiently distant perspective, might seem less significant than the revival of the fundamental Kantian idea of a necessary structure of the (knowable) world.

I want now, in the rest of this paper, to stand back and reflect upon the kind of enterprise that I have been engaged in so far. I began by asking why Russell, at the turn of the century, should have held the nature of the proposition to be a central philosophical issue. I went on to sketch a partial answer to this question in terms of the idealist background to Russell's thought, and to indicate some of the further ramifications which the issue of the nature of the proposition had in Russell's work early in this century. I shall now raise a question about my

---

[17] Russell to Lady Ottoline Morrell, 1916 (exact date unknown). Quoted in Russell, *Autobiography*, 57.

original question: what is one doing in asking such a question, and in offering the kind of answer that I have sketched?

It might be held that there is a straightforward philosophical problem about the nature of the proposition, a problem which can perfectly well be understood independently of the historical background against which it arises. If one holds this view of the matter, then one will naturally think that the question: why was Russell concerned with this problem? is simply a question about *Russell*—what features of his mind or his historical position led him to focus on this problem? The question with which I began the paper will thus seem to be a purely historical or even psychological question, interesting enough in its way, no doubt, but not relevant to the substantive philosophical issue of the nature of the proposition, or to any other substantive philosophical issue. Now I hope that the main body of this paper has done something to make this attitude unappealing. In particular, I hope to have made it plausible that asking *why* Russell was interested in the nature of the proposition is inseparable from asking what exactly it was that he was interested in when he was interested in the nature of the proposition; or asking, what is the issue of the nature of the proposition, as Russell understood it? To understand the question, 'What is a proposition?', as Russell asked it, one must have some idea of the context of the question—why it arises, what purpose the answer is to serve, the constraints within which this answer is to be sought, and so on. It is from such things that the question gets its life and its force.

The claim that I am making is a claim about what it is to understand Russell's concern with the nature of the proposition. Understanding here demands that we recapture Russell's presuppositions and motives, that we see what general views he takes for granted, or wishes to advance, or wishes to oppose; and that we see how he interpreted these views and how he connected them with one another and with other views. To identify the problems at stake, and the arguments being put forward, we have to articulate the framework within which the problems arise and the arguments operate. In particular, we have to see how the historical context gives rise to this framework. A claim of this sort, about what is involved in understanding something, is also a claim about the nature of the thing that is to be understood. Although I spoke of Russell's question on the one hand, and of the context of that question on the other, I do not mean to suggest that these can be thought of as separate and independent items. My claim is, on the contrary, that Russell's question is that question which it is only in virtue of its context. The context is, if you like, partially constitutive of the question.

The complexity and context-dependence which, I have claimed, hold of Russell's problem of the nature of the proposition are, I think characteristic of many philosophical views or problems. I have not, of course, substantiated this general view here; at most I have sketched a single illustration. I shall, nevertheless, say something about the interest which I take this view to have. In particular,

I shall say something about the difference that this view makes to our understanding of the relation between philosophy and its history. A crucial part of understanding this relation is, I take it, to explain why the study of the history of philosophy should be thought of as being itself a philosophical activity. One answer to this which is, I think, quite widely accepted, is that there are certain philosophical problems which we are concerned to solve, and that studying classic philosophical texts helps us to find solutions to them. This is the sort of view that John Mackie, for example, advances in the introduction to his book on Locke (*Problems*, 2). The 'main aim' of the book, he says there, 'is not to expound Locke's views, or to study their relations with those of his contemporaries or near contemporaries, but to work towards solutions of the problems themselves'. The philosophical problems here are taken as given. The emphasis is on solving these problems and, in this enterprise, we enlist the help of Locke, or Russell, or Kant, or of anyone whose work we find useful. Studying the history of philosophy, insofar as this is a philosophical activity, is, on this view of the matter, a cooperative endeavour aimed at solving philosophical problems. Seeing things in this way makes the historical aspect of the history of philosophy—the fact that the texts that we study were written at specific moments in the past—irrelevant to its philosophical uses. The cooperative endeavour would go forward in the same way whenever the works had been written.

I wish to propose a rather different way of thinking about the relation of philosophy to its history, which is suggested by the view of philosophical understanding which I have been discussing. The emphasis here is not so much on solving philosophical problems as on gaining a deeper understanding of what a given problem is, why it arises, what gives it its force, why it grips us or fails to grip us. The main body of the paper suggested the way in which an appeal to its historical background might give us a deeper understanding of Russell's problem of the nature of the proposition. But the real interest and philosophical point of these ideas emerges when we think of their application not to others but to ourselves and our own philosophical activity. Where do the problems that grip us come from? What gives them their force, and why do they grip us? To confront questions of this sort is to attempt to understand our own philosophical position in terms of our philosophical history. Our own philosophy no more takes place in an historical vacuum than did Russell's and, like Russell's, our own philosophical position is in part to be understood in terms of its historical context. Self-understanding, on this view, is one of the motives to a study of the history of philosophy.

It may, however, be questioned whether this view of the history of philosophy as a search for historical self-understanding does justice to the philosophical importance that I wish to claim for it. Similar historical enterprises have been undertaken for a variety of subjects, including the more prestigious sciences; yet the practitioners of those sciences do not seem to find this historical knowledge of any relevance to their scientific work. An examination of episodes in the history of physics, say, can teach us something about what physics is. But the sort of thing we can learn here seems to be of interest to philosophers of physics but not, in their professional capacity, to physicists themselves.[18] Why is philosophy not like this? We cannot answer this question by appealing to the fact that a philosopher of physics is not a physicist, whereas a 'philosopher of philosophy' (if there were any) would be a philosopher. One objection to this answer is that it appeals to institutional arrangements and departmental boundaries without considering their rationale; it thereby simply fails to meet the question. A second objection is that the answer suggests that an interest in the nature of philosophy is, or ought to be, the concern of a number of specialists within philosophy, rather as the philosophy of physics is; this picture clearly misrepresents the matter. A more nearly satisfactory answer involves substantive and controversial claims. In particular, I wish to claim that the nature of philosophy is something which is always liable to arise in the course of ordinary philosophical argument. Philosophy is a subject for which the meaningfulness of its terms and the correctness of its procedures is always an issue; the distinction between philosophy and metaphilosophy is therefore not a useful one, because meta-level issues constantly arise within the practice of the subject.[19] These claims are claims about the nature of philosophy, and are to be established not by direct argument but by the accumulated weight of examples which bear it out; in other words, these claims are to be established historically.

   We are thus in a curious, but not paradoxical, position. I argued that one reason for a philosophical interest in the history of philosophy is that we learn from it something about the nature of philosophy. But the claim that what we can learn in this way is relevant to the practice of philosophy is itself one that must itself be established historically. The weakness of this position is that it will do nothing to persuade those who hold that the lessons of the past do not apply because we have, at last, found the true method and made philosophy a science—which I take to mean, among other things, that it can safely proceed in a relative ignorance of its own history and without worries as to its nature. To those who are capable of believing this there is nothing that can be briefly said, except perhaps to observe that their idea, that philosophy has broken with its past and become a science, is itself one that has a long history. Mark Twain observed that giving up smoking

---

[18] Compare Kuhn, *The Essential Tension*, 120: 'Among the areas to which the history of science relates, the one least likely to be significantly affected is scientific research itself.'

[19] Compare Cavell, *Must We Mean What We Say?*, p. xviii: 'I would regard this fact—that philosophy is one of its own normal topics—as in turn defining for the subject . . .' The Foreword to this book has been a recurrent source of inspiration and instruction to me in my attempts to think about the nature of philosophy, and its relation to its history.

was easy, he had done it a hundred times; the same might be said of philosophy's attempts to repudiate its past and establish itself on a new, and scientific, footing. This does not, of course, show that the latest attempt will not be successful, but it does suggest that the appropriate attitude is a sceptical one.

I claimed that the nature of philosophy is always liable to become an issue in ordinary philosophical argument; and I said that this claim could only be established historically. Short of doing this historical work, however, there are ways of thinking about the claim which may be helpful. One such way, which I shall call the negative way, can best be approached through the most pessimistic attitude towards philosophy. The pessimist contrasts philosophy with the most obviously successful sciences—especially physics. As philosophers have long insisted, physics is successful in ways in which philosophy is not. In the light of this contrast, the pessimist goes on, there is every reason why philosophers should question the meaningfulness of philosophical terms and the correctness of philosophical procedures, for the (relative) failure of philosophy gives reason to think that those terms are meaningless, and those procedures incorrect. On this pessimistic view, philosophy is and ought to be a self-reflective subject because it is at best an open question whether this subject has any claims to be regarded as a branch of knowledge at all. Some of the ideas on which this pessimistic view is based must be accepted. First, philosophy is not a science, not a technical subject; if it is thought of as a science it will certainly appear as a most unsuccessful one. Secondly, the terms in which the past is subjected to philosophical criticism, and a new philosophical doctrine advanced, are specific to that new philosophy. (To adapt an idiom of Kuhn's, we may say there is no 'normal philosophy; Kuhn, *The Structure* of *Scientific Revolutions*.) A less pessimistic attitude towards these same facts would emphasize the idea that in philosophy we seek to question the fundamental presuppositions of various kinds of human knowledge and activity. A subject of this sort must inevitably be concerned with its own fundamental presuppositions; and once these are at stake they will clearly play a special role, for to question them is implicitly to question all the other philosophical conclusions that we may have reached.

A second, and positive, way of thinking about the self-reflective character of philosophy appeals to the connection between philosophy and self-knowledge. Thought of in this way, philosophical criticism is directed, in the first instance, not against the ignorance of others but against the confusions to which one is oneself constantly vulnerable. What one can hope to gain from philosophy is not, primarily, positive doctrine but rather a clearer mind and a deeper insight into one's position in the world. If these Socratic ideas appeal to us at all, then it will seem unsurprising that the philosophical enterprise should itself be subject to philosophical examination and criticism. If, indeed, we accept that philosophy has to do peculiarly with self-knowledge, we might well find it obvious from the start that the history of philosophy is a part of philosophy itself. One way in which we can understand our own philosophical position is historically, by seeing how it has developed through time. At this point it becomes clear that thinking about Russell and his break with idealism does more than provide us with an example of an interesting philosophical moment. Russell's break with idealism is a decisive point in the development of what is sometimes called the analytic tradition in twentieth-century philosophy. Many of us are in some more or less remote sense the heirs of Russell, as also perhaps of Frege and the young Wittgenstein. Here I include those who find the approach of these authors deeply misguided, and who struggle to free themselves from it and to develop alternatives; as the example of Russell and idealism itself shows, a philosophical position must be understood in terms of what it is most fundamentally reacting against, as well as of the positive aim that it hopes to achieve. In studying Russell's break with idealism we are, therefore, studying a crucial moment in the historical background to our own philosophical period. My subject in this paper has been an issue in the history of philosophy, but my ulterior aim has been philosophical self-knowledge. What I hope I have conveyed in these concluding remarks is the idea that philosophical self-knowledge and an understanding of our own philosophical history are intimately connected.[20]

[20] Versions of this paper were read at the University of Pennsylvania, the University of California at Berkeley and the University of Chicago, as well as Johns Hopkins University. I should like to thank the audiences at each of these institutions for their comments. I have also benefited from discussions with Stefan Collini, Christine Korsgaard, Dan Lloyd, Susan Neiman, Hubert Schwyzer and, especially, Burton Dreben about earlier drafts. Part of the work on this paper was supported by the American Council of Learned Societies, under a programme made possible in part by the National Endowment for the Humanities.

2

Beginning with Analysis

In a book published in 1900, based on a series of lectures given in the previous year, Russell says: 'That all sound philosophy should begin with an analysis of propositions, is a truth too evident, perhaps, to demand a proof' (Leibniz, p. 8). Like many appeals to self-evidence (or, in more recent jargon, to 'intuition'), this is a highly tendentious assertion. It suggests that the ideas of a proposition and of analysis are obvious and straightforward notions, which can thus serve as a starting point of philosophy. These views have had significant influence in the subsequent development of analytic philosophy—as the very name of that tradition suggests. The idea of a proposition, and of the analysis of propositions, has often been treated as if they were quite uncontroversial, no more than common sense. This attitude, I think, is quite wrong. Any given conception of propositions and analysis is in fact inextricably tangled in metaphysics. The idea of 'finding and analysing the proposition expressed' by a given sentence is one that makes sense only within a given philosophical context, which imposes constraints on the process; the philosophical context cannot itself, therefore, be based on a neutral or uncontroversial notion of analysis.

My thesis is thus a very general claim about the role of propositions and analysis in analytic philosophy. My subject, of course, is much narrower, and can only suggest the plausibility of the general thesis. What I shall chiefly discuss are Russell's changing views about propositions, and also the correlative idea of analysis, in the period, roughly, from 1900 to 1914. Those views illustrate my thesis with great clarity, because Russell seldom completely covers up or smooths over the difficulties which face his view at any given time; he simply treats them as problems to be solved, and moves on. His views change quite markedly over time, because at each point he encounters difficulties which require shifts, which in turn throw up further difficulties, so that a stable view remains as remote at the end as at the beginning. It is not that there is a knock-down argument against any of Russell's views, or that his views are in any very straightforward sense incoherent; it is rather that in Russell's hands the notion of a proposition simply begins to collapse of its own weight.

I shall start by talking about the notion of a proposition very generally, and then about the views that Russell puts forward in *The Principles of Mathematics*; later Russellian doctrines will emerge as we go.

It should strike us as noteworthy that each of Frege and Russell has as central to his thought the idea of an abstract entity which represents, or perhaps *is*, the content of a declarative sentence. For Russell, of course, this is the notion of a proposition; for Frege it is that of a *Gedanke*. Part of the reason for this may be that both Frege and Russell were mathematicians, and began their serious philosophical careers by attempting to give an account of mathematics, where the idea of the abstract content of a sentence seems to be at home.[1] As W. D. Hart puts it: 'Frege . . . may have drawn on his mathematical education for some of his philosophical ideals. The theorem is an ideal of mathematical statement. It is typically a single sentence meant to be strong enough to stand by itself: what it says should be impersonal, unambiguous and impervious to context; above all, it should be true utterly without qualification' (Hart, 'Clarity', 199). Although my focus is on Russellian propositions, I shall mention points of contrast with Fregean *Gedanken*. The fact that these contrasts exist, and are significant, suggests that articulating what may seem to be the commonsensical notion of the content of a declarative sentence is by no means a straightforward task.

As a first step in articulating the notion of a proposition we may say that it is to be an abstract entity which is, so to speak, like a sentence only more so. The properties of a proposition are to be those properties which might be thought to characterize declarative sentences, except that where a sentence has those properties in a messy or unclear way, the proposition has them in a purified form. Truth or falsehood is the most obvious of these properties. Declarative sentences, one might suppose, are what have truth-values. But a declarative sentence may be vague or ambiguous, and so of uncertain truth-value; it may be true only approximately, or to some extent; it may change its truth-value from one occasion of utterance to the next. A proposition, by contrast, is true or false eternally and without qualification. It is, we might say, a bearer of truth-values suitable for the theorems of mathematics. Similarly, a sentence is the object of understanding, but may be misunderstood, or only more or less understood. A proposition, by contrast, if grasped, is grasped completely. The metaphor of grasping here is Frege's. Russell, as we shall see, speaks of being acquainted with a proposition or—slightly later—of being acquainted with the constituents of the proposition and uniting them into a judgment by means of a mental act of judging. The point, however, is the same: the vagueness and unclarity which we might associate with understanding sentences is replaced by a definite, clear-cut, all-or-nothing idea. So sentences come to be seen as simply the more or less

---

[1] I do not, of course, want to claim that *only* a mathematician could have had the idea of the content of a sentence as an independent abstract entity. Indeed Russell attributes it to Moore (see the Preface to *Principles*; and see Moore's 'The Nature of Judgement', 176–93). It is, however, in the context of views about mathematics that this conception of a proposition seems most natural, and most powerful.

defective expressions of propositions, abstract entities which are the real bearers of content and vehicles of truth-values; propositions lie behind our sentences, and give them such meaning as they have.

One immediate presupposition of the idea of a proposition is that we can usefully and significantly talk of a proposition as an entity, which may be considered in isolation. This is a sort of atomism of sentences or propositions: that a sentence conveys what it conveys as a discrete unit, independent of the discourse with which it is surrounded. Taken as a quite general claim about sentences, this seems to me quite implausible. It is, of course, open to someone to claim that this sort of atomism holds of propositions, even though it does not hold of sentences. I shall not, however, try to argue these points here; my focus will be on issues more relevant to Russell's attempt to find a conception of the proposition which would satisfy him.

To this point I have been talking about the origin of the idea of a proposition as a sort of abstract super-sentence. And just as sentences have a grammatical structure, so propositions too, at least on Russell's conception, have a structure. A proposition, as Russell conceives the notion, contains constituent parts; it consists, indeed, of certain constituents in a certain, definite arrangement.[2] He seems, indeed, to think of a proposition as made up of its constituents in a quite literal sense, almost as a wall is made up of bricks. Now one crucial point about Russell's conception of propositions in *The Principles of Mathematics* is that he assumes that in most cases the structure of a proposition very closely reflects the structure of the sentence which expresses it. Thus in section 46 of *Principles* he says, for example:

The correctness of our philosophical analysis of a proposition may be checked by the exercise of assigning the meaning of each word in the sentence expressing the proposition. On the whole, grammar seems to bring us much nearer to a correct logic than the current opinions of philosophers . . .

A potential problem here is seen in the phrase '*the* sentence' expressing a given proposition. Russell individuates propositions extremely finely, but even on his view a given proposition can be expressed by more than one sentence. Nothing

---

[2] There is a contrast here even with Frege, whose views are close to Russell on these matters. A Fregean *Gedanke* does not appear to consist of definite constituents in a definite arrangement. Frege is not wholly consistent on this point, but he sometimes puts forward the view that a *Gedanke* can be analysed in different ways, equally correct. Thus the *Gedanke* expressed by a subject-predicate sentence (or perhaps by a given utterance of the sentence) might on one occasion by analysed as made up of the sense of a proper name and the sense of a first-level predicate, and on another occasion as made up of the sense of a first-level predicate and the sense of a second-level predicate. On this view, to ask: but which are the real constituents of the *Gedanke*? would be to ask a misleading question. Thus Frege says explicitly: 'We must notice, however, that one and the same thought (*Gedanke*) can be split up in different ways and so can be seen as put together out of parts in different ways.'—'A Brief Survey of my Logical Doctrines', in *Posthumous Writings*, 201–2.

rules out the possibility that one proposition should be expressed by two sentences with different grammatical structures. And what then of the assumption that the structure of a proposition is more or less isomorphic to that of the sentence which expresses it? At the time of *Principles*, however, this problem does not seem to occur to Russell; on his later view, as we shall see, the problem does not arise, because he abandons the assumption that there is generally an isomorphism between a sentence and the proposition which it expresses.

Let us now take up another fundamental feature of Russellian propositions, which is shared by Fregean *Gedanke*. Even from our brief sketch, it is clear that propositions are context-independent; they do not depend for their content or their truth-values upon their context of utterance. Indeed this feature is so fundamental that the way I expressed it is misleading. A proposition, as an abstract entity, *has* no context of utterance. A more accurate way to put the point is that Russell assumes that our utterances express propositions, vehicles of content and bearers of truth-values, which are abstract, independent of context. A sentence which expresses a given proposition is spoken or written in a given context, and may express the proposition that it expresses only because of that context; but nothing analogous can be said of propositions themselves.

The sentences of mathematics, as we have seen, seem to lend themselves naturally to Russell's way of thinking: it is not hard to see how one might take such a sentence as expressing a content which is eternal, context-independent, and free of the contingencies of our means of expressing it. This is true also of theoretical sentences of the more abstract natural sciences. But such sentences are more the exception than the rule. Very few of the sentences that we actually utter say what they say, and have the truth-values that they have, independent of the contexts in which they are uttered. Most are dependent for their contents and their truth-values upon their contexts of utterance. This is most obviously true of sentences containing so-called indexical or token-reflexive expressions, such as 'I', 'here', 'now', and 'this'; sentences containing such expressions are obviously dependent, for their truth-values, upon the identity of the utterer and the time and place and circumstances of utterance. Sentences of this sort are sometimes treated by philosophers as a sort of oddity, but in fact they account for most of the sentences actually uttered. The phenomenon of indexicality, however, is more widespread than our examples perhaps suggest. Clearly sentences containing tensed verbs also fall under this heading; so do sentences containing proper names, for many people may share a single name, with uses of the name being disambiguated by the context of utterance.

The phenomenon of indexicality has often been treated as posing special difficulties or puzzles, or at any rate as requiring discussion additional to that afforded the general nature of language. This is one aspect of the influence that the notion of a proposition has had on much subsequent analytic philosophy.

Context-independent utterances are in fact quite unusual, especially in the spoken language. Yet very often that type of utterance is, so to speak, treated as the norm, so that deviations from it are what require special explanation and treatment. In particular, the issue is often one of finding a systematic way of representing the context-dependent as context-independent, ie. finding systematic rules to indicate what context-independent contents our context-dependent sentences in fact express. The assumption here is that each of our sentences can be thought of as expressing a context-independent content, and perhaps also that we only fully understand the workings of a sentence when we see how to convert it into a context-independent equivalent.

There are, however, arguments which suggest that except in quite special cases the notion of the content of a sentence cannot be peeled off from the context of utterance of the sentence; consideration of these arguments will lead us to a feature of Russellian propositions which we have not yet mentioned, a feature which also distinguishes them from Fregean *Gedanke*. These arguments, at least in the form that I shall discuss them, are to be found in the work of F. H. Bradley,[3] the idealist against whom much of Russell's polemic is directed. Although the point can be made more generally, I shall indicate how the argument goes by talking about sentences that make reference to particular parts of time. The claim here is that such sentences are in fact dependent for their meaning and their truth-value on their contexts of utterance, even if they do not contain any overtly indexical expressions.

Consider an example such as 'It is raining at Heathrow at 1600 GMT on 23 February, 1974'. The sentence is Quine's, nearly enough, and it is intended as an example of what Quine calls a standing sentence—one that is not dependent for its truth-value on the occasion of its utterance.[4] We have familiar ways of keeping track of the years: we say how many years have elapsed from some notable event, the accession of an emperor, perhaps, or the birth of a saviour. But how, from a more distant perspective, is that notable event itself to be located in time? Given that the same system is still in use, there is no problem, for we can locate the starting point indexically, relative to me-here-now: we begin our system of numbering years with a year which is one thousand nine hundred and ninety-three years before the year in which I am writing *this*. For the same reason, once the system is established it does not in fact matter if the given event did not take place in the year that is supposed—the system functions because it is in general use, not because of distant history. But if a given system were no longer in use, and if we did not know the relation of that system to the one we use, we should have to rely on a description of the event, and we have no guarantee that such a description would suffice to identify it uniquely.

---

[3] See Bradley, *Principles of Logic*, especially book 1, ch. 2; see also Strawson, *Individuals*, especially chs. 2 and 3.   [4] Quine, 'The Nature of Natural Knowledge', 67–81; see especially p. 75.

Still, it may be said, the system that we have for keeping track of time is perfectly adequate. Given not only its intended audience, but anyone who is ever at all likely to read it, surely Quine's sentence will do perfectly well to convey what it conveys independent of time and circumstances of utterance. This is correct; for all human purposes, we can achieve context-independence. But it is far from clear that the qualification, 'for all human purposes', is one that we can assume when talking about Russellian propositions, for these are abstract eternal entities, altogether independent of human beings. By those standards, it may seem that any sentence referring to a particular part of time or of space is unavoidably context-dependent. (Nothing here counts against *Quine's* use of the notion of a standing sentence, which has no such metaphysical pretensions or ambitions as Russell's notion of a proposition.)

The claim that this argument points towards is that *none* of our sentences, except perhaps for the abstract sentences of mathematics and theoretical science, are in fact context-independent. But then how can we think of the notion of content, in such a way that it avoids these difficulties? The argument suggests that we cannot, and hence that for most sentences it is incoherent to think in terms of the content of the sentence, as something that can be wholly abstracted from the context in which the sentence is used, and treated as an independent abstract object.

Now in *The Principles of Mathematics* the notion of a proposition which Russell takes as paradigmatic is in fact not vulnerable to this sort of argument (whereas Frege's notion of a *Gedanke* may be). The crucial point here is that the entities which are the subject matter of the proposition are, on Russell's conception, paradigmatically, *contained* in the proposition. Thus the proposition expressed by the sentence 'Socrates is mortal' *contains* the actual person, Socrates. More to the point of the example used above, a proposition about some particular moment of time will contain that moment of time. Thus Russellian propositions are hybrid entities. On the one hand, they are, like Fregean *Gedanke*, abstract entities representing or embodying the content of a declarative sentence. On the other hand, unlike their Fregean analogues, these abstract entities can contain concrete entities, such as people and moments of time.

It is not explicit in what Russell says that he adopts this conception of a proposition, as an abstract entity which may contain concrete entities, in order to counter Bradley's argument.[5] It is, however, quite plausible that Russell designed his notion of a proposition to meet the threat of Bradley's argument. And a closely connected, more general, anti-idealist point is explicit. On a Fregean conception, which has become widely accepted, propositions or their analogues

---

[5] In G. E. Moore's early work it is clear that his analogue of the notion of a proposition, which was an important influence on Russell, evolves out of disagreement with Bradley. It is, however, not explicit that the disagreement is at the point relevant to my discussion here. See Moore's 'The Nature of Judgment'.

contain entities (*Sinne*, for Frege) other than the objects they are about; they are about those objects in virtue of some relation which their constituents stand in to them. We might generically call this relation *designation*.[6] On Russell's conception, however, propositions paradigmatically do not contain ideas or senses which in some way designate the reality that the proposition is about; the proposition itself contains that reality, and does not merely designate it. It is clear that Russell is deeply distrustful of the idea of designation. Thus he holds that in grasping a proposition the mind is in direct contact with the entities that it thinks or speaks about. Intermediate entities, such as Fregean *Sinne*, would be a denial of this direct contact; for Russell, however, it is only our being in direct contact with entities outside the mind that makes it possible to speak or think of them at all.[7]

According to *The Principles of Mathematics*, then, propositions paradigmatically have two fundamental features. First, a proposition will, in general, have the same structure as the sentence expressing it. We noted one problem here, arising from the possibility that two sentences of different structures may express the same proposition. A further issue concerns the qualification 'in general'. Russell holds back from saying that the normal case is universal; what sorts of factors could justify departing from the norm? The answer to this question is by no means clear.

The second fundamental feature is, to put it negatively, the denial of designation: that propositions, at least paradigmatically, do not contain entities (such as Fregean *Sinne*) which *designate* the things they are about; propositions, rather, *contain* those things. The paradigm of a proposition is that expressed by 'Socrates is mortal'. This proposition has exactly the structure of the sentence. Also it contains Socrates, and the property of mortality. A crucial consequence of the denial of designation is that for Russell at this point there is no independent notion of a *fact*: since the proposition that Socrates is mortal contains Socrates and the property of mortality, it simply *is* the fact that Socrates is mortal. Facts, for Russell, are true propositions. It follows immediately from this that we cannot explain what it is for a proposition to be true by appealing to the holding of a corresponding fact, or indeed in any other way. Truth and falsehood are for Russell (as for Moore and for Frege) 'incapable of analysis' (Russell, 'Meinong', 76); this point, as we shall see, comes to play an important role in Russell's finally abandoning the doctrine of propositions (see below pp. 45–7).

This kind of paradigm seems to make the notion of a proposition quite straightforward and attractive. Even at the time of writing *Principles*, however,

---

[6] Frege uses the word *bedeuten*; there are, however, great difficulties in Frege's philosophy with the view that there is some *one* relation here.

[7] See the exchange of letters with Frege, Frege to Russell, 13 November, 1904, Russell to Frege, 12 December. Published in Frege, *Nachgelassene Schriften*, vol. ii; and translated in Frege, *Philosophical and Mathematical Correspondence*. See also Russell's 'Knowledge by Acquaintance', 221–2.

Russell could see that it would not work in general. It is a paradigm that exerts great influence, but it cannot be universally applied. What works well for sentences such as 'Socrates is mortal' does not seem to work at all for the sentence 'I met a man', as Russell himself points out. Suppose the sentence is true; I did meet a man—Quine, let us say. Still 'I met a man' does not seem to say the same as 'I met Quine', so it ought not to express the same proposition. Worse, suppose the sentence is false, that I did not meet a man. False sentences too ought to express propositions, but clearly if I did not meet a man there is no one who even seems to be a good candidate for being the constituent of the proposition corresponding to the words 'a man'. In short, the sentence 'I met a man' seems absolutely to resist assimilation to the paradigm mentioned above. How then can Russell treat such sentences? The answer lies in Russell's notion of *denoting*, and the theory of denoting concepts, a theory articulated in *Principles* and subsequently rejected in 'On Denoting'. A *denoting concept* is an entity with the following useful and agreeable property: when it occurs in a proposition, the proposition is not about it (the denoting concept), but rather about some other entity, that denoted by the denoting concept. Thus in the case of the sentence 'I met a man', the words 'a man' correspond to a constituent of the proposition, but that constituent is not Quine or any other man. It is, rather, the denoting concept *a man*, which denotes a curious sort of disjunctive combination of all men. This entity is stipulated to have exactly the properties needed to yield the required result, that the proposition is true if I met at least one man, and false if I met no men.

   In general Russell holds that the presence in a sentence of any description, ie. any phrase formed with 'a' or 'the' or 'all' or 'any' or 'some' or 'every', indicates the presence, in the corresponding proposition, of a denoting concept. It is perhaps an advantage of this theory that it enables us, in general, to preserve the idea of the isomorphism of structure between sentence and proposition: a phrase such as 'a man' or 'every man' corresponds to a constituent of the proposition, namely the relevant denoting concept. There are also, however, drawbacks to the theory. One is its formidable complexity, and the vexing philosophical difficulties which it seems to throw up at every turn. In some cases these difficulties result in an undermining of the isomorphism of structure between sentence and proposition: thus Russell distinguishes two propositions which may be expressed by 'Socrates is a man', namely that more accurately expressed by 'Socrates is a-man', and that more accurately expressed by 'Socrates is-a man' (see *Principles*, 54, second footnote).

   A second, more obvious, drawback to Russell's theory of denoting concepts is of course that the theory of denoting concepts relies on the idea of designation which Russell's paradigmatic conception of the proposition avoided; indeed we might almost say that 'denotation' is just another word for designation. It is this,

I think, that lies behind many of the philosophical problems that Russell has with denoting; in particular it is at work in his arguments against the notion in 'On Denoting'.

Russell introduces the theory of denoting concepts to extend his conception of propositions so that it covers cases which do not seem to fit his paradigm. He also uses it in response to another issue, which plays little role in his thought at first, but later comes to dominate it. This issue we might broadly call epistemological. The primary focus here is not so much on how we can *know* this or that proposition, but rather on how we can *understand* propositions. I call the issue epistemological, even though it is not directly concerned with knowledge, because it is concerned not with what propositions there are, or what they are like, but with our relation to them.

Russell's fundamental epistemic relation—the means by which, on his view, the mind can escape from its own boundaries—is *acquaintance*, a relation of direct and presuppositionless contact between the mind and objects outside it. Clearly to say we are acquainted with things does not explain how the mind escapes its own boundaries, it simply asserts that it does. But that's the point. For Russell there can be no complexity to our contact with outside things, no story to be told: we simply are in contact with them, and that's that. It is not a defect but a virtue of acquaintance that there is nothing more to be said about it beyond the little I have indicated. Now in *The Principles of Mathematics* Russell pays very little attention to issues of knowledge and understanding. He seems, however, to presuppose that to understand a proposition is to be acquainted with it, and thus with its constituents.

This view of understanding is in tension with the conception of propositions that we have discussed. It seems to be true that I understand the proposition expressed by 'Socrates is mortal', and on Russell's account this proposition contains Socrates. According to his inchoate view of understanding, it would follow that I am acquainted with Socrates. As soon as one considers such a claim carefully it is likely to seem quite implausible, so that there must be something wrong with the theory that implies it. In *The Principles of Mathematics*, however, Russell's attention is elsewhere, and this sort of fact does not seem to worry him. At that time he seems to accept that we are acquainted with Socrates, and with the King of France, and with anything else that one can mention (later, as we shall see, he focuses more on such issues, and takes a narrower view of the objects of acquaintance). In one instance, however, Russell does give careful consideration to the question of our ability to understand. This instance is the case of propositions about infinitely many objects, eg. the false proposition expressed by 'All prime numbers are odd'. If we were to construe this proposition according to the Russellian paradigm, it would contain all the prime numbers, ie. it would be a proposition of infinite complexity. Russell is agnostic about the question whether there *are* such propositions, but he does say that, in any case, we are not acquainted with any: 'all the propositions known to us', he says, 'are of finite complexity' (*Principles*, 145).

How, then, does Russell account for our ability to understand the proposition that all prime numbers are odd? The answer is that he invokes the theory of denoting concepts. Our false proposition about the primes does not contain all of the prime numbers, and does not need to. What it contains in their place, so to speak, is the denoting concept *all prime numbers*. In virtue of containing this denoting concept, the proposition is about all the primes. And this idea can be used to explain how we can understand the proposition. It may be implausible to suppose that I am acquainted with each of the prime numbers, but it is open to Russell to claim that I *am* acquainted with the denoting concept, *all prime numbers* (indeed one of the advantages of denoting concepts is that it is open to Russell to claim almost anything about them).

In the period immediately after *The Principles of Mathematics* issues of understanding come to be increasingly prominent in Russell's writings. This can be seen most clearly in a number of works which he left unpublished—perhaps because he found no theory of such matters which satisfied him even for a short period. In the manuscript 'On Meaning and Denotation', written when Arthur Balfour was Prime Minister of England, Russell says that the two phrases 'Arthur Balfour' and 'the present Prime Minister of England' in some ways function the same: each can be used to talk about a certain man. In other ways, however, he says there is a significant difference between the two phrases:

When we make a statement about Arthur Balfour, he himself forms part of the object before our minds, ie. of the proposition stated … no one who does not know what is the designation of the name 'Arthur Balfour' can understand what we *mean*: the object of our thought cannot, by our statement, be conveyed to him. But when we say 'the present Prime Minister of England believes in retaliation', it is possible for a person to understand us completely without his knowing that Mr. Arthur Balfour is Prime Minister, and indeed without his even having heard of Mr Arthur Balfour. (Russell, *Collected Papers*, iv. 315–16)

Perhaps even more striking in this regard is the earlier manuscript, 'Points About Denoting'. Here Russell distinguishes the meaning of a proposition from its denotation: the meaning of the proposition that the Prime Minister of England in 1904 advocates retaliation would contain a denoting concept which denotes Balfour; the denotation of the proposition would contain Balfour himself. Using this distinction, Russell very clearly articulates what I shall call *the principle of acquaintance*: 'It is necessary, for the understanding of a prop[osition], to have *acquaintance* with the *meaning* of every constituent of the meaning, and of the whole; it is not necessary to have acquaintance with such constituents of the denotation as are not constituents of the meaning' (*Collected Papers*, iv. 307).

The manuscripts from which the above passages are drawn cannot be dated precisely, but internal evidence shows that they were written after *The Principles of Mathematics* and before 'On Denoting', ie. while Russell held the theory of denoting concepts. What they clearly indicate is that during this period Russell increasingly subjected the analysis of propositions to epistemological constraints: roughly, it became an explicit and self-conscious criterion of an acceptable analysis that it show that the proposition is made up of constituents with which we are acquainted. Putting it this way may be misleading, because it makes it sound as if the notion of *acquaintance* which we are invoking is itself fixed and clear-cut, whereas in fact this notion is no firmer than is the notion of the analysis of propositions. The principle of acquaintance is articulated—for the first time in Russell's work, as far as I know—in the manuscript 'Points About Denoting'. It is not, however, a fixed and definite principle which Russell denied until that time, and then began to accept for some reason. There is probably no time, during the period we are concerned with, at which Russell would have *denied* the principle. What changes is that Russell becomes increasingly interested in epistemological questions. He articulates the principle, and begins to use it to determine how propositions are to be analysed (or, more accurately, what proposition we may take a given sentence to express). Whereas in *Principles* Russell had been willing to accept that we are acquainted with almost anything, he later takes an increasingly stringent view of the objects of acquaintance. This is not a sudden change, but takes place gradually over the ten or more years following the completion of *Principles*.

What is crucial about this from our point of view is that the epistemological constraint which the principle of acquaintance embodies, and especially the notion of acquaintance itself, cannot be the *result* of analysis. They are, rather, requirements imposed from the outside on that notion. Once imposed they drastically affect what counts as a satisfactory analysis, and hence also what propositions are like, ie. they function as constraints upon the notions of a proposition and of analysis. At any given moment Russell tends to take a given group of constraints for granted, and speak as if analysis were a neutral process; but the way the constraints shift makes it clear that this is not so.

Russell only briefly explores his increasing epistemological concerns in the context of the theory of denoting concepts. 'On Denoting', written in 1905, rejects that theory in favour of a quite different view. Before we discuss that development, however, it is worth noting that the shift to the view of 'On Denoting' is neither necessary nor sufficient for this increasing concern with epistemology. If Russell had not made that shift, his new concerns would have led, rather, to an increasing application of the theory of denoting concepts. A sentence such as Russell's 'Arthur Balfour advocates retaliation' is in fact understood by those who are not (in Russell's sense) acquainted with Balfour; so surely

Russell would have come to the view that most proper names stand not for their bearers but for denoting concepts (indeed Russell does explicitly take this step in the case of proper names which fail to name anything).[8] This kind of development—the increasing epistemic constraints imposed on the analysis of propositions—would presumably have continued. If so it would have led him to see denoting no longer as the exception, introduced to account for a relatively small number of particularly troubling sentences, but as the usual case. The paradigm of a proposition containing the object which it is about, a paradigm which exercised great influence on Russell in *Principles* was being undermined by epistemic considerations in the period before 'On Denoting'. Russell's increasing epistemic concerns led him to rely more heavily on the theory of denoting concepts. The reliance on the theory of denoting concepts, however, is also, as we pointed out, a reliance on designation: the denoting concept denotes (or designates) its object. This by itself provides Russell with a reason to be suspicious of the theory of denoting concepts, and this suspicion is a crucial part of the background to the rejection of that theory in 'On Denoting'.

There are, of course, other factors at work in 'On Denoting'. One is simply the internal difficulties of the theory of denoting concepts as Russell attempted to articulate and develop it. These difficulties may be traced out in unpublished manuscripts in the period leading up to 'On Denoting', and issue in a notoriously complex and difficult argument in that essay. Another factor is the need to come up with an analysis of propositions which meshes in the right way with the logic that Russell had developed. It ought, one might think, to follow *by logic* from the proposition that John is the man who broke the bank at Monte Carlo that someone broke the bank at Monte Carlo, that if James is distinct from John then James did *not* break the bank at Monte Carlo, and so on. If we analyse propositions using the theory of denoting concepts, however, these inferences are obscure, and do not appear to be a matter of logic at all. The analysis put forward in 'On Denoting', by contrast, makes them straightforward inferences in (what we would call) first-order logic with identity. So here, then, is another constraint on analysis: that it ought, as far as possible, to assimilate obviously correct inferences to valid inference patterns of logic.

Clearly there is a great deal more that could be said about Russell's reasons for making the change from the theory of denoting concepts to the view put forward in 'On Denoting'. I shall not, however, discuss this matter any more here.[9] More relevant to our concerns is the fact that according to the method of analysis put forward in 'On Denoting' most propositions have a structure which is very

---

[8] See 'The Existential Import of Propositions', 398–401; reprinted in Russell, *Essays in Analysis*, 98–102; see especially p. 100.

[9] For some discussion on this matter, see the present author's *Russell, Idealism, and the Emergence of Analytic Philosophy*, ch. 6, especially pp. 249–54.

unlike the grammatical structure of the sentences which are usually used to express those propositions. Russell now completely rejects the isomorphism between sentence and proposition which *Principles* had assumed as the usual case, if not the invariable rule. Thus take the sentence which in our earlier discussion functioned as a paradigm of such isomorphism: 'Socrates is mortal'. When Russell comes to apply the method of analysis implicit in 'On Denoting' to (ordinary) proper names, he draws the conclusion that this sentence does *not* express a subject-predicate proposition. It expresses, rather, a proposition whose large-scale structure is that of an existential quantification. This is a striking result. The structure of a sentence is no longer to be taken as a guide to the structure of the underlying proposition. On the contrary: Russell's work from this point on is full of warnings that the superficial structure of language is misleading, and does *not* reflect the underlying structure. There is thus a sort of dialectic. The idea of a proposition's having a structure is clearly drawn from the fact that sentences have structure; a proposition is initially conceived of as having a structure isomorphic with that of the sentence which expresses it, the ontological composition of the proposition mirroring the semantic composition of the sentence. But then it is claimed that most or all of our actual sentences do not in fact succeed in reflecting the real structure of the proposition; this real structure becomes something hidden, which we try to find.

This development highlights one presupposition of the idea of philosophical analysis, as we find it in Russell (and in Moore, and in many others). That idea requires not merely that propositions be articulated, that they have a certain structure, but also that this structure may be reflected, more or less accurately, by sentences which express that proposition. It makes clear sense to say of a sentence that it contains an existential quantifier, say. It is, however, far less clear what could be meant by saying that a proposition, an abstract entity, contains a quantifier. Yet Russell must be able to say such things. The claim of Russell's theory of descriptions—'that paradigm of philosophy' in the words of Ramsey, in a description endorsed by Moore (Ramsey, 'Foundations of Mathematics', 263)—is not merely that for certain purposes it may be *convenient* to rewrite definite descriptions according to a certain protocol, say, to make sure that within a given formal language we are never left with names that fail to refer. The claim is, rather, that propositions expressed by sentences containing definite descriptions *actually have* a structure which is accurately, or more accurately, expressed by the rewritten version. This rewritten version is itself, of course, a sentence, and a sentence which draws on the resources of (what we would call) first-order logic with identity. And of course the claim is that such propositions always *did* have that structure, even before the discovery of first-order logic. This no doubt accounts in part for the confidence, even arrogance, that one sometimes finds in Russell's writings: only now, after centuries of confusion, do we have the tools which enable us to discover the real structures underlying our discourse.

The aim of philosophical analysis, seen in this light, is to find that sentence which most accurately reflects the real structure of the proposition that we are interested in. We can illustrate this conception of analysis by talking briefly about Moore's so-called paradox of analysis. The paradox is roughly this: in analysing a sentence, we simply pass from one sentence expressing a proposition to another sentence expressing the same proposition. If the first sentence really did express the proposition, surely this transition cannot represent philosophical progress. Yet—and this is where the paradox comes—there *does* seem to be philosophical progress, at least in some cases of analysis. Now the answer which our framework suggests is that we are not, in general, aware of the structure of the propositions that we grasp; and that one sentence which expresses a proposition may correspond more closely to the structure of the proposition than another sentence which expresses the same proposition. Then philosophical progress consists in passing from a sentence which does not reflect the structure of the underlying proposition, or does so only very loosely, to a sentence which comes closer to reflecting that structure, or even to one that is completely isomorphic to it. It may be a discovery to find the structure of the proposition which a given sentence expresses. What is actually discovered, or produced, however, is a new sentence, which is claimed to reflect the structure of the underlying proposition. The point to emphasize is thus that all of this depends upon the idea that a proposition has a structure, and that a *sentence* can reflect that structure more or less closely. Yet if propositions really are abstract entities, they are completely unlike sentences; so a crucial assumption is made when we assume that a sentence may reflect the structure of a proposition.

This idea of underlying structure, of the deep structure that backs up and makes possible the sentences we utter, has had a formative influence on philosophy—and, indeed, on linguistics—since Russell. Certainly this idea can be found, at least in a limited context, in Frege. In Russell, however, we see the idea full blown and quite generally applied. As Wittgenstein says in the *Tractatus*, in a passage that seems to allude to the theory of descriptions: 'Russells Verdienst ist es, gezeigt zu haben, dass die schienbare logische Form des Satzes nicht seine wirchliche muss' (*Tractatus* 4.0031: It is Russell's service to have shown that the apparent logical form of a proposition does not have to be its real one).

Although of fundamental importance, this idea of philosophical analysis is also very problematic. The obvious problem is that what we actually have to deal with are not propositions but utterances of sentences. If we cannot assume that the proposition expressed by a sentence has the same structure as the sentence itself, then we need some other guide to the structure of the proposition. If two philosophers consider a given sentence, and one says that its analysis is so-and-so, and the other says it is such-and-such, how can this dispute be settled? Saying that analysis is a process of finding a sentence which accurately reflects the structure of the underlying proposition is of no help, for each philosopher can claim to have done that. Russell, at least at certain points, would have claimed to be able to perceive the proposition, in some non-sensuous sense of perception (for this reason he would perhaps have disagreed with the statement that what we actually have to deal with are not propositions but utterances of sentences). But reliance on non-sensuous perception hardly recommends itself as a method of settling disputes, for each party can simply claim to 'perceive' the given proposition as having the structure that he or she attributes to it. Clearly this will not help to settle any dispute about the real structure of the proposition.

I talk in this way of the dispute being unsettleable not from some dogma that every real question must be settleable, but rather because it emphasizes a crucial point. The idea of philosophical analysis—the process of trying to find the structure of the proposition that underlies a given sentence—is empty until some constraints are imposed upon it. We must have some idea of what constitutes a satisfactory analysis, some criterion of success, before the idea has any content at all. Thus for Russell, as we saw, one criterion of success came to be that a final analysis of a sentence should enable us to assimilate its behaviour in inference to established procedures of logic. A second criterion is that embodied in the principle of acquaintance: the analysis must show that a given proposition is made up only of constituents with which we are acquainted. As Russell says at the end of 'On Denoting': 'in every proposition that we can apprehend (ie. not only those whose truth or falsehood we can judge of, but in all that we can think about) all the constituents are really entities with which we have immediate acquaintance.' Russell there speaks of this as a *result* of the theory of descriptions, but this seems to me quite misleading; it is something more like the aim of the theory—the result being that the aim is indeed achieved, or anyway a step towards its achievement taken, at least to Russell's satisfaction. (In speaking of this as a criterion of the success of the analysis it is important also to bear in mind that it is not at all obvious or uncontroversial which entities we are in fact acquainted with, or even whether the idea of acquaintance is a sensible one at all. As we have seen, Russell changed his mind significantly and frequently on the question of just which entities we are acquainted with.)

The increasing weight given to the epistemic factor creates further difficulties for Russell. One is simply that, as Russell interprets the notion of acquaintance after 1905, the principle of acquaintance embodies a demand that he cannot meet. It requires that any sentence I understand can be shown to express a proposition composed only of elements with which I am acquainted; as Russell becomes increasingly stringent in his account of the things we are acquainted with, this demand seems less and less plausible. A second point is perhaps even more troubling, for it threatens the motivation behind the idea of a proposition. I said that according to 'On Denoting' the sentence 'Socrates is mortal' expresses a proposition of existential form. But this is not quite accurate. According to Russell's view, when the Greek equivalent of the sentence was uttered by Socrates himself it presumably expressed a proposition of *subject-predicate* form, a proposition of which Socrates himself is a constituent. For those of us not acquainted with Socrates, however, the sentence, as we have mentioned, expresses an existentially quantified proposition. More significantly, even for those of us now living, however, there is no one proposition that is expressed by the sentence. Which proposition it expresses will vary from person to person. For any given person, his or her utterance of the sentence will express a proposition containing constituents, in some way related to Socrates, with which the utterer is acquainted. Since different people are acquainted with different entities, it may be that no two of us express the same proposition when we utter the sentence.

This is a very remarkable conclusion. The notion of a proposition, as we saw at the outset, was to be an abstract entity which summed up the content of a sentence in a wholly impersonal and context-independent way. Part of the motivation for the notion comes from the idea that, as Frege puts it, there is not your Pythagorean Theorem and my Pythagorean Theorem, but simply *the* Pythagorean Theorem (Frege, 'Der Gedanke', 68). This still holds, on Russell's new view, for the theorems of mathematics, but it does not hold for much else. In the case of 'Socrates is mortal', for example, it *does* seem as if there is your proposition and my proposition. Russell has some work to do to explain how it can be that if you say 'Socrates is mortal' and I say 'Socrates is not mortal' we have in fact contradicted one another; and it is by no means obvious that he succeeds in giving a satisfactory explanation of this fact—yet it is this sort of fact which in some sense underlies the whole idea of the content of a declarative sentence which Russell's talk of propositions aims to articulate. Thus the epistemic constraints which give content to the notion of analysis, as Russell employs it, also threaten to undermine the intuitive foundation of the idea of a proposition.

Russell becomes increasingly sceptical about the existence of propositions, and finally concludes that there are no such things. The chief reasons for this, however, do not have to do with the issue just discussed but with points touched on earlier. We saw above that Russell's paradigmatic conception of a proposition, as containing the entities it is about, allows no room for a distinction between facts and true propositions: facts simply *are* true propositions on this conception. But propositions, of course, can be false as well as true; if facts are simply true propositions then we cannot explain the distinction between truth and falsehood in what might seem to be the most natural way, ie. by saying that true propositions express facts, and false ones do not. As we saw, indeed, Russell in 1904 thinks that we cannot *explain* the distinction between truth and falsehood at all: it must simply be taken for granted, as the starting point of explanations.

Even in 1904, the way that Russell expresses the indefinability of truth and falsehood, and the conclusions that he draws from it, suggest that it is a view about which he is deeply uneasy. Thus, as if hankering after an explanatory notion of a fact, he says: 'it *seems* to remain that, when a proposition is false, *something* does not subsist which would subsist if the proposition were true' (Russell, 'Meinong', 75). And most strikingly, he says: 'this theory [ie. the view that truth and falsehood are undefinable] *seems* to leave our preference for truth a mere unaccountable prejudice.' And he concludes the essay by saying: 'as for the preference which most people . . . feel in favour of true propositions, this must be based, apparently, upon an ultimate ethical proposition: "It is good to believe true propositions, and bad to believe false ones" ' (*op. cit.*, p. 76). He adds a joke whose cleverness is unlikely to allay the unease he clearly feels about this position, saying of his ultimate ethical proposition: 'This proposition, it is to be hoped, is true; but if not, there is no reason to think that we do ill in believing it' (*loc. cit.*).

Even though Russell is here *advocating* the view that truth and falsehood are indefinable, one senses that he is not fully convinced; the consequences that he draws from it are, as he states them, simply too implausible, and he cannot get rid of the feeling that the truth of a true proposition is due to the existence (or subsistence) of something which would not exist if that proposition were false—ie. he cannot get rid of the feeling that there are (proposition-independent) facts, or entities which will play the same role.[10] He later expresses this worry in a way that connects with another theme we have mentioned: his increasing stringency about just what entities we are acquainted with. He begins, that is to say, to have doubts about whether we are in fact acquainted with propositions—in particular, with false propositions. Writing in 1913, for example, he says 'It seems plain that a false proposition is not itself an actual entity' (Russell, *Theory of Knowledge*, 109). What this indicates is a shift from a view which takes *proposition* as the fundamental notion of metaphysics to takes *fact* as fundamental. While the notion of a proposition was fundamental, it was merely a curiosity that some propositions, the true ones, are also called facts, while others are not. But when the notion of a fact becomes fundamental, true propositions can be retained by equating them with facts, but false propositions become problematic, at best.

---

[10] It seems likely that Russell's inclination to think that there are *facts* which are independent of propositions—and, indeed, to take the notion of a fact as fundamental—was strengthened by his reading of the pragmatists. In particular, he used the notion of a fact to express his opposition to the pragmatist view of truth. See 'James's Conception of Truth'.

At some time between 1906 and 1910, then, Russell abandons the idea that there are propositions in the sense which he had previously advocated.[11] *Principia Mathematica* makes free use of the notions of proposition and propositional function, and presupposes that we can quantify over such entities; yet according to the doctrine of that work there simply are no propositions. Instead of the theory of propositions, Russell attempts to develop the multiple relation theory of judgement, according to which a belief is not a relation between a mind and a proposition, but rather a relation between a mind and various objects—exactly those objects which, according to the old view, are the constituents of the proposition. Here too he is confronted by insuperable obstacles, which result in his abandoning the book in which he had intended to set out the new theory.[12]

I began this essay by claiming that the notion of a proposition, and the concomitant notion of analysis, should not be taken as uncontroversial or commonsensical notions, to be presupposed at the beginning of philosophical discussion. My attempt to sketch the development of Russell's notion of a proposition has been in service of this thesis. The idea that there are propositions, and that they can be analysed, already makes crucial philosophical assumptions. And the idea of analysis itself gets us nowhere until we put constraints upon the process. Even those who would agree with Russell about the importance of philosophical analysis might put different constraints on the process, and so come up with quite different results. Both the vindication of the process, and the constraints to be put on it, must be the result of philosophical thought. They are presuppositions of the process of philosophical analysis, and cannot themselves be justified by appeal to it. Whatever else philosophical analysis may be, it cannot be a *starting point* for philosophy.

These comments on philosophical analysis can be put in a broader context by contrasting Russell's views on the subject with those of his most distinguished living successor: Quine. Quine speaks of the definition of ordered pair, either by the method of Wiener or by that of Kuratowski, as a 'philosophical paradigm' (surely a conscious echo of Ramsey's comment on Russell's theory of descriptions). Right away we see a difference between Quine and Russell. Wiener's method is not the same as Kuratowski's. (According to the former, for example, the empty set is a member of a member of any ordered pair; not so according to the latter.) But then which method is correct? Which most closely reflects the

---

[11] Russell's 'The Nature of Truth' puts forward an early version of the multiple relation theory of judgment as a possible alternative to his earlier conception of propositions; Russell is there agnostic as to which view is the correct one. In 1910, when Russell reprinted the essay in his *Philosophical Essays*, the first two sections are published under the title 'the Monistic Theory of Truth'; the third section, where the multiple relation theory had been expounded, is replaced by a new essay 'On the Nature of Truth and Falsehood', in which the earlier agnosticism is replaced by an advocacy of the multiple relation theory. That theory is also advanced in the first volume of *Principia Mathematica*; see especially pp. 43 ff. [12] *Theory of Knowledge*.

underlying structure of propositions in which reference is made to ordered pairs? For Quine, unlike Russell, these are misleading questions, better rejected than answered. The definition of ordered pair, he says,

… is paradigmatic of what we are most typically up to when in a philosophical spirit we offer an 'analysis' or an 'explication' of some hitherto inadequately formulated 'idea' or expression. We do not claim synonymy. We do not claim to make clear and explicit what the users of the unclear expression had in mind all along. We do not expose hidden meanings. … We fix on the particular functions of the unclear expression that make it worth troubling about, and then devise a substitute, clear and couched in terms to our liking, that fills these functions. Beyond those conditions of partial agreement, dictated by our interests and purposes, any traits of the explicans come under the head of 'don't-cares'. (Quine, *Word and Object*, 258–9)

Quine's appeal to the definitions of Wiener and Kuratowski clearly represents a continuation of a trend that Russell, along with Frege, began: the use of technical methods in philosophy. What is striking, however, from the present point of view, is how the technical methods stand aloof from the philosophical disagreement. Quine uses Russell's analysis of definite descriptions. The technical method is the same, yet the philosophical purpose, the philosophical gloss, is about as different as it could be. From Quine's point of view, his version of, or substitute for, philosophical analysis is a way of preserving the insights of Russell and others without their excess metaphysical baggage. From the point of view of Russell, and indeed of many current authors, Quine has thrown out the baby with the bathwater. Who is correct is obviously not an issue that can be settled here. Indeed, one aim of this paper is to call into question the very idea of correctness as applied to such questions, or the idea that they can be settled. The methods that one might suppose could be employed to decide such questions, such as Russell's method of philosophical analysis, turn out to have philosophical presuppositions, and internal difficulties, which makes them far from neutral. It thus seems to me an evident truth that sound philosophy cannot hope to *begin* with an analysis of propositions.[13]

---

[13] I am indebted to Stewart Candlish, Thomas Ricketts and, especially, Burton Dreben for their comments on earlier versions of this essay.

3
Logic in Russell's Logicism

Russell, as is well known, was a logicist.[1] He believed, and attempted to demonstrate, that mathematics is reducible to logic. What is perhaps less clear is *why* Russell was a logicist—what philosophical purpose was served by his belief in this doctrine, what motive lay behind his attempt to reduce mathematics to logic. An investigation of this point will, I think, enable us to see more clearly what logicism amounts to in Russell's hands. Russell's logicism was originally intended as part of some kind of argument against Kant, and post-Kantian idealism, but how exactly does this argument go? Russell, unlike the logical positivists, does not seek to use logicism to show that mathematics is analytic; his use of logicism against Kant is quite different from that of the positivists. But how, then, does Russell think that logicism is anti-Kantian? A fairly clear answer to this question emerges from an examination of the earliest phase of Russell's logicism (i.e. that dominated by *The Principles of Mathematics*). In section I, I attempt to articulate this answer. My discussion of the motivation of Russell's early logicism is intended as the starting point of a discussion of Russell's conception of logic, and this is the subject of section II. The significance of the reduction of mathematics to logic depends, of course, upon the conception of logic that is in play. An understanding of the significance that Russell attributed to logicism in the early years of this century will therefore provide us with insight into the conception of logic that he held at that period, and into his reasons for holding it. Russell's conception of logic is antithetical to one crucial element, at least, in the modern view of logic. I shall call this element the model-theoretic conception. I shall try to show that the differences between Russell's conception of logic and this modern conception are closely connected with his use of logicism as an argument against Kant (as he interpreted Kant) and against idealism. In particular, if Russell's conception of logic were the model-theoretic one, his argument against Kant would not have the force that he took it to have. Both the motivation that I attribute to Russell's early logicism, and the conception of logic upon which it relies, are threatened by the paradox which bears Russell's name. The theory of types, which was Russell's response to the paradox, undermines logicism as

---

[1] Given the length of Russell's active philosophical life, and the multiplicity of positions that he held, few claims about his views can be made without qualification as to time. I mean primarily his views in the first decade of the last century, when he did all of his serious work on logicism—*The Principles of Mathematics*, 'Mathematical Logic as Based on the Theory of Types' and the *Principia* itself.

Russell had originally conceived it. These very complex issues will be briefly discussed in section III.

I

Russell thought of logicism as anti-Kantian. This is clear both from his discussion at the time (see *Principles, passim*) and from his later statements. Thus he says, in *My Philosophical Development*:

The primary aim of *Principia Mathematica* was to show that all pure mathematics follows from purely logical premises and uses only concepts definable in logical terms. This was, of course, an antithesis to the doctrines of Kant, and initially I thought of the work as a parenthesis in the refutation of [Kant].

(A similar passage, repeating the phrase 'a parenthesis in the refutation of Kant', is to be found in Russell's 'Autobiography', in the Schilpp volume on Russell.)[2] But how, exactly, did Russell take logicism to be part of an argument against Kant? Most fundamentally, Russell's logicism was intended as a refutation of Kant's view of mathematics. Russell, as we shall see, does not deny the Kantian claim that mathematics is synthetic *a priori*. He does, however, deny the claim that mathematics is based on what Kant had called the forms of our intuition, forms which impose spatiality and temporality upon the objects which we intuit. Russell insists that mathematics is wholly independent of space and time. Logicism was to constitute a basis for this insistence in the following way. If one accepts, as Kant did, that *logic* is independent of space and time (and of our forms of intuition), then logicism will show that the same is true of mathematics. One crucial property which logicism shows to be transferable from logic to mathematics is thus the property of being independent of space, time and the forms of intuition.[3]

Kant, according to Russell, held the opposite opinion only because of his ignorance of mathematics and, in particular, of the new logic.[4] The logic available

---

[2] 'My Mental Development', in Schilpp (ed.), *The Philosophy of Bertrand Russell* 13.

[3] The contrast between Kant and Russell here is complex; their agreement on the synthetic status of mathematics masks two points of disagreement (as well as a more basic conflict over the significance of the distinction between the analytic and the synthetic, which I shall discuss later). Kant holds that being analytic and being independent of space and time are co-extensive properties of judgements (see especially *Critique of Pure Reason*, A 158 = B 197, where Kant makes it clear that all synthetic judgements are dependent on intuition and thus on space and time; analytic judgements, by contrast, are repeatedly said to be dependent only on concepts, and thus not on intuition). Logic, for Kant, has these two properties: it is independent of space and time and it is analytic. For Kant, however, the status of logic is different from that of mathematics, which lacks both properties. Russell, by contrast, argues that logic and mathematics have the same status. Both, he insists, are independent of space and time. For Russell, however, being independent of space and time is not co-extensive with being analytic; he denies that either logic or mathematics has this latter property.

[4] Russell's general view of Kant is largely endorsed by Michael Friedman in his 'Kant's Theory of Geometry'. Friedman's work is, however, far more sympathetic to Kant than is Russell's.

to Kant was syllogistic logic, which lacks even the full power of monadic quantification theory. Given this logic, the theorems of Euclid, say, do not follow from Euclid's axioms by logic alone. As Russell sees the matter, this fact is at the basis of Kant's theory of mathematics:

There was, until recently, a special difficulty in the principles of mathematics. It seemed plain that mathematics consists of deductions, and yet the orthodox accounts of deduction were largely or wholly inapplicable to existing mathematics. Not only the Aristotelian syllogistic theory, but also the modern doctrines of Symbolic Logic . . . In this fact lay the strength of the Kantian view, which asserted that mathematical reasoning is not strictly formal, but always uses intuitions, i.e. the *a priori* knowledge of space and time. Thanks to the progress of Symbolic Logic, especially as treated by Professor Peano, this part of the Kantian philosophy is now capable of a final and irrevocable refutation (*Principles*, section 4).

A decisive advance here was Russell's development of polyadic quantification theory, and the associated understanding of quantifier dependence.[5] One result of this was a logic which, unlike syllogistic logic, could handle the reasoning which is involved in mathematics, for example, in deriving theorems from axioms. A second result concerns the understanding of the calculus. The work of Dedekind, Cantor and Weierstrass allowed the crucial notions of the calculus to be given precise definitions. These definitions require the use of nested quantifiers if they are to be put in rigorous form; quantifier dependence is crucial here. These definitions make no appeal to space, time or motion; nor do they rely upon the notion of an infinitely small quantity, or infinitesimal.[6] This second point too Russell sees as an advance which undermines Kant's theory of mathematics:

It was formerly supposed—and herein lay the real strength of Kant's mathematical philosophy—that continuity had an essential reference to space and time, and that the Calculus (as the word *fluxion* suggests) in some way presupposed motion or at least change. In this view, the philosophy of space and time was prior to that of continuity, the Transcendental Aesthetic preceded the Transcendental Dialectic, and the antinomies (at least the mathematics ones) were essentially spatio-temporal. All this has been changed by modern mathematics (*Principles*, section 249).

These results of polyadic quantification theory are impressive, especially to a mathematician educated to think that logic means syllogistic logic. Impressive

[5] I say 'Russell's development' because, in spite of what Russell says in the passage quoted, this notion is not to be found in any explicit form in Peano's work. On the other hand, Russell's treatment is itself less explicit than that of Frege, but I assume that it is independent of the latter. The best source for Russell's development of (a theory equivalent to) polyadic quantification theory is 'The Logic of Relations'.

[6] Since our concern is with the post-Kantian idealists, as well as with Kant, it is important to note that the use of the infinitesimal in mathematics was explicitly discussed by Hegel, who found it to be contradictory. See especially *Hegel's Science of Logic*, which is a translation by A. V. Miller of Hegel's *Wissenschaft der Logik*, section 2, ch. 2, C.

as they are, however, these results do not amount to logicism. They may show that modern logic is necessary for a (non-Kantian) understanding of mathematics, but they do not show that it is sufficient; they do not amount to a reduction of mathematics to logic. For this we need to take into account the fact that logic, for Russell, is not (what we call) first-order logic but is, rather, higher-order logic, as powerful as set theory. This fact is something that I shall discuss later. The present point is that it makes possible the full reduction of mathematics to logic. Two issues in particular are worth emphasizing. First, given the Russellian analogue of set theory, the arithmetic of the real numbers can be understood in terms of the natural numbers. Second, it appears to be possible to reduce the arithmetic of the natural numbers, in turn, to logic— given Russell's generous conception of what is to count as logic. This is in contrast to the view that the natural numbers are special entities, governed by their own laws, laws which might admit of, or even require, explanation in terms of the form of our intuition. From Russell's point of view, then, modern logic and mathematics show that the reliance upon spatio-temporal notions, which is characteristic of Kant's theory of mathematics, is not required at any point for an understanding of geometry or of the calculus, or of any part of mathematics.[7] Kant's theory of mathematics is thus refuted by logicism, the view that mathematics is reducible to logic.

The use of logicism against Kant's view of mathematics may seem to be a relatively narrow point. It is not clear, on the face of it, why the success of this claim of Russell's should carry any weight as a general argument against Kantianism, or as an argument against Kant's idealist successors, most of whom were far less concerned with mathematics than was Kant himself. But in Russell's hands the refutation of Kant's view of mathematics served as the basis for a more general attack on Kantianism and on post-Kantian idealism. The attack is against what Russell at least took to be a single doctrine, crucial to both Kantianism and post-Kantian idealism. We can formulate this doctrine as follows: our ordinary knowledge (of science, history, mathematics, etc.) is, at best, true in a conditioned and non-absolute sense of truth. This formulation obscures several points, having to do in particular with the differences between Kant and the idealists, and with idealist (and Russellian) interpretations of Kant.

---

[7] The case of geometry deserves special mention. The argument that geometry is logic requires the distinction between pure geometry and applied geometry: the former is simply a branch of mathematics, whereas the latter, for Russell, is part of physics (roughly, it tells you which geometry in the first sense is applicable to the real world). No such distinction was accepted by Kant, for example: his view is that there is only one sense of geometry, and that it gives knowledge of the real (physical) world.

The issue of geometry makes it clear that Russell's logicism is not exactly the same as Frege's. Frege was also willing to accept a version of Kant's claim that geometry depends upon the forms of our intuition. This difference in content stems in part from a difference in philosophical context and motive. Frege was not concerned with post-Kantian idealism; his target was naturalism and psychologism. See Sluga, *Gottlob Frege*, especially ch. I.

More subtly, perhaps, the idea that this doctrine is objectionable suggests that there is an absolute or unconditioned sense of truth which can be contrasted with conditioned truth. These matters will require some discussion.

Kant held that our knowledge is not unconditioned. It is confined to the world of appearances, which cannot be thought of as ultimately real and independent of us. One important basis for this claim is embodied in the argument of the antinomies, that if the world is taken to be 'a whole existing in itself', i.e. as independent of our representations of it, then contradictions can be derived. Kant's conclusion is that the world is not such a whole. This is the doctrine of transcendental idealism, that the world is empirically real but transcendentally ideal. All of our knowledge thus has this status: it is knowledge only of the world as it appears to us, and if construed more strongly than this is contradictory. The idea of the unconditioned, or of a world of things-in-themselves, plays a purely negative role here; our knowledge is *not* unconditioned, is *not* of things-in-themselves. (This is not to deny that these ideas may play a positive role in other parts of Kant's philosophy.)

The post-Kantian idealists rejected Kant's distinction between the phenomenal world, or world of appearances, and the noumenal world, or world of things-in-themselves. This distinction is closely connected with other Kantian dualisms which the idealists rejected: that between sensibility and the understanding, and that between the analytic and the synthetic (one of the connections, at least, will emerge in our later discussion; see note 26). The fact that the idealists rejected the distinction between the phenomenal world and the noumenal world meant that they drew un-Kantian conclusions from Kant's arguments against the consistency of regarding the world we know as a thing-in-itself. The idealists claimed that these arguments (and others) show that the ways in which we ordinarily think of the world are inconsistent. Ordinary 'knowledge', if thought through with full rigour, leads to contradictions. For the idealists, these contradictions do not result from a special metaphysical way of construing our ordinary knowledge, as if it were about things-in-themselves rather than about appearances. For the idealists the contradictions simply are implicit in (what we take to be) our ordinary knowledge. For this reason, they do not infer from the contradictions that we should eschew metaphysics. They infer, rather, that the categories of thought used in ordinary 'knowledge' are inadequate, and that we must attempt to find categories of thought that are not vulnerable to such inconsistencies. The only truly consistent way of thinking—that which yields 'absolute knowledge'—is to be found in the metaphysical conception of the world as a single organic whole, every part of which is internally related to every other. (This idealist position is perhaps most obviously articulated in the Heglian dialectic; but something like this is, I think, a distinguishing characteristic of post-Kantian idealism in general.) The idea of absolute knowledge affords the idealists a perspective from which all of our ordinary (i.e. non-metaphysical) claims to knowledge can be judged and found to be at best relatively or conditionally true.

For the idealists, then, real truth is absolute truth, which in turn means unconditioned truth. This makes it natural for the idealists to read Kant as if he too held that conditioned truth is second-rate, somehow not real truth—even though for Kant there is no other sense of 'true' than the sense in which it refers to conditioned truth. Now the important point, from our perspective, is that Russell more or less took for granted this idealist reading of Kant. Given the idealist orthodoxy in which he was educated, this is hardly surprising. The point, however, goes deeper than Russell's reading of Kant. Russell also took for granted the conception of truth from which this reading stems. Truth, for Russell, was absolute and unconditioned. Like the idealists, but unlike Kant, he held that there is an absolute sense of truth, and that it is to this that human knowledge should aspire. Unlike the idealists, however, Russell held this to be the only sense of truth, anything else being just a polite word for falsehood. From Russell's point of view, then, the crucial doctrine common to Kant and to his successors is the claim that all of our ordinary knowledge is true in a second-rate sense. What we call 'knowledge' is only relatively true, not absolutely true, true only from an empirical point of view, not from a transcendental point of view. (From this point I shall, where convenient, ignore the fact that this claim cannot be straightforwardly attributed to Kant. Equally, I shall sometimes speak of Kant as an idealist, as Russell does without hesitation.) Russell objects to this claim because he thinks it tantamount to saying that all of what we ordinarily take as knowledge (including mathematics) is false.

Russell uses logicism to argue against the crucial idealist and Kantian claim that our ordinary knowledge cannot be absolutely or transcendentally true. There are, I think, two rather different arguments that connect logicism to the refutation of this claim, though only one of them is explicit in Russell's texts. The first, and explicit, connection has to do with the arguments that Kant, and to some extent other idealists, used as a basis for the claim that the world as we ordinarily understand it is not wholly consistent. (I am here presupposing an idealist interpretation of Kant—in particular that for Kant it is our ordinary understanding of the world, and not only a metaphysical construal of that understanding, which is inconsistent.) For Kant, as I have already said, one important basis for this idea is to be found in the antinomies. The first two antinomies are spatio-temporal, and claim to show that if space and time are taken as real—as features of the world as it really is, rather than merely of the world as it appears to us—then contradictions follow. This claim, if accepted, seems immediately to show that the world as we take it to be cannot be fully real, for the world as we take it to be is spatial and temporal, and these features, it seems, give rise to contradictions. This point seems to have been more or less taken for granted by many of Kant's idealist successors. Hegel, for example, says:

These Kantian Antinomies will always remain an important part of the critical philosophy; they, more than anything else, brought about the downfall of previous metaphysics and can be regarded as a main transition into more recent philosophy.[8]

More striking than this, perhaps, are the flattering terms in which Hegel refers to Zeno, calling him, for example, 'the originator of the dialectic' (*der Anfänger der Dialektik*).[9] For one post-Kantian idealist, in particular, the supposed contradictions in the notion of space were of the highest importance. This was Russell himself, who argued, in the late 1890s, that space, if considered as devoid of matter, gives rise to contradictions: '. . . empty space . . . gives rise to the antinomy in question; for empty space is a bare possibility of relations, undifferentiated and homogeneous, and thus wholly destitute of parts or of thinghood.'[10] This claim, which was elaborated in his *Foundations of Geometry*, was intended to be the first step in an elaborate 'dialectic of the sciences', which would take scientific knowledge as the subject of a Hegelian-style dialectic.[11] The result of this dialectic would be to show that all such knowledge is merely relative, i.e. not fully true as it stands. So when, a few years later, Russell argues against (what he took to be) Kant's claims of the inadequacy of the notions of space and time, it is perhaps with the fervour that is said to characterize recent converts.

In *Principles*, in any case, Russell's claim is that space and time are consistent, and that modern (i.e. nineteenth-century) mathematics demonstrates this beyond doubt. More accurately, perhaps, he claims that modern mathematics makes available consistent theories which may represent the truth about space and time; whether they in fact do so is a matter on which he is willing to remain agnostic. The crucial point is that mathematics makes consistent theories of space and time possible.[12] The importance of this point to Russell can be gathered

---

[8] *Hegel's Science of Logic*, 190; cf. also pp. 197–8.

[9] The context of this quotation is as follows: 'Zeno's distinctive characteristic is the dialectic. He is the master of the Eleatic school, in which pure thought comes into its own in the movement of the concept in itself, and in the pure spirit of inquiry; he is the originator of the dialectic.' Hegel, (*Vorlesungen über die Geschichte der Philosophie*) (*Lectures on the History of Philosophy*), 295; the translation is my own.

[10] *An Essay on the Foundations of Geometry*, 191. It is worth noting that Russell sees nothing new in the idea that there are contradictions in space; it is, he says 'an ancient theme—as ancient, in fact, as Zeno's refutation of motion' (p. 188). One of Russell's arguments (on pp. 189–90) closely resembles F. H. Bradley's discussion on pp. 31–2 of *Appearance and Reality*, and has more distant affinities with Zeno's argument and with Kant's second antinomy.

[11] Besides *Foundations of Geometry*, see also 'On the Idea of a Dialectic of the Sciences' notes of Russell's dated 1 January, 1898. These were not published at the time, but are in *My Philosophical Development*, 43–53.

[12] Russell puts forward this claim in opposition to Kant. The idea that it conflicts with Kant's view relies, as I have indicated, upon an interpretation of Kant which I do not wish to endorse. The alternative interpretation sees Kant as claiming that the mathematical theories of space and time are, on their own terms, consistent, and that inconsistency arises only from the metaphysical interpretation given to these theories. The important point here, however, is *Russell's* interpretation of Kant.

from the fact that the notion of space, which is hardly an obvious subject for a book on the foundation of mathematics, is the subject of Part VI of *The Principles of Mathematics*, and occupies nearly 100 pages of that book. This part of the book concludes with a discussion of Kant's antinomies, and claims that they are 'disproved by the modern realization of Leibniz's universal characteristic' (section 436). Russell's claim that there are consistent mathematical theories of space and time draws, as one would expect, upon the treatment of real numbers and of continuity made available by Cantor, Dedekind and (especially) Weierstrass. It is important, however, to see that it also depends upon the central claim of Russell's logicism, that mathematics is wholly independent of the Kantian forms of intuition. It is only if mathematics is in this way independent of space and time that it can be used, in non-circular fashion, as an argument for the consistency of the latter notions. Russell thus takes the central claim of logicism, and the claim of the consistency of space and time, as crucial to his opposition to Kant:

> The questions of chief importance to us, as regards the Kantian theory, are two, namely, (1) are the reasonings in mathematics in any way different from those of Formal Logic? (2) are there any contradictions in the notions of space and time? If these two pillars of the Kantian edifice can be pulled down, we shall have successfully played the part of Samson towards his disciples (*Principles*, section 433).

This, then, is the first and most explicit way in which Russell takes logicism as part of a general argument against Kant and post-Kantian idealism. Logicism shows that consistent theories of space and time are available; the spatio-temporal world need not be written off as contradictory and not fully real.

Less explicit in the text of Russell's work, but hardly less important, I think, is the idea that mathematics functions as a particularly clear counterexample to the crucial idealist claim about knowledge which I briefly discussed earlier. A direct consequence of the Kantian version of the claim is that our knowledge is confined to what can be given in intuition, i.e. to actual or possible objects of sensible experience. Since these objects are partially constituted by our minds, a second consequence of the Kantian view is that our knowledge is conditioned by the nature of our cognitive faculties. The post-Kantian idealist analogue of this general claim is that all of our ordinary, non-metaphysical knowledge is at best relatively true. As against these very general idealist claims as to the inadequacy of our ordinary (non-metaphysical) knowledge, Russell sets out, in *Principles*, to show that mathematics is true—not true just as one stage in the dialectic, or more or less true, but true absolutely and unconditionally; not just true if put in a wider context, or if seen as part of a larger whole, but true just as it stands; not, to revert to the Kantian idiom, true from the empirical standpoint but false from the transcendental standpoint, but simple TRUE, with no distinctions of standpoint accepted. Mathematics, for Russell, is thus to function as a counterexample to a claim which he sees as crucial to any form of idealism, Kantian or post-Kantian.[13] The claim that mathematics is independent of space and time is again important, here for two reasons. First of all, as before, space and time were themselves held by the idealists to be inconsistent or only 'relatively true'. If mathematics were based on these notions it would be subject to the same doubts. Second, if mathematics were based on space and time, it would not be *unconditionally* true; its truth would be confined to the sphere of the spatio-temporal.[14]

For Russell in the early years of this century, then, logicism was the basis for a complex argument against idealism, of both the Kantian and the non-Kantian varieties. It is worth contrasting this argument with that of the logical positivists,[15] for whom logicism also formed part of an argument against Kant, but an argument of a very different sort. For the positivists, the essential claim about logic was that it was analytic, in the sense of being true by meaning or true by convention; they held that truths which are analytic in this sense were empty of content, and made no claim on reality. Logicism, on this account, enables one to maintain the *a priori* and non-empirical status of mathematics while denying that there is any genuine *a priori* knowledge. Because mathematics is logic it is analytic, and because it is analytic it is empty of content; so one can insist that it is not genuine knowledge. This, in turn, enables one to maintain the empiricist claim that sense experience is the source of all genuine knowledge. Mathematics, which threatened to provide a counterexample to this principle, is shown by logicism not to do so. All of these points can be seen in, for example, Carnap's discussion of the impact that Wittgenstein's *Tractatus* had on the Vienna Circle.[16]

---

[13] At this point we can see that it is in fact crucial to Russell's purposes that mathematics be genuine knowledge; this is one of the reasons that he insists that mathematics and logic are both synthetic in character. Kant holds logic to be analytic, and not genuine knowledge; he asserts, for example, 'no one can venture with the help of logic alone to judge regarding objects, or to make any assertion' (*Critique of Pure Reason*, A 60B 85). Since Kant holds logic to apply beyond the spatio-temporal, he might be thought to hold it to be (in his sense) 'unconditioned' (as Parsons points out, the applicability of logic to things-in-themselves is implicit in Kant's view that we can *think* of things-in-themselves; see 'Kant's Philosophy of Arithmetic', 115–19). But since logic is analytic, it is not unconditioned *knowledge*, and so not a counterexample to his general position.

[14] Russell sometimes offers a different sort of argument, which I do not emphasize, against Kant's view of mathematics. If mathematics depends upon the forms of our intuition, and this is a psychological feature of the human mind, then it looks as if mathematics is dependent upon psychology. Russell does not always clearly distinguish this anti-psychologistic argument from his anti-idealist arguments. See e.g. *Principles*, section 430.

[15] At this point I am of course simplifying a very complex story. In particular, the view of Carnap in *Logische Syntax der Sprache* does not depend on logicism in anything like the sense which I am presupposing. See Michael Friedman, 'Logical Truth and Analyticity in Carnap's *Logical Syntax of Language*'.

[16] Carnap's 'Autobiography', in Schilpp (ed.), *The Philosophy of Rudolf Carnap*, 46–7:

Wittgenstein formulated . . . [the view] that all logical truths are tautological, that is, that they hold necessarily in every possible case, therefore do not exclude any case, and do not say anything about the facts of the world . . . [T]o the members of the Circle, there did not seem to be a fundamental difference

Given this account of logicism and its philosophical significance, it is clear why logicism can be thought of as an anti-Kantian doctrine. Kant held that our knowledge of mathematics is *a priori* even though the truths of mathematics are synthetic rather than analytic. One of the motives of his philosophy as a whole was to explain the possibility of this (supposed) kind of knowledge—to answer the question which he at one stage described as 'the proper problem of pure reason', namely: 'How are synthetic *a priori* judgments possible?'[17] If logicism shows that mathematics is analytic, then it shows that at least in one clear case, perhaps the clearest, Kant's motivating question is simply based upon a mistake. More generally, as was indicated above, logicism seems to clear the way for the anti-Kantian view that all knowledge is straightforwardly based on a single source, and that source is sense experience.

For the positivists, then, the point at which logicism told against the Kantian view had to do with the issue of the sources of knowledge—in particular, whether knowledge must be thought of as having the mind as one of its sources. Given the Kantian assumption that knowledge is correlative with what is known, the issue is at the same time the issue of whether the world that is known must be thought of as partially constituted by the mind. Russell's use of logicism against Kant is quite different. One sign of this is the fact that he does not hold that mathematics is empty of content or analytic or tautologous. It is clearly Russell's view that mathematics is genuine knowledge, and this is essential to the use that he makes of logicism. A deeper sign of the difference between Russell and the positivists is that for the former the terms 'analytic' and 'synthetic' bear no real philosophical weight. He does say that mathematics (and logic) are synthetic,[18] but these remarks function simply as a denial of what he sees as the absurd view that the propositions of mathematics follow from the law of contradiction, and nothing else.[19] The claim that mathematics is synthetic is not, in Russell's hands, part of

---

between elementary logic and higher logic, including mathematics. Thus we arrived at the conception that all valid statements of mathematics are analytic in the specific sense that they hold in all possible cases and therefore do not have any factual content.

What was important in this conception from our point of view was the fact that it became possible for the first time to combine the basic tenet of empiricism with a satisfactory explanation of logic and mathematics.

[17] Section VI of the introduction to the *Critique of Pure Reason*. This section was added in the second or 'B' edn of the Critique, but contains nothing that is not consistent with the 1st edn text; the passage is at B 19.

[18] See e.g. *Principles*, 434. This view was one which Russell held consistently throughout the period leading up to *Principia* (and, in fact, until he came under the influence of Wittgenstein's new views on the status of logic; see p. 81, below). For a later reference, see *The Problems of Philosophy*, 79, 83–4. In the former of these passages, Russell makes clear his view that deduction can give *new* knowledge, i.e. knowledge not contained in the premises.

[19] The notion of analyticity is not discussed at all in *Principles*, which is one sign of the lack of importance that it had in Russell's thought. He does discuss it, as one could hardly avoid doing, in his book on Leibniz. His discussion there contains a number of arguments against the philosophical significance of the notion.

a theory of mathematics. Nor is it part of a theory of analytic and synthetic knowledge. Russell has no such theory, and no concern at all with the distinction between the analytic and the synthetic except to reject it as philosophically unimportant. The fundamental point here is that Russell in *The Principles of Mathematics* completely rejects the Kantian concerns with the sources of knowledge, and with anything recognizable as epistemology at all. Underlying the arguments against Kant and the idealists is a shift of focus, due as much to Moore as to Russell, from epistemology to ontology, from knowledge to truth.[20] He believes, or writes as if he believes, that in favourable cases the mind has direct and unmediated contact with abstract objects: we simply perceive them, in some non-sensuous sense of 'perceive' which is held to be unproblematic and presuppositionless. Metaphysics is no longer subservient to epistemology; knowledge now appears as merely our access to what we know, not as constitutive of it. (We can perhaps recognize in this the sort of view that Kant found objectionable in Leibniz and Wolff; certainly it has the same results, that metaphysics proceeds without epistemological constraints, and threatens to run riot.)

First and foremost among the things with which the mind has direct contact, in Russell's view, are *propositions*. These are abstract entities, neither linguistic nor mental. The notions of truth and ontology (being) are very closely connected with that of a proposition. Propositions are the bearers of truth and falsehood; the absoluteness and objectivity of truth requires the objectivity and independence of propositions. Propositions have constituents; everything that is, is a constituent of propositions, and everything that can be a constituent of a proposition must have some sort of ontological status (in Russell's words, it *is*, even if it does not exist). The notion of a proposition is thus central to Russell's

---

[20] It must seem paradoxical to speak of the author of *Our Knowledge of the External World*, the advocate of reduction of physical object-statements to sense-data statements, as anti-epistemological in his orientation. Various considerations mitigate this paradox. One is that all of Russell's works in the epistemological vein are written after the completion of *Principia*; there was a shift in his concerns around this time, perhaps traceable in part to the lectures that Moore gave in 1910–11 (later published as *Some Main Problems of Philosophy*). A second is that the notion of a sense-datum can be seen, in a curious way, as the natural outcome of the view that we have a direct and unproblematic relation to the objects of our knowledge. If one holds this view then it may seem obvious, upon reflection, that the objects of our knowledge are not such things as tables and trees. The fact of sensory illusion seems to show this (it may be said, indeed, that one who holds the view of knowledge that I have mentioned is the appropriate target for the argument from illusion). Thus one searches for suitable objects of knowledge—relata which can preserve the relation of knowing as a direct and unproblematic one. The result is the notion of a sense datum, as conceived by Russell and Moore—not as a subjective or mental entity, but as an objective non-mental thing with which our minds are in direct and unmediated contact. The non-mental nature of Russellian sense-data is of course crucial to this way of understanding matters, and is often overlooked. A third fact is probably most important of all from the present perspective. Russell's epistemological worries do not rapidly extend themselves to serious questions about our knowledge of abstract objects. Here the answer is that we simply are in direct contact with them, that we 'perceive' them in some non-sensuous fashion, continues to satisfy him at least until the 1920s. This is the point which is most relevant to the discussion of logicism and also, although less obviously, to his anti-Kantianism.

philosophy. Elsewhere (Chapter 1 above) I have discussed its general role in his break with idealism, and I shall not repeat this discussion here. In the next section, however, we shall see that this notion plays a role both in the use that Russell wishes to make of logicism and in his conception of logic.

II

Given that Russell's use of logicism as part of an argument against Kant and the idealists is as I have described it, what does this imply about Russell's conception of logic? To play the philosophical role that Russell had in mind, logic must, above all, be *true*. Its truth must be absolute, unconditioned and unrestricted. These features may appear to be uncontroversial, even trivial, but in fact they mark a crucial difference between Russell's conception of logic and what I have called the model-theoretic conception. Logic, for Russell, was a universal language, a *lingua characteristica*, not a mere calculus which can be thought of as set up within a more inclusive language.[21] He thus conceives of logic as universal and all-inclusive. I shall endeavour to explain both this conception of logic and its connection with Russell's use of logicism against the idealists.

The idea of logic as made up of truths already marks a difference between Russell's conception and the model-theoretic conception. According to the latter, logic is made up of a formal system which contains schemata which are subject to interpretations, where each schema has a truth-value in each interpretation. The crucial notion is thus *truth in all interpretations* or validity. For Russell, by contrast, the crucial notion is simply truth. Logic on his conception does not consist of schemata whose truth-values wait upon the specification of an interpretation; it consists of propositions which have a content and a truth-value on their own account.[22] Propositions, as we have already said, are taken to be objective non-linguistic and non-mental entities; they have their truth-values independently of our language, of our acts of synthesis or of any interpretation. The propositions of logic, as Russell constantly implies, contain variables and logical constants, and nothing else (see e.g. *Principles*, ch. I); this implies, and Russell clearly accepts, that variables and logical constants are themselves non-linguistic entities.

---

[21] For discussions of this conception of logic, see van Heijenoort, 'Logic as Language and Logic as Calculus'; and Goldfarb, 'Logic in the Twenties: The Nature of the Quantifier'.

[22] This point is closely connected with that made by Frege, when he insists that his logic *expresses a content*. See especially 'Über den Zweck der Begriffsschrift': 'my aim [in the *Begriffsschrift*] was different from Boole's. I did not wish to present an abstract logic in formulas, but to express a content through written symbols.' To say that a statement of logic expresses a content is presumably also to say that it is true or false on its own account, without the need for an interpretation.

The notion of an interpretation, and the correlative idea of an uninterpreted formalism, are wholly alien to Russell's thought at this period. He simply never mentions such ideas; the conception of logic as universal is not something that Russell articulates and defends, but something that he seems to take entirely for granted. He does, however, defend one feature of his conception. On Russell's conception of logic, there is no question of our specifying what the variables are to range over; they range over everything. It is thus a part of his conception that there is no room for the specification of a universe of discourse. (We might say that the only universe of discourse, on Russell's conception of logic, is *the* universe, the actual universe, comprising everything that there is. To say this, however, is to reject the notion of a universe of discourse within which the range of the variables is confined.) Thus the propositions of logic are wholly general: they contain variables, and the variables range over everything. Russell's argument against the idea of (restricted) universes of discourse is revealing, and I shall examine it at some length.

The basic argument is one that Russell repeats several times in his work in the first decade of the century. One version goes as follows:

> it is quite essential that we should have some meaning of *always* which does not have to be expressed in a restrictive hypothesis as to x. For suppose 'always' means 'whenever x belongs to class i'. Then 'all men are mortal' becomes 'whenever x belongs to the class i, then, if x is a man, x is mortal'; i.e. 'it is always true that if x belongs to the class i, then, if x is a man, x is mortal'. But what is our new *always* to mean? There seems no more reason for restricting x, in this new proposition, to the class i, than there was before for restricting it to the class *men*. Thus we shall be led on to a new wider universe, and so on *ad infinitum* . . . .[23]

The point of this argument is that if we are to have a restricted universe of discourse (i.e. something other than simply *the* universe), then we must establish this universe of discourse by means of a statement which says what the variable is to range over. But in *that* statement there is no reason to suppose that we are using a restricted universe of discourse. Nor, indeed, can we be doing so unless there is yet another statement in which the restrictions on the first statement are made explicit; and then, of course, exactly the same point will apply to the second statement. Thus it is, on this view, possible to use restricted variables, but the use of such variables presupposes the use of unrestricted variables, which simply range over everything that there is. Thus we can conclude that it is the unrestricted variable which is fundamental. We can also conclude that only propositions using such variables should be thought of as propositions of logic, at least by Russell's standards of what is to count as logic.

[23] This version is from 'Mathematical Logic as Based on the Theory of Types', 71. For other versions see e.g. 'On "Insolubilia" and their Solution by Symbolic Logic', 2056, and *Principles*, section 7.

A proposition which uses a restricted variable is made within the context of some other statement which establishes the universe of discourse. Its meaning, and its truth if it is true, are thus conditional upon that other statement. To say this, however, is to say that it is not unconditionally true. By Russell's standards it thus has no right to be thought of as a proposition of logic; such propositions must be unconditionally true, and this in turn require that they contain all their conditions within themselves.

This argument of Russell's takes it for granted that the statement which establishes the universe of discourse is on the same level as the assertion which is made once the universe of discourse is established. Thus the former can be taken as antecedent and the latter as consequent in a single conditional statement. Russell, that is, assumes that all statements are on the same level; this contrasts with the model-theoretic view that we must distinguish the schemata of the object-language from the statements of the meta-language. Intrinsic to Russell's conception of the universality of logic is the denial of the metalinguistic perspective which is essential to the model-theoretic conception of logic. This makes a crucial difference to the way in which one thinks of logic. Consider, for example, the question of the completeness of a system of logic, which is so nat-ural for us. This question relies upon the idea that we have, independently of the logical system, a criterion of what the system ought to be able to do, so that it relies upon the essentially meta-theoretic notion of an interpretation, and of truth in all interpretations. These meta-theoretic ideas, however, are foreign to Russell's conception of logic; the question of the completeness of a system in the modern sense simply could not arise for him.[24] Logic for him was not a system, or a formalism, which might or might not capture what we take to be the logically valid body of schemata; logic for him was, rather, the body of wholly general truths.

The fact that Russell does not see logic as something on which one can take a meta-theoretical perspective thus constitutes a crucial difference between his conception of logic and the model-theoretic one. Logic, for Russell, is a systematization of reasoning in general, of reasoning as such. If we have a correct systematization, it will comprehend all correct principles of reasoning. Given such a conception of logic there can be no external perspective. *Any* reasoning will, simply in virtue of being reasoning, fall within logic; any proposition that we might wish to advance is subject to the rules of logic. This is perhaps a natural, if naive, way of thinking about logic. In Russell's case, however, we can say more than this to explain why he should have held such a conception. Given the philosophical use that Russell wishes to make of logicism, no other conception is

[24] For the development of the issue of (semantic) completeness in its modern sense, see the paper of Goldfarb's cited in n. 21, and also the introductory note by Burton Dreben and Jean van Heijenoort to Gödel's proof of completeness, in vol. i of Gödel's *Collected Works*.

available to him. If logic is to be unconditionally and unrestrictedly true, in the sense that Russell must require it to be, then it must be universally applicable. This in turn implies that statements about logic must themselves fall within the scope of logic, so the notion of a meta-theoretical perspective falls away. If this were not so, if logic were thought of as set up within a more inclusive metalanguage, then by the standards which Russell and the idealists share, it would appear that logic is not absolutely and unconditionally true. Logic, on this modern picture, is not unrestricted, for it is set up in a more inclusive language which must fall outside its scope. Nor can the truth of logic, conceived of in this way, be thought of as absolute and unconditioned, for it is dependent upon the metalanguage within which it is set up. There is no reason to believe that Russell ever considered anything like the model-theoretic conception of logic—at least as a conception of *logic*—but if he had done so, the use he wishes to make of logicism would have given him reason to reject it in favour of the conception of logic as universal.

My claim here, of course, is a claim about Russell and about the argumentative situation that he found himself in. Given that situation, I want to say, he would have found this view of logic necessary to sustain his attack on the idealists.[25] We can reinforce this idea by seeing that the conception of logic as universal, and some arguments for it, have analogues in certain idealist lines of thought. What I have particularly in mind here is the argument which the post-Kantian idealists used against the Kantian notion of the thing-in-itself. The Kantian thing-in-itself, as the idealists understood the notion, provides a contrast with all knowledge that is possible for us. What we know are appearances, which are conditioned by our forms of sensibility and by the (schematized) categories of the understanding. The thing-in-itself is, by definition, that which is independent of us and our cognitive faculties; it is therefore something of which we can have no knowledge. Kant's claim, of course, is that although we can—almost by definition—have no knowledge about things-in-themselves, we can nevertheless think of them, and may, indeed, have rational grounds for belief about them. He does, moreover, presuppose that we can at least know that there are things-in-themselves, even though we can have no (other) knowledge about them. These views of Kant's were widely attacked by his idealist successors; it is the basis of the attack that is of concern to us. If things-in-themselves are really wholly beyond the reach of our knowledge, how could we know even that there are such things? More broadly, since the categories of the understanding are surely conditions of *thought* as well as of knowledge, how can we even have thoughts or

---

[25] I say 'would have' rather than 'did' because there is no reason at all to believe that Russell articulated the sorts of considerations that I am giving. In particular, there is, as I have said, no reason to think that he considered any other conception of logic as possible.

beliefs about things-in-themselves?[26] These objections are clearly expressed by McTaggart:

The thing-in-itself as conceived by Kant, behind and apart from the phenomena which alone enter into experience, is a contradiction. We cannot, we are told, know what it is, but only that it is. But this is itself an important piece of knowledge relating to the thing. It involves a judgment, and a judgment involves categories, and we are thus forced to surrender the idea that we can be aware of anything which is not subject to the laws governing experience.[27]

McTaggart is attacking Kant for being insufficiently serious and literal about the idea of generality. If the categories really are the categories, then they must apply to everything. There is nothing that we can conceive of as being exempt from them, and no position from which we think without employing them. In particular, they must apply to the critical philosophy, and thereby to the very statement of the categories themselves.

Russell, I wish to suggest, might have accepted similar arguments against the idea of a perspective external to logic, from which we can establish logic. On Russell's conception, logic applies to everything—including the very statements which establish logic. This point can be very clearly seen in certain passages in *Principles*. Russell denies that we can prove the independence of a truth-functional axiom by finding an interpretation for the negation of that axiom together with the other axioms. The general technique is clearly well-known to him, but he argues that it is not available in this specific case. If we deny an axiom of this sort, reasoning itself becomes impossible:

it should be observed that the method of supposing an axiom false, and deducing the consequences of this assumption, which has been found admirable in such cases as the axiom of parallels, is here not universally available. For all our axioms are principles of deduction; and if they are true, the consequences which appear to follow from the employment of an opposite principle will not really follow, so that arguments from the supposition of the falsity of an axiom are here subject to special fallacies, *Principles*, (section 17).

This view, moreover, seems to be one that Russell held not only in *Principles* but also later, at the time when he was completing *Principia*.[28]

---

[26] At this point the idealist interpretation of Kant is again arguably mistaken. In particular, the view that things-in-themselves are independent of all our cognitive faculties seems to neglect Kant's distinction between sensibility and the understanding, and between the schematized and the un-schematized categories. At least in some places, Kant's view seems to be that things-in-themselves are independent of sensibility (and therefore of the schematized categories), but not of the understanding (and the un-schematized categories). See especially *Critique of Pure Reason*, A 253–4 = B 309–10.

[27] *Studies in Hegelian Dialectic*, 27. I cite McTaggart not only because he is clear and (on this point) representative, but also because we know that Russell took him seriously, read his work, and was influenced by his interpretation of Hegel. See e.g. *My Philosophical Development*, 38.

[28] See Russell's letter to Jourdain, dated 28 April 1909: 'I do not prove the independence of primitive propositions by the recognised methods; this is impossible as regards principles of inference, because

Russell's conception of logic as universal is connected with another crucial feature of his view of the subject. For Russell, logic has direct and immediate metaphysical or ontological implications. If the propositions of logic are indeed general truths, then certain things follow from them about what the world must be like. To put it another way: logic has metaphysical implications, which must be correct if logic is true. This is suggested by an important passage in the Preface of *Principles*, where Russell acknowledges his indebtedness, in metaphysical issues, to G. E. Moore:

> On fundamental questions of philosophy, my position, in all its chief features, is derived from Mr G. E. Moore. I have accepted from him the non-existential nature of propositions (except such as happen to assert existence) and their independence of any knowing mind; also the pluralism which regards the world, both that of existents and that of entities, as composed of an infinite number of mutually independent entities, with relations between them which are ultimate, and not reducible to adjectives of their terms or of the whole which these compose. Before learning these views from him, I found myself unable to construct any philosophy of arithmetic, whereas their acceptance brought about an immediate liberation from a large number of difficultes which I believe to be otherwise insuperable. The doctrines just mentioned are, in my opinion, quite indispensable to any even tolerably satisfactory philosophy of mathematics . . . Formally my premises are simply assumed; but the fact that they allow mathematics to be true, which most current philosophies do not, is surely a powerful argument in their favour (*Principles*, p. xviii).

The 'philosophy of arithmetic' which Russell found himself able to construct after (but only after) accepting certain metaphysical views from Moore is of course logicism; logicism has these presuppositions because they are presuppositions of logic itself.

Russell, then, sees logic as requiring the existence of propositions as non-spatio-temporal and non-mental entities; the existence of infinitely many distinct and independent entities; and the existence of non-reducible relations holding among these entities. These claims are fundamental to a whole metaphysics, which is sketched by Russell and Moore in conscious opposition to idealism. Why should logic have any such implications? This question can be approached through the technical considerations that we have already touched on. The propositions of logic, for Russell, contain only variables and logical constants; and the variables range over everything in the (actual) universe. So the letter '*p*' in (say) '*p* v *q*' and the letter '*F*' in '*Fx*' are treated as free variables, in the same way as '*x*' is treated as a free variable in '*Fx*'. This has the immediate

you can't tell what follows from supposing them false: if they are true, they must be used in deducing consequences from the hypothesis that they are false, and altogether they are too fundamental to be treated by the recognised methods.' This portion of the letter is printed in Grattan-Guinness (ed.), *Dear Russell—Dear Jourdain*, 117.

implication that the propositions of logic assert not merely that there are objects over which the objectual variables range, but also that there are propositions over which the propositional variables range, and predicates or their analogues over which the predicate variables range. The truth-functional part of logic requires that each proposition be determinately true or false; if the truth of logic is to be absolute, objective and completely general, then all true propositions must be objectively and absolutely true. Russell, I think, took this to imply that propositions themselves must be non-mental entities, which exist independently of any mind.[29] The quantificational part of logic, similarly, requires that there are predicates which are determinately true or false of objects (and never both); if logic is to be wholly general, each predicate must be determinately true or false of *each* object. These implications are, as Russell fully realized, claims which would be rejected by his idealist opponents. His position is that the power of logic, and the insight that it affords us into mathematics, ought to persuade us to accept the metaphysical presuppositions on which logic rests.

Russell's position here is closely connected with another issue which I have mentioned in passing: the fact that for him logic is (what we would call) higher-order logic, and first-order logic not even a natural fragment of logic. To put the point a different way: for Russell, higher-order logic is implicit in first-order logic, and involves nothing new in principle. In its mature form, in *Principia Mathematica*[30] or in 'Mathematical Logic as Based on the Theory of Types', Russell's logic quantifies over propositional functions as well as over individuals. It is, of course, because of this fact that Russell is able to achieve the power of set theory without assuming that there are sets; it is also because of this fact that some commentators have claimed that Russell's mature logic is no more logic properly so-called than is set theory.[31] From the present perspective, the question is whether the universality of logic is compatible with, or even implies, the idea that we can, as a part of logic, quantify over propositional functions. Such quantification involves us in existential claims; do such claims introduce a new and special subject matter (the theory of propositional functions)? My claim is that from Russell's point of view the introduction of quantification over propositional functions into logic is, in itself, quite compatible with the universality of logic, and arguably even implied by it. The necessity for avoiding the

---

[29] See *Our Knowledge of the External World* for some discussion of this point.

[30] Whitehead and Russell, *Principia* vol. I. All my references are to material printed in the 1st edn and reprinted 'unchanged except as regards misprints and minor errors' in the 2nd (introduction to the 2nd edn, p. xiii); my pagination, however, is that of the 2nd edn. I make the simplifying assumption that it is Russell, rather than Whitehead, who is responsible for the parts of *Principia* that are my concern.

[31] See Quine, *Philosophy of Logic* 64–8. Elsewhere Quine argues at some length that Russell's strategy of taking propositional functions as fundamental, and classes as defined, has no advantages (and some disadvantages) compared with that of taking classes as fundamental outright. See especially *Set Theory and its Logic*, ch. XI.

paradoxes, however, leads as we shall see in section III, to steps which are not compatible with the universality of logic. My emphasis here, however, will be on the first and positive claim, that if one grant Russell the conception of logic as universal, and waive the issues raised by the paradoxes, then one can argue that the theory of propositional functions is indeed part of logic whereas set theory, say, is not. In the end Russell may be wrong to think that he has a coherent conception of logic according to which *Principia* is logic, for in the end the paradoxes cannot be ignored. But there is, I think, more to be said for this Russellian view than most of his critics acknowledge.

Let us begin by taking it for granted that what we call first-order logic is indeed logic. Presupposing the Russellian notion of a proposition, we can say that first-order logic requires that we analyse propositions in a certain way. We must show that there is something shared by the propositions that Caesar killed Caesar and that Brutus killed Brutus, which is not shared by the proposition that Caesar killed Brutus. This much is necessary to show e.g. that the first two imply '($\exists x$) (x killed x)' whereas the third does not (although all three imply '($\exists x$) ($\exists y$) (x killed y)'. But what is this 'something shared'? Given the non-linguistic nature of a Russellian proposition, it can hardly be a merely linguistic entity (an open sentence); it is, rather, what Russell calls a propositional function.[32] What the first two propositions have in common, which the third does not, is that they are values or instances of the propositional function $\hat{x}$ *killed* $\hat{x}$. It is for these sorts of reasons, not simply because of a need for an analogue of set theory, that Russell's logic requires that there be propositional functions. The crucial point is that even doing first-order logic requires that we accept that there are propositional functions. The formal reflection of this fact is that the primitive proposition (axiom) of *Principia* which assures us of the existence of propositional functions is laid down as part of the transition from truth-functional logic to quantification theory. (The primitive proposition states: 'If, for some a, there is a proposition ϕa, then there is a [propositional] function $\phi \hat{x}$, and vice versa. Pp.' Since the transition from truth-functional logic to quantification theory is done twice over, in different ways, this proposition has two different numbers: *9.15 and *10.122.) The transition from first-order logic to higher-order logic in *12, by contrast, requires no primitive propositions concerning the existence of propositional functions, and, indeed, no new primitive propositions at all. (The axiom of reducibility does occur in *12 but, as we shall see in section III, it is not required

---

[32] Here I presuppose that propositional functions are not linguistic entities, a claim that has been doubted by a number of commentators. See *Principia*, ii, p. xii, where a distinction is made between a propositional function and the *symbolic form* of a propositional function. The context of this passage may make it less than conclusive. The general tenor of Russell's discussions of propositional functions, both in *Principles* and in *Principia*, however, is that they have the same status as propositions, and are indeed exactly like propositions except that propositional functions have variables in one or more places where the corresponding proposition has an entity.

for Russell's higher-order logic; the need for it arises from the project of reducing mathematics to this logic). Hence from Russell's point of view the distinction between first-order and higher-order logic is of no particular significance. Since quantification over objects of any sort requires that we accept that there are propositional functions, introducing quantification over these latter entities does not, by Russell's lights, involve any new principle; higher-order logic merely makes explicit what is in fact implicit in first-order logic.[33]

Let us contrast this Russellian view with that of a modern logician, who thinks that the distinction between first-order and higher-order logic is an important distinction of principle. Quine sees the schemata of first-order logic as made up of schematic predicate letters and quantified (or quantifiable) variables. The latter have true generality. When the schema is interpreted, they become variables ranging over some specified domain of entities (the universe of discourse of the interpretation in question). The former, however, do not have this sort of generality. When the schema is interpreted, each predicate letter is replaced by a particular predicate. The generality which seems to attach to a predicate letter, unlike that of a genuine variable, is simply a matter of the multiplicity of possible interpretations which are available; within any given interpretation, however, the predicate letter is simply interpreted as a particular predicate, which is in turn thought of as a linguistic entity. Quine has emphasized the importance of the contrast between a schematic letter and a true variable in a passage which deprecates the use of the notation of higher-order logic, rather than that of set theory:

This notation has the fault . . . of diverting attention from major cleavages between logic and set theory. It encourages us to see the general theory of classes and relations as mere prolongations of quantification theory, in which hitherto schematic letters are newly admitted into quantifiers and other positions that were hitherto reserved for 'x' and 'y' etc . . . . The existence assumptions, vast though they are, can become strangely inconspicuous; they come to be implicit simply in the ordinary rule of substitution for predicate letters in quantification theory, once we have promoted these letters to the status of genuine quantifiable variables . . . along with somewhat muffling the existence assumptions of the theory of types, [the notation] fostered a notion that quantification theory itself, in its 'F' and 'G', was already a theory about classes or attributes and relations. *It slighted the vital contrast between schematic letters and quantifiable variables.*[34]

The contrast which is crucial to Quine's position is, however, not available to Russell. The notion of a schematic letter is an essentially meta-theoretic one, which relies upon the idea that logic consists of schemata which are subject to

---

[33] It is important to note that propositional functions are not *constituents* of propositions (see *Principia*, 54–5); this fact is crucial to the basis of type theory. But we must acknowledge propositional functions if we are to have any account of generality.

[34] *Set Theory and its Logic*, 257–8; my italics.

interpretation. Given Russell's conception of logic as universal, and as consisting of propositions which have a meaning and a truth-value just as they stand, the notion can make no sense to him. To understand Russell's position we therefore have to invert all of Quine's points. Given Russell's conception of logic, higher-order quantification theory—and thus the Russellian analogue of set theory—really *is* a mere prolongation of quantification theory, and the existence assumptions of this theory really *are* implicit in the ordinary rules for quantification theory. Quine's remarks occur in the context of a discussion of Russell's use, in *Principia* and elsewhere, of propositional functions rather than classes as fundamental entities. Quine's position is that it would be on every score preferable to assume classes or sets as fundamental, rather than to define them in terms of propositional functions. From the perspective afforded by a Russellian conception of logic, however, Quine's implicit attack on Russell is misdirected. Given this conception, the ontology of propositional functions (or at least of some entities corresponding to predicate variables) really is implicit in ordinary quantification theory and, indeed, in all ordinary propositions. The ontological assumptions here may indeed be vast, but they are not special assumptions about some special subject matter, as the assumption of the existence of classes would be. This, from a Russellian point of view, provides a reason to think that the theory of propositional functions is logic, as the theory of classes would not be.

This contrast between Russell and Quine enables us to see more clearly what is involved in Russell's conception of logic. Russell's conception of logic cannot be characterized simply in terms of the rejection of what I have called the model-theoretic conception of logic, for Quine's position does not depend upon his holding that conception. Quine, indeed, does not appear to hold this conception; he does not, that is to say, accept that logic consists of a formalism which is subject to various interpretations.[35] One salient feature of Russell's conception of logic is thus not merely its rejection of the view of logic as formalism and interpretation, but its insistence upon the unconditional and presuppositionless character of logic. For Russell, anything whose existence must be presupposed in order to establish or state logic is itself a part of logic. If logic demands that there be propositions, or relations, then as a matter of logic there are; so also for propositional functions.[36] In discussing Russell's use of logicism against idealism we saw

---

[35] See for example Quine's *Philosophy of Logic*.
[36] Here again there is a clear contrast between Russell and Kant (and equally between Frege and Kant). For Kant, logic has no objects of its own, and does not even deal with objects; its concern is with the understanding and its form (see especially *Critique of Pure Reason*, preface to the 2nd edn, at B ix). Russell's propositions and propositional functions, by contrast, are logical objects (as are Frege's *Wertverlaüfe*). One way to understand the significance of Russell's paradox, and related paradoxes, is as showing that Kant was right on this issue, and Russell and Frege wrong. The assumption that there are logical objects, when combined with the generality which both Russell and Frege took as characteristic of logic, leads to paradox; see section III, below.

something of the basis for this idea of presuppositionlessness. It is, perhaps, a matter of indifference whether one thinks of this as intrinsic to the universalist conception of logic, or as merely a feature of Russell's universal conception of logic. A second salient feature of Russell's conception of logic is that he takes it for granted that our concern is not with language. The 'entities corresponding to predicate variables', on Russell's account, are not linguistic entities. This assumption stems from Russell's general attitude that it is propositions which are of real concern, and that the study of language (as distinct from the propositions which it expresses) is of no intrinsic philosophical significance. (This attitude is seen most clearly in *Principles*. It is somewhat modified by the rejection of the *Principles* theory of denoting, which leads to the view that certain expressions must be understood as incomplete *symbols*; and by the theory of types, according to which certain *symbols* lack significance. Even in *Principia*, however, this attitude survives. It is manifest in the explicitness and emphasis with which Russell says he is talking about symbols when he is, as if he sees talking about symbols as an odd thing to do. See e.g. i. 11, 48 n. and 66–7.) This Russellian attitude is connected with a further feature of his early logic, to which I now turn.

Logic, for Russell, is not a subject to be studied syntactically. Russell, indeed, shows no sign of having a conception of syntax as a tool which might be used for this task. There is, of course, a contrast here with what I have called the model-theoretic conception of logic. According to that conception, logic consists of a formalism subject to various interpretations, and a formalism is an object defined and studied by syntactic means. One does not, however, have to hold the model-theoretic conception of logic in order to think that logic can be studied syntactically. Even on something like a universalist conception, one might think that at any rate certain significant fragments of logic could be set up and studied by syntactic means, and results proved which would show something about logic in the universal sense. This suggests that the contrast between the universalist conception of logic and the model-theoretic conception is too crude. Many philosophers, I suspect, hold both and are more or less conscious of the differences and the connections between them. Certainly it seems reasonable to attribute something like this two-fold attitude to Quine. The use of syntactic methods in the way that I have suggested appears, moreover, to be compatible with the view that in the fundamental sense logic is universal and presuppositionless. A philosopher who comes close to exemplifying this two-fold approach is Frege, and at this point it will be helpful briefly to compare his view of logic with that of Russell.

Much of what I have said of Russell's conception of logic as universal could also, I think, be said of Frege's conception of logic (although the motivation of Frege's logicism is, as I have already remarked, rather different from Russell's). What I have said of Russell's propositional functions, for example, could equally well be said of Fregean *Begriffe*. (There is of course a difference arising from the presence, within Frege's system, of a sharp distinction between *Begriffe* and *Gegenstände*. This has the consequence that no analogue of set theory, and hence also no danger of paradox, arises for Frege until we add to his system the statement that to every *Begriff* there is a corresponding *Gegenstand*—axiom V of *Grundgesetze*. For Russell, by contrast, no such axiom is necessary.) There is, however, one general difference between Russell's conception of logic and Frege's. Russell's conception of logic is based on a metaphysical view which could be, and to some extent was, articulated quite independently of logic. Russell, as we have seen, held himself to be indebted to Moore for the metaphysics of propositions and their constituents, of being and truth. This metaphysics is independent of the logic which Russell erected upon it (which is not to say that it has any plausibility when considered apart from Russell's logic). For Russell, then, the metaphysics was independent of and prior to the logic. For Frege, at least according to the interpretation that I find most compelling,[37] the opposite is true. For Frege, logic, in the sense of the inferences that we do in fact acknowledge as correct, is primary; metaphysics is secondary, and articulated in terms which presuppose logic.

What is the significance of this difference for the conceptions of logic held by Frege and by Russell? Since Frege took logic, the body of correct inferences, as prior to metaphysics, he was bound to be concerned to delimit this body in terms which made no metaphysical presuppositions. It is for these reasons, I think, that Frege gives something very like a modern syntactic account of logic. Frege's standards of formal rigour approach those of the more rigorous of modern logicians. For this reason the notion of a formal system seems to be at least implicit in Frege's work. (If one takes this notion to imply a meta-theoretic perspective, then of course Frege does not have it. His concern with rigour was an internal concern, an object-language concern: he wanted to do deductions and assure himself that they were gap-free.) For these reasons too it is easy to suppose that Frege holds something like the modern conception of logic, implying at least the possibility of a meta-theoretic approach. This, I think, is a mistake. Frege's use of syntax has a different origin from that of a modern logician; although his work seems to exhibit similar standards of rigour, the reason for the rigour is different.

To look at Russell's work with the expectation of finding anything like syntactic rigour, however, is to be disappointed. As Gödel has said of *Principia*:

It is to be regretted that this first comprehensive and thoroughgoing presentation of mathematical logic . . . is so greatly lacking in formal precision in the foundations . . . that it presents [*sic*] in this respect a considerable step backwards as compared with Frege. What is missing, above all, is a precise statement of the syntax of the formalism.

---

[37] See especially Ricketts, 'Objectivity and Objecthood'.

Syntactical considerations are omitted even in cases where they are necessary for the cogency of the proofs, in particular in connection with the 'incomplete symbols'.[38]

Our earlier discussions suggest that Russell's lack of concern with syntactic rigour is not a matter of carelessness. Why should Russell have any concern with syntax? Not in order to define an uninterpreted formalism which can then be subject to various interpretations, or to be able to treat a system of logic meta-theoretically, as itself the object of mathematical study. Both of these reasons are ruled out, for Russell, by his lack of a genuinely meta-theoretical perspective. Nor, on the other hand, does Russell have a reason of Frege's sort. Russell's philosophical-logical views do not need to be based on a neutral, and therefore syntactic, notion of correct logical inference, for Russell's metaphysics is independent of logic and therefore available for use in defining the notion of logic. The definition is given in terms of the notion of a proposition, of the constituents of a proposition, and of truth. These notions are, as we have already seen, ones to which we have direct and immediate access, through a non-sensuous analogue of perception. Thus there is no need for a syntactic approach, from Russell's point of view. This is not to say that anything in Russell's conception of logic in fact rules out such an approach, though this conception of logic does show something about the significance of the results which can be obtained in this way. What it does indicate is that the syntactic approach is not a natural one for someone with Russell's conception of logic; there is no particular reason why it should have occurred to Russell. Nor, indeed, do I think that it did. From Russell's point of view, therefore, there is no reason that the proofs of *Principia* should obey standards of rigour at all different from those of any ordinary working mathematician. By these standards the proofs of *Principia* can be faulted, but the faults are confined. The view of *Principia* as pervasively lacking in rigour stems from the assumption that the appropriate standards of rigour are syntactic. But this is not the authors' view of the matter—otherwise it would be wholly inexplicable that they should claim that their proofs are in fact unusually rigorous.[39] The fact that Whitehead and Russell employ standards of rigour which are not those of either Frege or of the modern logician is not something that we have to accept as

---

[38] 'Russell's Mathematical Logic', in Schilpp (ed.), *The Philosophy of Bertrand Russell*, 126.

[39] In the preface to the 1st edn of *Principia*, Whitehead and Russell say that '[t]he proofs of the earliest propositions are given *without the omission of any step*' (p. vi; my italics). The reasons they give for this care are also important. They do not appeal to any abstract standards of syntactic rigour, but to more practical considerations: 'otherwise it is scarcely possible to see what hypotheses are really required, or whether our results follow from our explicit premisses', and 'full proofs are necessary for the avoidance of errors, and for convincing those who may feel doubtful as to our correctness' (ibid.). How far they are from wishing to put forward a formal system in the modern sense may also be gathered from the Preface and from the discussion, in the introduction to the 1st edition, of their use of symbolism. They say in the introduction, for example, 'In proportion as the imagination works easily in any region of thought, symbolism (except for the express purpose of analysis) becomes only necessary as a convenient shorthand writing to register results obtained without its help.' (p. 3).

inexplicable (or explicable only by the dubious supposition of Russell's carelessness). Once we have a correct understanding of Russell's conception of logic we shall also understand what his standards of rigour are, and why they are not those of Frege, or of the modern logician.

What I have said above about Russell's standards of rigour in logic can, I think, be generalized. Much of what Russell says about logic differs from what a modern logician would say. But we do Russell an injustice, and impede our own understanding, if we do not see that these differences are explicable in terms of a coherent (if perhaps ultimately untenable) conception of logic which is quite different from the modern one. This conception of logic, in turn, is directly connected with the philosophical motivation of Russell's logicism. When we see why logicism mattered so much to Russell, we see also that his conception of logic *must* have been quite different from ours.

III

Although I have, in the preceding sections, drawn to some extent on *Principia Mathematica*, what I have said of Russell's conception of logic, and especially of the motivation of his logicism, is clearly more inspired by *Principles* than by *Principia*. How does the picture change when we focus on the later work? One important general shift is that the anti-idealist motivation ceases to play any overt role. Russell was as much of an anti-idealist in 1910 as in 1902, but the issue no longer seems urgent to him; he looks on that battle as long since won. A second change is philosophically more interesting. In *Principia* Russell expounds, and relies upon, the theory of types; this alters the picture suggested by *Principles* in ways that are extremely complex. In what follows I shall simply attempt to indicate some of the changes most relevant to the present perspective.

The theory of types has two effects which are worth distinguishing. First, it threatens the conception of logic that I have attributed to Russell; here the crucial facts are that Russell's logic after 1907 has to contain explicit type restrictions, and the axiom of reducibility. Second, it makes it dubious, at best, whether what Russell attempts to reduce to logic is indeed mathematics; here the chief difficulty is the necessity, in *Principia*, for what Russell calls (misleadingly, as we shall see) the axiom of infinity and the axiom of choice (I shall largely confine my discussion to the former.)[40]

---

[40] Like the so-called axiom of infinity, the so-called axiom of choice is not mentioned in *Principles* but is recognized in *Principia* as required for mathematics; like the axiom of infinity, again, it is not in fact taken as an axiom of *Principia* but is used as an hypothesis as required (see below, pp. 77–8. I shall not discuss the axiom of choice for two reasons. First, the philosophical issues which the need for this 'axiom' raises are raised also by the need for the axiom of infinity, which is perhaps more interesting for our purposes. Second, the fact that the axiom of choice is not discussed in *Principles* is not due to some

Let me begin with the axiom of reducibility. There is a clear contrast here between *Principles* and *Principia*; in the earlier work no such axiom is mentioned. In *Principles* there is no need for the axiom of reducibility or any analogue of it. The axiom of reducibility is required in *Principia* because of two features of that work, which conflict if the axiom is not assumed. First, propositional functions are employed to do the work of classes, whose existence need not be presupposed (in this respect *Principia* is unlike *Principles*). Second, to avoid the threat of paradox, there are complex distinctions of category among propositional functions; in particular, these distinctions prevent us from generalizing over all the propositional functions which are true or false of a given entity. The two features threaten to conflict because if propositional functions are to play the role of classes, it is essential that we be able to generalize over all propositional functions which are true or false of a given entity; otherwise the reduction of mathematics to logic (including the theory of propositional functions) becomes quite impossible. The axiom of reducibility removes this difficulty, more or less by stipulation. The crucial consequence of the axiom is that distinctions of ontological category among propositional functions true or false of a given object—i.e. distinctions of order—can be ignored for mathematical purposes.[41] The axiom achieves this effect by stipulating that for every propositional function, of whatever order, there is a *co-extensive* propositional function of the lowest order.[42] Thus in mathematics, where only the extensions of propositional functions concern us, we can achieve the effect of generalizing over all propositional functions true or false of a given object simply by generalizing over those of the lowest order. By this method, the needs of mathematics are reconciled with Russell's type theory.

difference between that work and *Principia* which implies that the issue does not arise in the former. It is, rather, simply that Russell was not aware, when he wrote *Principles*, that the axiom had to be assumed as an independent principle. As he himself says in the introduction to the 1937 edn, he 'did not become aware of the necessity for this axiom until a year after the *Principles* was published' (p. viii). I see no reason to doubt his later statement on this point. By contrast, the need for the axiom of infinity in *Principia* but not in *Principles* indicates a crucial difference between these works, as we shall see.

[41] The word 'order' is consistently used in this sense in the introduction to the 2nd edn of *Principia*. Ramsey adopts this usage, and confines the word 'type' to distinctions among propositional functions which are based on distinctions among the entities to which they can be significantly applied; see 'The Foundations of Mathematics', especially pp. 23–8. In his usage, there is thus a clear distinction between type and order, and many later authors have followed him in making this distinction. In the first edition of *Principia*, however, Russell's use of the words 'type' and 'order' does not consistently follow this rule. In particular, he often uses 'type' for both kinds of distinctions among propositional function (e.g. in 9.14, which will be discussed below, pp. 76–7). Although I follow Ramsey's use of the word 'order' here, my later discussion, like that of the 1st edn of *Principia*, uses the word 'type' in a non-Ramseyan way to include distinctions of order.

[42] Two propositional functions are said to be co-extensive if they are true of exactly the same things; the extension of a propositional function consists of those things of which it is true. If the notion of the extension of a propositional function were taken as fundamental, it would provide us with an analogue of set theory with no more ado. Russell's method of dispensing with the assumption that there are classes (or sets or extensions) is to define class symbols in such a way that a sentence involving such a symbol expresses a (more complex) proposition about propositional functions.

If *Principia* is to count as a reduction of mathematics to *logic* then the axiom of reducibility must, of course, be a logical truth. It is, however, very far from clear that counting this axiom as logically true is consistent with the conception of logic that I have attributed to Russell. In one sense the axiom is so consistent: it can be stated using only logical expressions. It is, however, very hard to see how the sort of rationale that I gave for thinking that the theory of propositional functions is part of logic could be extended to show that this axiom is a truth of logic. That rationale was, roughly, that the assumption that there are propositional functions is required to make sense of logical relations in which any proposition stands, whatever its subject matter; thus this assumption is required not to explain some special class of statements—those about classes, say—but to explain the possibility of propositions and their logical relations in general, regardless of their subject matter. Clearly, however, no such rationale will justify the idea that the axiom of reducibility is a truth of logic. The truth of the axiom is not required to explain the possibility of propositions, and of logical relations between propositions, of all kinds, without regard to subject matter. On the contrary: the existence assumption embodied in the axiom is clearly required only for the special purposes of mathematics and the theory of classes. Counting the axiom of reducibility as part of logic thus seems quite inconsistent with the conception of logic that I have attributed to Russell.

A similar difficulty arises in rather a different way from the fact that *Principia* contains, and must contain, explicit statements of type restrictions. The difficulty here does not arise from the mere fact that there are type restrictions. I have suggested that it is a truth of logic (on the Russellian conception) that there are propositional functions; it is also a truth of logic that no contradiction is true. If propositional functions must, to avoid contradiction, be subject to type restrictions, then it must also be true (and presumably also a truth of logic) that there are type distinctions among propositional functions. The difficulty arises not from the mere fact that there are type distinctions; it arises from the fact that these distinctions have to be stated within *Principia*. The crucial fact here is that according to the conception of logic which I have attributed to Russell there can be no genuine meta-perspective on logic: logic applies to every statement, and thus also to statements which are intended to limit the scope of the variable used in other statements.

We saw this point stated explicitly in 'Mathematical Logic as Based on the Theory of Types' (see p. 61, above). The point recurs in the introduction to *Principia*, where Russell again argues that the unrestricted variable is fundamental, but goes on to qualify the claim:

We shall find that the unrestricted variable is still subject to limitations imposed by the manner of its occurrence, i.e. things which can be said significantly concerning a proposition cannot be said concerning a class or relation, and so on. But the limitations to which the unrestricted variable is subject do not need to be explicitly indicated, since they are the limits of significance of the statement in which the variable occurs, and are therefore intrinsically determined by this statement (*Principia*, 4).

The picture that this suggests is that the limitations imposed by type theory do not need to be stated but will, in a later terminology, make themselves manifest. Certainly this is what *Principia* requires, for statements of the limitations imposed by restrictions of type are, as we shall see, liable to be in violation of type theory.[43] But the expectations aroused by this statement are not fulfilled. *Principia* does contain statements of type restrictions. These statements, moreover, do not occur merely in the expository prose, which has perhaps a purely heuristic function. On the contrary: the numbered sentences which are the heart of *Principia* themselves contain notions which are required to set up type theory, and which threaten to violate it. Thus *9.131 is a definition of 'being the same type as'; and the primitive proposition (axiom) *9.14 makes essential use of the notion, asserting 'If "ϕx" is significant, and if a is of the same type as x, "ϕa" is significant, and vice versa.' (for reasons already noted, p. 67, above, the proposition stated in *9.14 occurs again, with the number 10.121).

It is important to see clearly exactly why a statement establishing type theory—indeed the very notion 'is of the same type as'—violates type restrictions. If the clause 'a is of the same type as x' is not to be wholly otiose (and in fact it is not), then it must sometimes be true and sometimes false. That is, there must be an object, call it b, of which it makes sense to say that it is of the same type as some given object a, but where this is not true; and there must be another object, c, which is of the same type as a, and where this can also be said. But then there is one propositional function, that expressed by 'x is of the same type as a' which can be significantly applied both to b and to c (truly in one case, falsely in the other). But by a crucial tenet of type theory itself (expressed in the 'vice versa' clause of *9.14) it ought to follow from this that b and c are of the same type. Since 'is of the same type as' is transitive, this conclusion is directly contrary to the initial assumption that b is different in type from a but that c is of the same type as a.

The difficulty here clearly arises from the attempt to state type theory within type theory. The argument above constitutes a *reductio ad absurdum* of the idea that we can treat 'is of the same type as' as expressing a propositional function which must itself be subject to the restrictions of type theory. Yet the universality of logic, as I have articulated it, seems to demand that *every* proposition fall within the scope of logic, and that every propositional function be subject to type theory. Once again, the demands of type theory seem to be inconsistent with the

---

[43] This point was perhaps first made by Wittgenstein; see 'Notes on Logic', in *Notebooks* 1914–16, 98, 101.

conception of logic that I have attributed to Russell. On this issue there is a clear contrast between Russell's conception of logic and the model-theoretic conception. On the latter conception we have available a metalanguage in which we can state type distinctions for the object language; the question whether our statements in the metalanguage violate the type distinctions of the object language simply does not arise. It is also worth noting that the difficulty that I raised for Russell might be resolved by combining the universalist conception of logic with a syntactic approach to type theory, so that type restrictions would not state anything about (non-linguistic) entities, but would simply lay down conditions of well-formedness on combinations of symbols. I shall not, however, investigate this possibility here.[44]

I turn now to the issues raised by the so-called axiom of infinity. Again, it is worth noting that no such axiom is mentioned in *Principles*. The main body of that work advances a view which lacks any distinctions of logical category. It is, according to that view, thus provable that there are infinitely many entities: '... if *n* be any number, the number of numbers from 0 up to and including *n* is *n* + 1, whence it follows that *n* is not the number of numbers. Again, it may be proved directly, by the correlation of whole and part, that the number of propositions or concepts is infinite.' (section 339). The first of these arguments is directly analogous to that used by Frege to show that his definition of natural number ensures that there are infinitely many natural numbers.[45] The correctness of this argument in Frege's logic, however, is directly connected with those features of that logic which make it contradictory. So also in the case of Russell's *Principles*. One way to make this point is to say that it is only because of the lack, in the view conveyed in most of *Principles*, of any type distinctions that the argument works; once type distinctions are introduced to avoid paradox, the argument fails. Unlike Frege, Russell is aware of the need for type distinctions, or some analogous way of avoiding the paradox. He is, however, not satisfied by the systems of types that he considers, and most of *Principles* proceeds as if Russell had never discovered the paradox. Certainly this is true of the present point. The issue of the axiom of infinity does not arise in *Principles* because Russell believes—or is willing to write as if he believes—that the infinitude of entities is provable by the general methods of logic.

In *Principia*, by contrast, type theory makes it impossible to prove that there are any infinite classes unless there are infinitely many *individuals*. This matter,

---

[44] A syntactically specified version of *Principia* would also be clearly inadequate for mathematics because of Gödel's incompleteness theorem, which states that any (consistent) formalism fails to prove some arithmetical truth. *Principia* is not syntactically specified, and it is by no means evident that one should think of it as a (rather careless) formalism at all. It is thus by no means clear that *Principia*, as its authors intended it, is vulnerable to an argument based on Gödel's theorem.

[45] Compare Frege, *Foundations of Arithmetic*, section 82.

Russell insists, cannot be settled by logic: 'This assumption [the axiom of infinity] . . . will be adduced as a hypothesis whenever it is relevant. It seems plain that there is nothing in logic to necessitate its truth or falsehood, and that it can only be legitimately believed or disbelieved on empirical grounds.' (*Principia*, vol. II, p. 183). Russell does not, however, assume the infinitude of individuals as an axiom (although he does use the expression 'the axiom of infinity'). He says, rather, that both this so-called axiom and the axiom of choice are to be taken 'as hypotheses', i.e. as antecedents to conditionals, wherever they are needed (besides the passage from *Principia* vol. II, p. 183, quoted above, see also vol. I, p. 482).

Russell's attitude towards the axiom of infinity does not threaten the conception of logic that I have attributed to him. It does, however, threaten the fundamental project of logicism: it might be said that *Principia* represents not so much the culmination of Russell's logicism as Russell's abandonment of logicism. It is, however, a subtle question, whether a form of (pseudo) logicism that is forced to take the axiom of infinity as an extra-logical assumption can play the philosophical role that I claimed Russell's early logicism played. One of the arguments that I attributed to Russell was simply that mathematics is an example of a body of absolute truth, whose truth was in no way dependent upon (or conditioned by) the spatio-temporal; this example undermines a crucial idealist doctrine. Stated like this, the argument no longer holds. Mathematics will no longer stand as an undeniable example of knowledge which is absolute, valid beyond the realm of the spatio-temporal, and non-trivial (i.e. obviously genuine knowledge). Mathematics, i.e. logic plus the axiom of infinity, is presumably dependent upon whatever evidence we may have for there being an infinitude of individuals, and individuals presumably exist in space and time (hence the statement in the passage quoted above that the infinitude of individuals is an empirical matter). It is, however, possible that the basic point of Russell's claim would still hold. Logic (not including the axiom of infinity) is not shown by the need for the axiom of infinity to be other than wholly general and absolutely true. It is perhaps less obvious than before that logic is an example of genuine knowledge, rather than being analytic in Kant's sense, but the point is at least arguable. It is thus possible that logic, including the theory of propositional functions but excluding the axiom of infinity, could play the anti-idealist role for which Russell originally cast mathematics. The fate of the other argument that I attributed to Russell is equally unclear. This argument had to do with the crucial role of mathematics in showing that consistent theories of space and time are available. Now if it were thought that the consistency of the infinite, and indeed the transfinite, depended simply upon the fact that their existence is a truth of logic, then clearly the need for an extra-logical assumption of infinity would be fatal. Or again, it might be thought that the crucial question posed by the need for an extra-logical assumption of the infinite is the consistency of this assumption (given the truths of logic); to this question Russell clearly has no answer. An interpretation somewhat more sympathetic to Russell, however, might claim that the power of his position comes from the fact that he is able to show that particular arguments purporting to show the inconsistency of the infinite are one and all erroneous. This fact continues to hold. The logic of *Principia*, though it cannot prove that there are infinitely many entities, can define the notion of the infinite; the understanding embodied in this definition is sufficient to show that traditional philosophical arguments against the infinite are misconceived.

The details of the impact of type theory upon Russell's conception of logic and of logicism are very complex. But even from the outline given above it is clear that the picture which I sketched of the motivation of Russell's logic and of the Russellian conception of logic is seriously threatened by the introduction of type theory. Should we infer from this that Russell's views on these matters shift between *Principles* and *Principia*? Is it incorrect to attribute the earlier picture to Russell at the time of *Principia*? I suggest that it is wrong in principle to insist that there must be a definite answer to a question of this sort. In the case of this particular question I suspect that no clear-cut answer would emerge, even if all the facts were known. The most significant facts in this case are, first, as we have seen, that the development of type theory does undermine Russell's earlier conception of logic and his philosophical claims for logicism; second, he does at times show at least some awareness of this; third, within the relevant period Russell does not find any other conception of logic, or any other view of the significance of logicism, which is remotely plausible. This third fact is in some ways the most significant, for it means that Russell continues, at least when his attention is not fully focused on the issue, to talk as if he still held the old conception of logic, and the old view of logicism. Insofar as any general philosophical conception of logic influences him at this time it is this one. He does not really discard the old picture, for he has nothing with which to replace it; on the other hand, he cannot continue to hold this picture with a clear conscience.

One way of thinking about this situation is as an example of what is, I think, a more general truth. When philosophy takes on a technical guise there is always the danger that the technical endeavour will take on a life of its own. One may become caught up in the technical endeavour, and cease to think very hard about whether it will still serve the purposes that originally motivated it, or any others. When the resulting mathematical achievement is *Principia Mathematica*, the neglect of philosophy may be pardonable, even laudable; commentators, however, should be wary of assuming that so great an achievement, simply in virtue of its magnitude, *must* have a philosophical point. It is entirely possible that changes in the enterprise, perhaps dictated by technical needs, cause it to lose contact with the considerations that gave it its original point. Something like this, I think, happened to Russell's logicism.

One piece of evidence in favour of the general reading that I am advancing is that Russell never attempts, in *Principia*, to give an account of logic, even when such an account seems to be called for. Thus his statement of the conditions that a logical system must satisfy, the analogues of completeness and consistency, reads like this:

The proof of a logical system is its adequacy and its coherence. that is: (1) the system must embrace among its deductions *all those propositions which we believe to be true and capable of deduction from logical premises alone* . . . and (2) the system must lead to no contradictions (*Principia*, 12–13, my italics; cf. also pp. v, 59–60).

The first of these two criteria is the analogue of completeness: our system of logic must be powerful enough. But Russell has no characterization of what *powerful enough* comes to, because he has no way of characterizing logic (which the system is presumably trying to capture). He cannot characterize it semantically, as suggested by the model-theoretic conception, for this conception is still wholly alien to this thought. Yet neither can he characterize it in terms of the universalist conception, for these terms do not fit the type-theoretic system of *Principia*. Instead he offers a statement of what a system of logic ought to be able to prove which is completely without content; as an account of logic it would be absurd. Taken quite literally it makes any (axiomatizable) theory at all reducible to logic, provided we can persuade ourselves to believe that that theory is reducible to logic or that its axioms are principles of logic; given our belief, logic just expands (so to speak) to embrace the relevant axioms. But what, then, is the content of the *belief* that such a theory is reducible to logic? What is it that we are trying to persuade ourselves to believe? Russell, so determinedly anti-psychologistic, would hardly advance a view according to which the scope of logic is dependent upon the beliefs which we have; what the passage indicates, I think, is that he simply has no account of logic which he can accept.[46] He realizes, more or less clearly, that his previous view of logic will not do, and so realizes that

---

[46] The question of the nature and status of logic occupied Russell after the completion of *Principia*. It appears that this was to have been one of the issues discussed in the unwritten third portion of Russell's projected 1913 book, *The Theory of Knowledge*. See *Collected Papers*, vol. vii, which contains as much as Russell wrote of the book, and also discusses his plans for the remaining portions.

some alternative account is required, but he simply has no coherent alternative to offer.

A second piece of evidence for the reading that I am advancing is the eagerness with which Russell later adopts a new view of logic—a view which he admittedly does not fully understand at the time. In the final chapter of his *Introduction to Mathematical Philosophy*, written in 1918, Russell discusses the nature of logic (and thus, given logicism, of mathematics) as follows:

All the propositions of logic have a characteristic which used to be expressed by saying that they were analytic, or that their contradictories were self-contradictory. This mode of statement, however, is not satisfactory . . . Nevertheless, the characteristic of logical propositions that we are in search of is the one which was felt, and intended to be defined, by those who said that it consisted in deducibility from the law of contradiction. This characteristic, which, for the moment, we may call tautology . . . (*Introduction to Mathematical Philosophy*, 203).

Russell eagerly claims that logic consists of tautologies (he is influenced in this by his earlier conversations with Wittgenstein; at the time he wrote this, however, he had not read the *Tractatus Logico-Philosophicus*). He insists upon this in spite of the fact that, as he says, he does not know how to define 'tautology' (p. 205). It ought to be a puzzle to us that so great a thinker as Russell can insist, in diametrical opposition to his earlier views, that logic has an essential characteristic which he cannot define, and cannot explain in a fashion which is at all illuminating. Without a clear understanding of the notion of tautology, how could he possibly have reason to believe that logic consists of tautologies? Part of the answer to this puzzle no doubt lies in the impact that Wittgenstein's personality had on Russell before the First World War, an impact that was evidently not dependent upon Russell's understanding of Wittgenstein's views. But a crucial part of the answer also must be Russell's recognition that his thought about the nature of logic was bankrupt: his old view will no longer work, he has nothing to take its place, and yet his work crucially depends on logic having some kind of special philosophical status. Under these circumstances he clutches at the word 'tautology', hoping, perhaps, that Wittgenstein will emerge from the trenches with a definition of the word which will enable it to play the role that Russell needs it for.

My conclusion, then, is not straightforward. If one focuses on *The Principles of Mathematics* a rather clear picture emerges of Russell's conception of logic and of the general philosophical motivation of Russell's logicism; the two are connected in complex ways which I have tried to indicate. This clear picture is, however, only possible because the main doctrines of *Principles* ignore the difficulties posed by Russell's paradox and related paradoxes. No doubt Russell thought that he would find a solution to the paradoxes which did not threaten anything which he took to be philosophically fundamental. This hope, however, was misplaced; the theory of types, I have argued, *does* undermine philosophically crucial aspects of Russell's early conception of logic. The magnificent structure of *Principia* is thus left without a clear and coherent philosophical motivation.[47]

[47] I should like to express my gratitude to the organizers of the conference in Munich where this paper was read, and to the Volkswagen Stiftung for making the conference possible. I cannot mention all those at the conference who gave me criticism, advice and encouragement, but I should like to thank them all, and especially Peter Clark and Bill Hart. For criticism of earlier drafts of this paper I am indebted to Francis Dauer, Michael Friedman, Warren Goldfarb, Leonard Linsky, Thomas Ricketts and, especially, Burton Dreben.

4

Russell's Substitutional Theory

The work in which the basis of *Principia Mathematica* was first presented (Russell, 'Mathematical Logic') contains one peculiarly baffling passage. After setting up a hierarchy of propositions. Russell says:

In practice, a hierachy of *functions* is more convenient than one of propositions. Functions of various orders may be obtained from propositions by the method of *substitution*. (Russell, 'Mathematical Logic', 77)

In what immediately follows, however, Russell seems to put forward not a method of obtaining functions but rather a method of eliminating them, replacing them by what he calls 'matrices':

If *p* is a proposition, and *a* a constituent of *p*, let '*p/a;x*' denote the proposition which results from substituting *x* for *a* wherever *a* occurs in *p*. Then *p/a*, which we will call a *matrix*, may take the place of a function; its value for the argument *x* is *p/a;x*, and its value for the argument *a* is *p*. . . . *In this way we can avoid apparent* [*i.e. bound*] *variables other than individuals and propositions*. . . .

    Although it is *possible* to replace functions by matrices, and although the procedure introduces a certain simplicity into the explanation of types, it is technically inconvenient. Technically it is convenient to replace the prototype *p* by Φ*a*, and to replace *p/a;x* by Φ*x*; thus where, if matrices were being employed, *p* and *a* would appear as apparent variables, we now have Φ as an apparent variable. (loc. cit.; long emphasis mine)

Russell is here alluding to a theory which he developed around 1906, and called 'the substitutional theory'. This theory should not be confused with what is today called 'the substitutional theory of quantification'. The modern theory has essentially to do with the substitution of names for one another within sentences or other linguistic objects; in Russell's theory, as we shall see, neither propositions nor the entities substituted within them are linguistic. (Russell's other name for the theory is also, in retrospect, unfortunate. He calls it 'the no-classes theory', but this is a term which he applies equally to the type theory of *Principia*. Since this name is ambiguous in this way I shall avoid it.) The purpose of this paper is to explain Russell's substitutional theory and, more especially, to explain why he developed it and why he subsequently discarded it. An account of

I am indebted to Burton Dreben for helpful discussions and advice; and to Susan Neiman for criticism of the final draft of this paper.

the philosophical pressures which led to the substitutional theory is an indispensable part of a general understanding of the philosophical context of *Principia Mathematica*: I hope to provide such an account. The substitutional theory turned out to be a blind alley, but an understanding of Russell's motives in exploring it will help to show the general direction in which he wished to proceed.

I

My aim in this section is to sketch enough of Russell's philosophy of the relevant period to make clear the constraints within which he hoped to be able to avoid the paradox which bears his name. I shall show that the need to escape from the paradox conflicts with Russell's most fundamental philosophical assumptions, giving rise to a tension within his thought. This enables us to understand the attraction which the substitutional theory had for Russell: it seemed to offer a way of avoiding the paradox without threatening his philosophy. As will become apparent in section III, however, the substitutional theory turned out to lack the advantages which Russell first attributed to it, so that in the end he abandoned it as 'technically inconvenient'. The tension in Russell's thought thus remains unresolved, and survives in *Principia*, where it tends to distort Russell's account of type theory, adding confusion to matters which would in any case not be straightforward.

My discussion in this section draws largely upon Russell's *Principles of Mathematics*. While his views changed between the publication of that book (1903) and the period which is our concern (say, 1905–7), these changes must, I believe, be understood as modifications of the basic framework of *Principles*.

(i) The Universality of Logic

The truths of logic, as Russell saw the matter, embody the correct principles of reasoning. This idea may seem uncontroversial, even obvious, but in fact it marks a crucial difference between Russell's conception of logic and that of the modern logician (post-Gödel, say). According to Russell's understanding of logic, all reasoning employs logic and is subject to logic. Logic can, therefore, have no metatheory: we cannot reason about logic from the outside, for all reasoning is, *ipso facto*, within logic. We can of course set up different formalisms, and study their metatheories; but nothing that we can treat in this way is *logic*. It is in this spirit that Russell denies the possibility of (the usual kind of) independence proofs for the axioms of logic:

[I]t should be observed that the method of supposing an axiom false, and deducing the consequences of this assumption, which has been found admirable in such cases as the axiom of parallels, is here not universally available. For all our axioms are principles of deduction; and if they are true, the consequences which appear to follow from the employment of an opposite principle will not really follow. . . . (Russell, *Principles*, 15)

One cannot deny an axiom of logic and see what follows, for the axioms of logic are the principles of correct reasoning, and the notion of one thing following from another is lost if one of these axioms is denied. If an axiom of logic is denied, reasoning itself becomes impossible.

This conception of logic, as embodying the correct principles of reasoning, and thus as universal, is quite different from the modern view of the subject. A central concept of modern logic is that of truth in an interpretation, where an interpretation will include the specification of a set as the universe of discourse, i.e. what the variables are to be interpreted as ranging over. The notion of an interpretation is a metatheoretic one, and one that is consequently foreign to Russell's thought. Russell's logic is not a formalism which awaits interpretation to give a meaning to its formulae. Rather, these formulae already have meaning, and the range of the variables in them is not some independently specified universe of discourse but, simply, *the* universe. A universal quantification thus makes a claim about all objects, and the question of its truth or falsity for a given interpretation does not arise: either the claim is true of all objects that there are or it is not. (Similar remarks are true also about Frege's conception of logic. Frege, like Russell, thinks of logic as universal, and thus as not subject to interpretation; hence his insistence that his logic, unlike Boole's, expresses a content, e.g. Frege, 'Über den Zweck der Begriffsschrift', 90–1. See also van Heijenoort, 'Logic as Calculus and Logic as Language'.)

An understanding of the way in which Russell thinks of logic enables us to explain features of his work which, from a modern point of view, appear as oddities or as trivial mistakes. One such feature is the fact that Russell can give no coherent account of the notion of a rule of inference. This is because the notion is an essentially metatheoretic one. If the rule of inference is just one more statement within the theory, then we require another rule of inference to show that the conclusion follows from the premises together with this state-ment; and the new rule is in turn subject to just the same argument (see Carroll, 'What the Tortoise said to Achilles'). Rules of inference are thus a source of difficulty for Russell. He speaks of 'a respect in which formalism breaks down' (Russell, *Principles*, 41), and retreats to the view that the validity of an inference cannot in the end be a matter of rules but rather 'must be simply perceived, and is not guaranteed by any formal deduction' (loc. cit.). It is to be noted that this same view of rules of inference holds sway also in *Principia*, although Russell is there somewhat less frank about its difficulties. The rules are, again, simply counted as among the primitive propositions of logic, and the consequence, again, is that no clear account of their use emerges (Whitehead and Russell,

Principia, e.g. pp. 94, 98, 106; this view of rules of inference is, I believe, a partial explanation of the notorious fact that *Principia* contains no explicit rule of substitution).

The universality of logic, as I have tried to indicate, follows directly from the conception of logic as embodying the correct principles of reasoning. This is a conception which Russell everywhere presupposes, but nowhere articulates; he does not seem to have been aware of it as an assumption, to which there might be alternatives. We cannot, therefore, explore Russell's arguments for the conception. What we can do, however, is to see how crucial a role it played in Russell's thought at this period. In particular, I shall argue that Russell's overarching project of reducing mathematics to logic gets its purpose—in Russell's eyes, at least—from this conception of logic.

If one thinks of the reduction of mathematics to logic as being simply the construction of a mapping, subject to certain constraints, between two uninterpreted formalisms, then it is clear that the philosophical interest of this achievement requires explanation. The obvious form of such an explanation is that the one formalism, considered either as uninterpreted or as subject to its natural interpretation, has some philosophically significant property, and that the reduction shows that, contrary to what would otherwise be supposed, the other formalism also has this property. Thus the logical positivists claimed that the logic of *Principia* was analytic, and that the reduction of mathematics to this logic showed that mathematics also is analytic. But this motive cannot be imputed to Russell, for he did *not* think that logic is analytic; he seems to take the reduction of mathematics to logic as showing that, since mathematics is synthetic a priori, logic must be so too (Russell, *Principles*, 457; *Problems*, 82–90). Nor can it be claimed that it is any epistemological characteristic—certainty, for example—which Russell ascribed to logic and hoped to transfer, via the reduction, to mathematics; Russell's paradox, and the difficulty of its solution, made it impossible to suppose that logic is more certain than mathematics. Russell even went so far as to claim that a part of our evidence for the axioms of logic comes from the fact that they enable us to derive the independently known truths of mathematics (Russell, 'On "Insolubilia" ' 194; see also Whitehead and Russell, *Principia*, 37).

Russell's reason for the reduction of mathematics to logic, therefore, cannot be to show mathematics to be analytic, or to increase the certainty of our knowledge of it. Russell's motive in this, his dominant intellectual project for nearly ten years, can only be understood in terms of the conception of logic that I have sketched. If logic consists of the correct principles of inference, and mathematics is reducible to logic, then mathematics is thereby shown to involve no assumptions which are not already involved in any thinking or reasoning at all. In particular—and this, I believe, takes us to the heart of the matter—mathematics is thereby shown not to depend upon any facts about the forms of our intuition of space and of time, and so the Kantian theory is refuted:

There was, until very lately, a special difficulty in the principles of mathematics. . . . Not only the Aristotelian syllogistic theory, but also the modern doctrines of Symbolic Logic, were either theoretically inadequate to mathematical reasoning, or at any rate required such artifical forms of statement that they could not be practically applied. *In this fact lay the strength of the Kantian view.* . . . Thanks to the progress of Symbolic Logic . . . this part to the Kantian philosophy is capable of a final and irrevocable refutation. (Russell, *Principles*, 4; my emphasis. See also p. 457.)

What I wish to emphasise, then, is not just that Russell held the conception of logic which I have described, but that this conception was a fundamental part of his philosophy: without appealing to this conception we are unable to explain the importance of what was most central to Russell's thought in this period, namely the reduction of mathematics to logic.[1] (Frege's motives in undertaking the logistic reduction must, I believe, be explained similarly, i.e. in terms of his conception of logic as universal. Frege spoke of logic as 'analytic', but this word did not play the same explanatory role in his philosophy as it did in, say, Carnap's.)

(ii) Terms, Concepts, and Propositions

In this sub-section I shall explain other aspects of Russell's underlying philosophy, especially his views about the nature of propositions and the status of their constituents. I begin with the notion of a *term*, as it occurs in *Principles*. The word 'term' is, according to Russell, 'the widest word in the philosophical vocabulary' (Russell, *Principles*, 43).[2] Anything you can think of or talk about is a term; hence, as Russell says, 'to deny that such and such a thing is a term must always be false' (loc. cit.). Ordinary concrete objects, abstract objects, and putative but non-actual objects are all terms; Russell's own examples include a man, a moment, a relation, a chimera, and the Homeric Gods (Russell, *Principles*, 43, 449). Terms are not the words which name these things, but are the things themselves.

---

[1] This claim is borne out by Jager, who neglects the conception of logic which I have emphasised, and seems to think that the only motive which the logistic reduction could have is that of showing mathematics to be analytic. Nonplussed by Russell's statement that logic is synthetic a priori, he fails to give any coherent account of Russell's motives. In particular, Jager denies that the reduction can be seen as in any way anti-Kantian, in spite of Russell's explicit statements that it is. See Jager, *The Development of Bertrand Russell's Philosophy*, 218–21.

I should emphasise that my discussion has glossed over several subtle issues, e.g. what Russell meant by 'analytic' and by 'synthetic a priori', and the role of the refutation of Kant's theory of mathematics within a more general attack upon Kant, as well as upon the idealist tradition which Russell saw as stemming from Kant.—These matters are given fuller treatment in Hylton, *Russell and the Origins of Analytic Philosophy*.

[2] Russell's use of the word 'term' in *Principles* is closely related to Moore's use of the word 'concept' in 'The Nature of Judgement'. See Russell *Principles*, pp. xviii, 44; and Moore, 'The Nature of Judgment'.

Thus not every term *exists*, in the ordinary sense of being in space and time; but every term *is*, or subsists, or has Being. In *Principles* Russell clearly believes that every name we can use succeeds in naming some term; but, as we shall see in section II, the possibility of a different view was already implicit in his philosophy.

Russellian terms unite to form Russellian propositions. Propositions are thus not linguistic entities, except when they are about words. Russell is, at this time, never interested in words for their own sake. When he mentions them at all, it is usually only to say that they are *not* his concern, as here:

Words all have meaning, in the simple sense that they are symbols which stand for something other than themselves. But a proposition, unless it happens to be linguistic [i.e. about words] does not itself contain words: it contains the entities indicated by words. Thus meaning, in the sense in which words have meaning is irrelevant to logic. (Russell, *Principles*, 47)

The term, or terms, which forms the subject-matter of a proposition will in the normal case be one of the terms *occuring* in the proposition, or, equivalently, one of the *constituents* of the proposition. Thus when Russell speaks of Socrates occuring in (say) the proposition that Socrates is human, this means exactly what it says: it is Socrates, the man himself, who is a constituent of the proposition (Russell, *Principles*, e.g. p. 43).[3] The general rule is that the terms which are the subject-matter of the proposition are also among its constituents. The only exceptions to this rule are provided by those propositions which contain denoting concepts. A denoting concept, such as *all numbers*, is a single term which stands in the rather mysterious relation of denoting to some other term or terms. The denoting concept *all numbers* stands in this relation to all the numbers. Denoting concepts differ from other terms in that when a denoting concept occurs in a proposition the subject-matter of the proposition is not that denoting concept itself, but is rather the term or terms which it denotes. Thus the proposition that Socrates is human both *contains* Socrates and is *about* Socrates, but the proposition that all numbers are prime contains the single denoting concept *all numbers*, but is about all the numbers. Russell introduced denoting as a mechanism whereby a proposition might be about infinitely many objects—as is the proposition that all numbers are prime—without containing infinitely many objects (Russell, *Principles*, e.g. p. 73); but once introduced the notion came, as we shall see, to be used in other ways and to other ends.

Terms unite to form propositions, but not just any combination of terms forms a proposition. We can attribute mortality to Socrates, but we cannot

---

[3] This view is so counter-intuitive that it may be hard to believe that Russell meant it literally, but the evidence that he did so is overwhelming. Moore, 'The Nature of Judgment', does something to explain the reasons for this view. See Hylton, *Russell, Idealism, and the Emergence of Analytic Philosophy*, for a full discussion.

attribute Socrates to mortality. This is the basis of a distinction which Russell makes among terms. Those terms which can only occur in a proposition as subject, never as what is attributed to the subject, he calls 'things'. All other terms are called 'concepts', and Russell holds that they can occur in propositions either as subject or as what is attributed to the subject (Russell, *Principles*, 44–5). This, for our purposes, is the crucial point. Unlike Frege's distinction between *Gegenstände* and *Begriffe*, Russell's distinction between things and concepts is not a distinction between what can occur only as subject and what can occur only attributively. 'Every term', Russell says, 'is a logical subject: it is, for example, the subject of the proposition that itself is one.' (Russell, *Principles*, 44). Some logical subjects can appear *only* as logical subjects, while others can appear both as logical subjects and attributively:

Socrates is a thing, because Socrates can never occur otherwise than as a term [i.e. as subject] in a proposition: Socrates is not capable of the curious twofold use which is involved in *human* and *humanity*. (Russell, *Principles*, 45)

One confusing piece of terminology should be noted here. Although everything is a term, Russell speaks of something occurring as a term in a proposition only if it is a subject of that proposition; similarly he speaks of the terms of a proposition, meaning its logical subjects (Russell, *Principles*, e.g. p. 45). The reason for this is that one of the things that Russell means by 'term' is logical subject; everything is a term because everything can be a logical subject, but in a given proposition only some among its constituents occur as terms, i.e. as logical subjects.

Russell does not simply assume that the distinction he draws among terms is the correct one. He explicitly considers the view, analogous to Frege's, that what can occur attributively cannot also occur as subject, i.e., as he puts it, that

a distinction ought to be made between a concept as such and a concept used as a term, between e.g. such pairs as *is* and *being*, *human* and *humanity*, one in such a proposition as 'this is one' and 1 in '1 is a number'. (Russell, *Principles*, 45)

Russell rejects this view, and his reasons for doing so are of the first importance. The basis for the rejection is that the view cannot be stated without presupposing its own falsehood. Consider the proposition that *human* is, and *humanity* is not, capable of occuring as a logical subject. In this proposition, *humanity* occurs as a logical subject; but this is just what the proposition says is impossible. So the fact that there is such a proposition shows that it cannot be true. It is worth quoting Russell at some length on this point:

. . . suppose that *one* as adjective differed from 1 as term. In this statement, *one* as an adjective has been made into a term; hence either it has become 1, in which case the supposition is self-contradictory; or there is some other difference between *one* and 1 in addition to the fact that the first denotes a concept which is a term. But in this latter hypothesis there must be propositions concerning *one* as term, and we shall still have to maintain propositions concerning *one* as adjective . . . yet all such propositions must be false, since a proposition about *one* as adjective makes *one* the subject, and is therefore really about *one* as a term. . . . This state of things is self-contradictory. (Russell, *Principles*, 46)

This argument presupposes that the statement that *one* as adjective differs from 1 as a term is subject to the same rules as are the statements we make using *one* as an adjective. The argument, that is, could be defeated by the claim that when we say that *one* is an adjective we are talking in the metatheory about a language in which *one* can only occur as an adjective; the fact that it occurred as a term in the metatheory would then not be damaging. But we have already seen that the universality of logic would, in Russell's eyes, rule out the possibility of any such appeal to a metalanguage not subject to the rules of logic. If this argument of Russell's is successful, it shows more than may at first sight appear. It does not in fact depend upon its being the same term which appears now as subject, now as adjective. All that is crucial to it is that a term will appear as subject in any proposition about it, e.g. that it cannot appear as logical subject, that it is a term, that it occurs in a proposition. So any proposition which says of anything that it is not a logical subject must be false: everything is a logical subject.

We can attain a different perspective on this argument by comparing it to the difficulty that Frege found himself in concerning the concept *horse*. As we have already seen, Russell's position is that everything can be a logical subject, whereas Frege's is that some things—*Begriffe*—cannot be. Russell takes as contradictory what Frege simply calls 'an awkwardness of language' (Frege, 'Über Begriff und Gegenstand', 46), namely that the concept *horse* is not a concept. Since a Fregean concept can never occupy the subject place in a proposition, the phrase 'the concept *horse*', which does occupy subject position, cannot refer to a concept. Thus for Frege the two phrases 'the concept *horse*' and '. . . is a horse' do not refer to the same thing: as Russell might put it, the concept taken as predicate is for Frege different from the concept taken as subject (this mode of expression is not, of course, Frege's). How, then, can Frege say, as he does, that 'the concept . . . is predicative' (Frege, 'Über Begriff und Gegenstand', 43)? The expression 'the concept' in this sentence, since it occupies subject position, refers to a concept taken as subject, not as predicate (as Russell might put it). But then the sentence, taken literally, is false. If Frege's theory is true, then, there is no way in which we can say that a concept is essentially predicative in nature, and so no way in which we can state Frege's theory itself.[4] For Russell this is enough to

---

[4] This is at least one of the origins of the doctrine of Wittgenstein's *Tractatus*: that certain facts about language are unsayable.

show that Frege's theory cannot be true: the theory consists of propositions which according to that theory itself cannot be propositions at all, and if they are not propositions, they certainly cannot be true.

Now it might be thought that these difficulties arise for Frege only because we take too naive a view of the matter. Russell argues that there cannot be entities which are incapable of becoming logical subjects, but this, it might be held, need not rule out a view like Frege's. Such a view requires a hierarchy of levels of concepts. Call the kind of concept that can be attributed to Socrates (whether truly or falsely) a 'first-level' concept. Then first-level concepts *can* be logical subjects; we cannot attribute other first-level concepts to them, but there are second-level concepts which can be attributed to them, and third-level concepts which can be attributed to second-level concepts, and so on. Thus there is nothing which cannot, at some level and in some sense, be a logical subject, nothing that we cannot talk about; yet no concept can have a first-level concept attributed to it. This view is, however, subject to the same objection as was the more naive view, although the objection naturally takes a more sophisticated form. The naive view was self-defeating because the attempt to say that a given concept could not be a logical subject involved making that concept a logical subject. The more sophisticated view is self-defeating in a parallel, if more devious, fashion.

Consider the statement that only first-level concepts can be attributed to Socrates. If this statement is to do what we want, it must imply that second-level concepts (and concepts of every higher level) can *not* be attributed to Socrates. But now consider the concept '. . . can be attributed to Socrates'. Assuming the universality of logic, this concept itself must occupy a determinate position in the hierarchy of concepts; but it cannot do so. The concept is true of first-level concepts, and so should be a second-level concept; but it is false of second-level concepts (and of concepts at every higher level), and so should be a third-level concept (and also a fourth-level concept, and so on). So it turns out that we cannot establish a hierarchy of concepts, because the statements by means of which we attempt to do so must be nonsensical if the hierarchy is correct.

Russell does not discuss Frege's hierarchy of concepts, but he does employ an argument with the same structure as the above. Considering the view that variables only range over some given universe of discourse, not over all objects, he says:

We might say that a given function Φx will always have a certain *range of significance* which will be either *individuals*, or *classes*, or . . . The difficulty of this view lies in the proposition (say) 'Φx is only significant when x is a class'. This proposition must not be restricted, as to its range, to the case when x is a class; for we want it to imply 'Φx is not significant when x is not a class'. We thus find that we are brought back after all the variables with an unrestricted range. (Russell, 'On "Insolubilia" ' 204–5)

What makes this of particular interest is that the theory of types is vulnerable to the same argument. *Principia* employs the notion '. . . is of the same type as . . .' not only in its expository prose but also in its numbered sentences: *9.14, for example, is a primitive proposition which states 'if "*Φx*" is significant, then if *x* is of the same type as *a*, "*Φa*" is significant, and vice versa.' (Whitehead and Russell, *Principia*, 133). Now '. . . is of the same type as *a*', where *a* is some individual, is a concept which is true of individuals. If the type restrictions are to be effective it must also be false, and thus significant, of non-individuals. But by the vice versa clause of *9.14, if a concept is significant as applied to two entities, the two must be of the same type. So if there is such a concept as '. . . is the same type as . . .', then there is only one type; but if there is no such concept then we cannot establish the type-hierarchy.[5]

(iii) The Paradox

The considerations thus far advanced were taken by Russell to establish two doctrines. The first is that concepts—the objective correlates of the predicates of sentences—are logical subjects or terms; given the universality of logic, the attempt to say of a particular concept that it is not a logical subject must presuppose that it *is* a logical subject. The second doctrine is that there can be no distinctions of type among logical subjects, i.e. that all terms are intersubstitutable *salva significationem*; again the crucial point is the universality of logic, which makes distinctions of type impossible, since the statement of such a distinction would itself violate the distinction.

These two doctrines together yield a contradiction—a version of Russell's paradox with predication substituted for class membership, and concepts or propositional functions for classes.[6] It was in fact in this form that Russell first stated the paradox in his letter to Frege, of the 16th June 1902:

Let *w* be the predicate, being a predicate which cannot be predicated of itself. Can *w* be predicated of itself? From either answer the opposite follows. (Russell, Letter to Frege, 125)

---

[5] The point that the statement of typerestrictions must violate type restrictions was made by Max Black (Black, 'Russell's Philosophy of Language'). Black, however, made the point only as an argument against the idea that type restrictions should be imposed upon ordinary language. My claim is that the unstatability of type theory within type theory was a problem for Russell in any case, and that this problem largely accounts for the difficulty he had in producing a theory which would avoid the paradox.

[6] Russell's reasons for taking propositional functions, rather than classes, as primitive in *Principia* seem to be twofold. First, propositional functions, unlike classes, are implicit in every proposition. This universality makes them good candidates for being logical entities, whereas classes, if assumed as primitive, would form a special subject-matter, the study of which would take us beyond logic. Secondly, Russell believed, or hoped, that type restrictions as applied to propositional functions had a naturalness that they would not have if applied directly to classes. Russell sometimes speaks as if it were the fact that classes are not assumed as primitive in *Principia* which enabled him to avoid the paradox (e.g. Russell, 'My Mental Development', in Schilpp (ed.), *The Philosophy of Bertrand Russell*, 14). A charitable exposition of Russell must understand this as a reference to the second of the above reasons, for if

Frege simply ignores this version of the paradox, and concentrates on the statement in terms of classes, because his hierarchy of concepts prevents the paradox for *Begriffe*. This is why the source of the contradiction in Frege's system is most naturally thought of as being the notorious axiom V of *Grundgesetze*, which states that the *Wertverläufe* (value-ranges) of two concepts are identical just in case the two concepts are co-extensive. Given that *Wertverläufe* are objects, this allows us to derive the contradiction. Each *Wertverlauf* must either fall under or fail to fall under any given concept—including that concept with which it is associated. So there is a concept expressed by '. . . is a *Wertverlauf* which does not fall under the concept with which it is associated'; and there is a *Wertverlauf* associated with this concept. Now we have only to ask whether this *Wertverlauf* falls under the concept with which it is associated, and the paradox results. In Frege's system the paradox thus stems from the assumption that there is an object associated with every concept, together with the identity-conditions for those objects. But for Russell the paradox arises without the use of any special assumption. For Russell there is no question whether concepts are *associated* with things that can play the role of logical subjects; concepts themselves must be capable of playing this role. The arguments which I have explored earlier in this section seem to prove that this must be so; yet if it is so, paradox seems to result.

There is thus a fundamental tension between, on the one hand, Russell's doctrine of the universality of logic, and, on the other hand, the need to avoid the paradox. The substitutional theory was an attempt to resolve this tension, and to avoid the paradox by means consistent with the universality of logic. The arguments we have examined show, or at least were taken by Russell to show, that concepts must capable of being used as logical subjects, and that there can be no distinctions of type among logical subjects. Given that there *are* concepts, the contradiction follows immediately: but, equally, our conclusions appear quite harmless if we deny that there are concepts. The argument that concepts must be capable of occurring as logical subjects did not show that there are any concepts, and would be quite consistent with this denial. A theory which did not assume that there are any concepts (or propositional functions) would therefore seem to offer Russell a way out of his dilemma: and this was the attraction of the substitutional theory.

II

In this section I shall, very briefly, explain the substitutional theory, and show how it exploits the notion of an incomplete symbol to attain an expressive power

propositional functions are not subject to typerestrictions a contradiction directly analogous to the class paradox arises. See Russell, 'On Some Difficulties in the Theory of Transfinite Numbers and Order Types', 154 n.; Quine, 'Russell's Ontological Development', 660–1.

which one might suppose impossible without the assumption of classes, or concepts. I shall not, however, attempt any rigorous development of the theory, much less a proof that it is, as Russell thought it to be, adequate to encode mathematics.[7]

It follows from what has already been said that the substitutional theory is to avoid the assumption that there are concepts. We are no longer to analyse propositions into a subject (or subjects) and what is said about the subject. Instead of this, the theory treats propositions as unanalysable. We still speak of propositions as containing entities, and we can substitute one entity for another in a proposition to obtain a possibly different proposition. But what is abandoned is the idea that p can be analysed into two elements, a and the property which p asserts to hold of a.[8] Writing at a time before he was fully committed to the substitutional theory, Russell put it like this:

> ... if we make statements of the form $F!x$ about a number of different values of x, we cannot pick out an entity F which is the common *form* of all these statements, or is the property assigned to x when we state $F!x$. (Russell, 'On Some Difficulties in the Theory of Transfinite Numbers and Order Types', 137)

The language here is the language of propositional functions, but it is, strictly speaking, superfluous. If we recognise propositional functions as entities which differ in type from objects, then we must *say* that they are of different type: and we have seen the trouble to which this leads. But a theory which does not recognise propositional functions as among the entities of the world is not committed to saying anything about them. Such a theory can be explained by talking only of propositions, and of substitutions of one entity for another within propositions. (The situation is perhaps a little more complicated than this way of putting it would suggest; this will emerge when I discuss the role of the idea of an incomplete symbol.)

The substitutional theory, then, assumes an ontology of entities, some of which are propositions, and the notion of substitution. The expression '$p/a;b$' is to mean 'the result of substituting a for b in p'. Strictly speaking, this notation is defined only in the context '$p/a;b!q$', which means 'q results from substituting

---

[7] Grattan-Guinness, 'The Russell Archives', goes further in some directions than I have done. Strictly speaking, a rigorous development of the theory is impossible, for Russell never presents the theory in rigorous form. His worknotes are full of attempts at an axiomatisation, but none seems to have satisfied him. The difficulties Russell encountered here are no doubt the 'technical inconvenience' of Russell, 'Mathematical Logic', 77.

[8] If Russell had worked out the implications of this view, his underlying philosophy would have changed very considerably. In 1900 Russell had written: 'That all sound philosophy should begin with an analysis of propositions is a truth too evident, perhaps, to demand proof.' (Russell, *Leibniz*, 8). Over the next decade the analysis of the proposition was his constant and central concern. The substitutional theory has the immediate consequence that propositions have to be accepted as basic, unanalysable entities.

b for a in p', but Russell frequently uses the shorter notation as either a name or an assertion of the q such that $p/a;b!q$. I shall follow Russell's usage on this point.

The notion of substitution is meant to apply to more than one entity at once, i.e. we want to be able to substitute b for a and b' for a', and so on. Now we could say that '$p/(a, a');(b, b')$' is to mean '$(\exists r) (p/a;b!r \And r/a';b'!q)$', and so on. But this would not be satisfactory. We want q to contain b' in just those places where p contains a'; but if a is a constituent of a', then $p/a;b$ will not contain a' at all. To define the sort of multiple substitution that we want we first define various notions:

$$a \text{ ex } p = \text{df. } (\forall x)(p/a;x!p)$$

This is read 'a does not occur in p', and simply means that a is not a constituent of p. The negation of this we abbreviate as 'a in p'. If two entities have no constituents on common, they are said to be independent of one another:

$$p \text{ ind } q = \text{df. } (\forall x)\sim(x \text{ in } p \And x \text{ in } q)$$

(See Russell, 'On the Substitutional Theory of Classes and Relations', 169 for these definitions.) Now we can define simultaneous substitution for two entities. Suppose we want to substitute c and d for a and b in p. If b is in a, choose an entity a' which is not in p, and which is independent of b and of d. First substitute a' for a, then d for b, then c for a'. If b is not in a, choose an entity b' which is not in p, and which is independent of a and of c. First substitute b' for b, then c for a, then d for b'. By this technique of choosing neutral entities, we can define simultaneous substitution for any given number of entities.

The power of the substitutional theory comes from the way in which it exploits the notion of an incomplete symbol. This notion, although not this name, first appears in 'On Denoting' (I shall abbreviate this article as O.D.), but the concentration on definite descriptions there makes the matter hard to grasp in its full generality. It seems to be widely believed that the main point of O.D. is to show that sentences such as 'The King of France is bald' or 'The round square does not exist' can be meaningful without our having to assume that there is (in some sense) such a thing as the round square or the King of France. Ayer certainly holds this view (Ayer, *Bertrand Russell*, 49–51), and Sainsbury seems to have this idea in mind when he says 'The theory of descriptions offered a release from the supposed need for nonexistent beings' (Sainsbury, *Russell*, 17). This idea is, however, quite mistaken, and it prevents us from achieving a clear view of exactly what change in Russell's philosophy is effected by O.D. We have seen that when a proposition is expressed by a sentence including a denoting phrase then, according to the view in *Principles*, the proposition is *about* what is denoted but *contains* the denoting concept. Thus, while the proposition that Socrates is mortal contains the man that it is about, the proposition that the

Queen of England is mortal does not contain the woman that it is about, but rather contains the denoting concept *the Queen of England*. But then the proposition that the Queen of England is mortal does not require that there *be* a Queen of England in any sense, merely that there be a denoting concept that purports to denote her. It thus appears that the mechanism of denoting—i.e. the theory which Russell held before O.D.—can be employed to do away with the need to recognise the King of France or the round square. Russell did not employ the theory of denoting in this way in *Principles*, but he came to do so before he wrote O.D.:

'The present king of England' is a complex concept denoting an individual; 'The present king of France' is a similar concept denoting nothing. The phrase intends to point out an individual, but fails to do so: it does not point out an unreal individual, but no individual at all. The same explanation applies to mythical personages, Apollo, Priam, etc. These words have a *meaning* . . . but they have not a denotation: there is no entity, real or imagined, which they point out. (Russell, 'The Existential Import of Propositions', 100)

Since this pre-O.D. theory enables Russell to avoid the view that there must be such an entity as the King of France, we cannot think of O.D. as designed to achieve this result.

The decisive move in O.D., then, is not the rejection of the view that denoting phrases must actually denote something if they are to have a use—for this was a view that Russell had already rejected, on a quite different basis. The decisive move is, rather, the rejection of the idea that denoting phrases function as logical units. According to the *Principles* view, a phrase such as 'the *F*' in a sentence corresponds to an entity, the denoting concept *the F*, in the propositions which correspond to the whole sentence. According to the theory of O.D., by contrast, there is no entity in a proposition which corresponds to the phrase 'the *F*'. If the sentence is, say, '*G* (the *F*)' (i.e. 'The *F* is *G*') then the form of the corresponding proposition is more accurately given by the sentence

$$(\exists x)(Fx \,\&\, (\forall y)(Fy \equiv y = x) \,\&\, Gx)$$

In this sentence there is no occurrence of the phrase 'the *F*'; and similarly, according to O.D., there is in the corresponding proposition no entity corresponding to the phrase 'the *F*'. This is why Russell calls such phrases 'incomplete symbols': by itself such a phrase does not stand for anything and thus, in Russell's terminology, has no meaning; but certain longer expressions, containing such phrases, do have meaning if taken as wholes. An incomplete symbol is thus a symbol which has been defined in certain contexts, but which does not itself stand for anything. We have already seen that there are pressures in Russell's thought which lead towards the view that expressions which stand for entities are everywhere intersubstitutable *salva significationem*, and this enables us to make a sharp contrast between these expressions and incomplete symbols, for the latter will make sense only in contexts for which they have been defined, and from which they are eliminable. This is why Russell says that an incomplete symbol is a phrase which 'by itself has no meaning at all, but by the addition of other symbols or words becomes part of a symbol or phrase which has meaning, i.e., is the name of something' (Russell, 'On the Substitutional Theory of Classes and Relations', 170).

The importance of this move is concealed rather than revealed by focusing on phrases of the form 'the *F*'. There are two connected reasons for this. The first, and more important, is that although phrases of the form 'the *F*' are only defined contextually, it turns out that they are in fact defined for *all* contexts in which we would naturally use a singular referring expression. Secondly, although a phrase such as 'the *F*' does not stand for the *F*, still, if an ordinary sentence containing the phrase is true, there must be an object which is uniquely *F*. By speaking here of an 'ordinary sentence', I mean to exclude both denials of existence ('There is no such thing as the *F*') and negations of wide scope ('It is not the case that: the *F* is *G*'). Excluding sentences of these kinds, i.e. considering only those which purport to affirm or deny something about the *F*, we can say that there must be a unique *F* if a sentence containing the phrase 'the *F*' is to be true.

The power of the notion of an incomplete symbol, which is concealed by its application to definite descriptions, is clearly shown by the use that Russell makes of it in the substitutional theory. The most crucial incomplete symbol (in its simplest form) is 'p/a'. This symbol does not stand for an entity, though both 'p' and 'a' do, and there is no entity which is p/a, whatever p and a may be (whereas for some instances of *F*, there is an entity which is the *F*, even though 'the *F*' does not stand for this entity). The symbol 'p/a' is defined, but only in certain contexts. We have already seen the definition of '$p/a;b!q$', but in this context 'p/a' does not even appear to name an entity—'the result of replacing *a* in *p* by' is clearly not the name of anything. The other contexts which are crucial for the theory are '$b \in p/a$' and '$p/a = q/b$'. Both of these are defined, and in such a way that it is clear that there is no entity named by 'p/a':

$$b \in p/a = \text{df. the } q \text{ such that } p/a;b!q \text{ is true}$$
$$p/a = q/b = \text{df. } (\forall x)(p/a;x \equiv q/b;x)$$

The definition of '$=$' between symbols of the form $p/a_1 \ldots a_n$ is a straightforward generalisation of the above:

$$p/a_1 \ldots a_n = q/b_1 \ldots b_n = \text{df.}(\forall x_1 \ldots x_n)(p/(a_1 \ldots a_n); (x_1 \ldots x_n)$$
$$\equiv q/(b_1 \ldots b_n); (x_1 \ldots x_n)$$

The extension of '$\in$' is a little more complicated, and two cases should be treated differently. First:

$$b_1 \ldots b_n \in p/(a_1 \ldots a_n) = \text{df the } q \text{ such that } p/(a_1 \ldots a_n);$$
$$(b_1 \ldots b_n)!q \text{ is true}$$

Secondly:

$$q/(b_1 \ldots b_n) \in p/(a_1 \ldots a_{n+1}) = \text{df. } (\forall r, c_1 \ldots c_n)$$
$$\{(q/(b_1 \ldots b_n)) = (r/(c_1 \ldots c_n)) \supset \text{the } s \text{ such that}$$
$$p/(a_1 \ldots a_{n+1}); (r, c_1 \ldots c_n)!s \text{ is true}\}$$

Symbols of the form 'p/a' or, more generally, symbols of the form '$p/a_1 \ldots a_n$', are thus defined for certain contexts. These are sentences in which symbols of this form appear to occupy subject-position and to be referring expressions. But the definitions show that these sentences are in fact only misleading ways of expressing propositions which are more accurately (though less briefly) expressed by sentences in which '$p/a_1 \ldots a_n$' does not occupy subject-position, or appear in any sense to refer to an entity. Thus the definitions show that some of these sentences may be true even though there is no such entity as p/a. Russell calls things such as p/a 'matrices', and attempts to show that they can perform all the functions which classes must perform if we are to reduce mathematics to the theory of classes. Now there are no such things as matrices. Symbols of the form 'p/a' enable us to talk, in certain contexts, as if there were; but these symbols get their significance not from standing for entities but simply because our definitions have given them a significance in those contexts. A symptom of this is that such expressions are eliminable wherever they are significant. It is natural to express this by saying, as Russell does, that a matrix is a mere symbol. Though Russell is certainly, by modern (or Fregean) standards, careless about use and mention, it would be a mistake to think that his use of this quite natural mode of expression indicates any real confusion. Still less should we take it as showing that Russell held matrices to be linguistic entities. This view makes nonsense of Russell's claim that 'a matrix is not an entity' (Russell, 'On the Substitutional Theory of Classes and Relations', 170), for one could hardly deny that the *expression* 'p/a' is an entity. To put the matter beyond all doubt, he does occasionally spell out his position more rigorously: 'When we say "so-and-so is not an entity", the meaning is, properly speaking, "The *phrase* 'so-and-so' is not the name of an entity." ' (loc. cit.).

Russell did not, in O.D., cast doubt on the idea that only a genuine entity can be the subject of a proposition. On the contrary, he actually removed some of the qualifications with which he had previously held this view. What is new with O.D. is the idea that in many or most sentences the grammatical subject does not correspond to an entity. The decisive break with *Principles* is not the rejection of the view that only entities which *are* in some sense or having Being can occur in propositions; Russell continues to believe this. The decisive break is rather that the grammatical form of the sentence is no longer to be taken as the logical form of the proposition. Thus we can make sense of sentences which appear to be about matrices—and we can claim that some of these sentences are true—without having to assume that there *are* matrices.

This is important because we can now avoid the paradox while still admitting that entities are everywhere intersubstitutable *salve significationem*. As Russell puts it, reverting to the terminology of propositional functions:

> . . . it is essential to an entity that it is a possible determination of *x* in any propositional function *Fx*; that is, if *Fx* is any propositional function, and *a* any entity, *Fa* must be a significant proposition. (Russell, 'On the Substitutional Theory of Classes and Relations', 171)

Now if p/a were an entity we should, according to this principle, have to admit that '$p/a \in p/a$' expresses a proposition; and thus the danger of paradox arises. But in fact 'p/a' is a symbol which our definitions allow us to eliminate only from certain contexts. If we try to read '$p/a \in p/a$' in accordance with our definitions we get something like 'the result of replacing *a* in *p* by the result of replacing *a* in *p* by'—and taken as a complete utterance this is clearly nonsense. What the matrix-notation allows us to do is to achieve the effects of a type-hierarchy while still maintaining that there are no distinctions of type among entities. The hierarchy is based on the impossibility of substituting more or fewer than *n* entities for *n* entities and still obtaining a proposition, i.e. on the fact that

$$p/(a_1 \ldots a_n);(b_1 \ldots b_m)!q$$

only makes sense if $n = m$. If we express all matrices in the form '$p/(a_1 \ldots a_n)$' and call *n* the *type* of the matrix, it follows that '$A \in B$' will not express a proposition unless *either* A is an entity and B is a type-1 matrix, *or* A is a type-*n* matrix and B is a type-$n + 1$ matrix. On the other hand, it follows from our definitions that if either of these conditions *is* satisfied then '$A \in B$' *will* express a proposition. We thus obtain a hierarchy of matrices which is entirely analogous to the hierarchy of classes (or propositional functions) in simple type theory. The crucial difference is that, because matrices are not entities, the restrictions on meaningfulness do not need to be stated. If we use our definitions to eliminate all uses of defined expressions, it will simply be evident whether or not the resulting sentence is significant. As Russell puts it:

> When a formula contains matrices, the test of whether it is significant or not is very simple: it is significant if it can be stated wholly in terms of entities. Matrices are nothing but verbal or symbolic abbreviations; hence any statement in which they occur must, if it is to be a significant statement and not a mere jumble, be capable of being

stated without matrices. (Russell, 'On the Substitutional Theory of Classes and Relations', 177)

The point here is simply that uses of matrix-expressions, except for their use in the original substitution context, '$p/a;b!q$', make sense only in virtue of our contextual definitions. So we ought to be able to eliminate all such uses to obtain a sentence which is 'stated wholly in terms of entities', i.e., a sentence in which all apparent referring expressions refer to entities. If we cannot do this, because a matrix-expression occurs in a context from which our definitions do not enable us to eliminate it, then the sentence does not express a proposition.

Let us speak of the *basic language* of the substitutional theory as the language of the theory without any of the expressions introduced by contextual definitions; and of the *extended language* as the basic language with the expressions introduced in this manner. Then we can make the point of the above paragraph by saying that in the basic language of the theory there are no type-restrictions upon significance. Every apparent subject-expression is a genuine subject-expression, and these are interchangeable *salva significationem*. In the extended language there will be type-restrictions among apparent subject-expressions, i.e. among matrix-expressions, but these restrictions will follow from the way in which matrix-expressions are introduced by contextual definitions, and will not need to be stated *ad hoc*. Any putative sentence of the extended language which violates type-restrictions will contain expressions introduced by contextual definition in a context from which our definitions do not enable us to eliminate them; or else will contain such expressions in contexts from which they cannot be eliminated without our substituting more or fewer than n entities for n entities in some proposition. In either case the attempt to restate the sentence in the basic language will make the failing evident, without the need to appeal to type-restrictions. Because the type-restrictions only hold among incomplete symbols, and not among genuine entities, they are, strictly speaking, superfluous; we do not need to worry whether type-restrictions of this Pickwickian kind are self-defeating, for our theory need never state them.

The substitutional theory thus allows us to simulate (some fragment of) the theory of classes without assuming that there are classes, or propositional functions; and since we avoid these assumptions we seem also to avoid the need for type-restrictions. Other means of simulating the theory of classes are restricted in power because they offer no means of expressing quantification over classes (e.g. Quine's theory of virtual classes; Quine, *Set Theory and its Logic*, 15–21); Russell's theory, however, allows us to do this. We cannot, of course, say 'For all one-place matrices, p/a, . . . p/a . . .' or 'For all matrices of one-place matrices, $p/(q/a)$, . . . $p(q/a)$ . . .', but we can achieve the effect of saying this. I assume we have the notion '*a* is a proposition'.[9] Then we can say:

$(\forall x, y)$(If x is a proposition & y in x then . . . . x/y . . .)
$(\forall x, y, z)$(If x is a proposition & y in x & z in x then . . . $x/(y, z)$ . . .)
$(\forall x, y, z)$(If x is a proposition & y is a proposition & y in x & z in y,
then . . . $x/(y/z)$ . . .)
and so on.

Thus quantification over matrices is eliminable by means of quantification over propositions of the requisite degree of complexity and their constituents.

Some idea of the power of the theory may be gathered from the way in which it can handle the definition of the ancestral of (the analogue of) a relation. Suppose we have a two-place matrix, $p_1/(a_1, a_2)(p_1$ might be, say $a_1 + 1 = a_2$, in which case $p_1/(a_1, a_2)$ is the analogue of the successor relation). We wish to find a matrix $q/(b_1, b_2)$ such that $q/(b_1, b_2);(x, y)$ is true just in case one of the following list of propositions is true:

$p_1/(a_1, a_2);(x, y)$
$(\exists z)(p_1/(a_1, a_2);(x, z)$ & $p_1/(a_1, a_2);(z, \text{y}))$
$(\exists x, z')(p_1/(a_1, a_2);(x, z)$ & $p_1/(a_1, a_2);(z, z')$ & $p_1(a_1, a_2);(z', \text{y}))$
$(\exists z, z', z'')(p_1/(a_1, a_2);(x, z)$ & . . .
. . .

In other words, we want $q/(b_1, b_2)$ to be the ancestral of $p_1/(a_1, a_2)$. Now consider the proposition:

$(\forall x, y)\{(x$ is a proposition & y in x & $(\forall z,w)(x/y;z$ & $p_1/(a_1, a_2)$;
$(z, w) \supset x/y;w)$ & $(\forall z)(p_1/(a_1, a_2);(b_1, z) \supset x/y;z)) \supset x/y;b_2\}$

If now we call this proposition q, then $q/(b_1, b_2)$ is the matrix that we want. (This way of defining the ancestral of a given relation is directly analogous to that in Whitehead and Russell, *Principia*, 543–4, except that we use matrices instead of classes.)

III

In this section I turn to the question of why Russell abandoned the substitutional theory. We have already seen that it is not because he finds the theory inadequate for mathematics: as late as 1908 he says that the theory is 'possible . . . although . . . technically inconvenient' (Russell, 'Mathematical Logic', 77; quoted

---

[9] Russell changes his mind about whether this notion is to be assumed as primitive or not. In any case, we must either assume it or find a way of defining it.

in full above).[10] Nor is it plausible to suppose that the technical inconvenience of the theory would by itself deter Russell; we have seen that the reasons which drove him to develop the theory were fundamental to his philosophy, and we should expect to find that the theory was abandoned for reasons no less fundamental.

One such reason, which has been held to explain Russell's abandonment of the substitutional theory, stems from his concern with the concept of truth. In the *Principles of Mathematics*, and throughout the three or four years immediately following its publication, Russell accepted the concept of truth as indefinable, and the fact that all propositions are either true or false as inexplicable. He even went so far as to say that our preference for true propositions over false ones could only be explained as 'an ultimate ethical proposition' (Russell, 'Meinong', 76). Not surprisingly, he came to find this unsatisfactory, and sought to explain truth in terms of the correspondence of the constituents of a proposition with reality. This theory, as Russell developed it, had the immediate consequence that, while the constituents of a proposition are real, propositions themselves are not. Expressions which appear to refer to propositions are incomplete symbols which have meaning only in a context in which we assert the proposition, or suppose it, or deny it, etc. Russell, that is to say, came to deny that propositions have any reality independent of our acts of judgement. This view is incompatible with the substitutional theory, which demands the independent existence of propositions for, as we have seen, the theory makes essential use of quantification over propositions.

Russell's concern with the nature of truth thus provides a possible reason for his abandonment of the substitutional theory, and it has been claimed that it is *the* reason (see Grattan-Guinness, 'The Russell Archives', 398–401). Closer consideration, however, suggests that this reason was at least not primary. One issue here is simply the timing of the two changes in Russell's views. Circumstances suggest that he abandoned the substitutional theory towards the end of 1906, or very early in 1907. The two articles of 1906 in which Russell advocates the theory are followed not by works in which he develops it further, but by a period during which he does not discuss such fundamental matters in print. The next time he does so, it is to put forward the type theory of *Principia Mathematica*, based not on substitution but on propositional functions (Russell, 'Mathematical Logic'). A paper which he read in March 1907 only alludes to these issues, but it is to propositional functions that it alludes, not to substitution (Russell, 'The Regressive Method of Discovering the Premises of Mathematics'). But if Russell did abandon the substitutional theory this early, it was not because he no longer

---

[10] *Pace* Quine, who claims that Russell abandoned the hope that the substitutional theory would be adequate for mathematics soon after the paper of February 1906. Quine, Introduction to Russell's 'Mathematical Logic as Based on the Theory of Types', 150–1.

believed in the reality of propositions. In another paper of 1907 he declares himself undecided as to the existence of propositions (Russell, 'On the Nature of Truth and Falsehood' section III), and it is not until 1910 that he publicly rejects them (Russell, *Philosophical Essays*, 147–58). A second reason not to take the rejection of propositions as explaining the abandonment of the substitutional theory is that by doing so we overestimate Russell's concern with the consistency of his various theories. Given the importance of the issues at stake, it would have been unsurprising if Russell had both developed a logic relying upon quantification over propositions and explained the nature of truth in a way which implies that propositions do not exist, leaving the reconciling of these two positions as an open problem to be solved later. Indeed we may say not only that Russell *might* have done this but that he did do it for, as Grattan-Guinness points out, *Principia Mathematica* itself relies upon quantification over propositions (Whitehead and Russell, *Principia*, 1910, 41–3; see Grattan-Guinness, 'The Russell Archives', 401).

Russell's abandonment of the substitutional theory is to be explained not in terms of a conflict between that theory and other parts of his philosophy, but rather in terms which are internal to the theory and to his reasons for adopting it. To put the matter very briefly, the substitutional theory as I have sketched it (the simple substitutional theory, as I shall call it) turns out to be vulnerable to paradoxes. These paradoxes are what we would call semantic rather than logical, but within the substitutional theory they arise without the use of any special assumptions. The theory can be modified so as to avoid these paradoxes, but, so modified, it lacks just those features which, I claimed, made it attractive to Russell. Given that the theory no longer possessed those features, we can understand why Russell might have abandoned it for reasons of technical convenience.

One example of the paradoxes to which the simple substitutional theory is vulnerable is the following. Some matrices have only propositions as members: p/a is such a matrix just in case $p/a;b$ is true only where b is a proposition. With each such matrix, p/a, we associate a proposition, p_a^*, which says that all the members of p/a are true, i.e. $(\forall x)(p/a;x \supset x$ is true$)$. Now let q be the following proposition:

$$(\exists p,a)(p_a^* = (\ (\forall x)(p/a;x \supset x \text{ is true}) \ ) \ \& \sim (p_a^*, \in p/a) \ ).$$

Then q/p_a^* is a matrix all of whose members are propositions. So we associate with it a proposition, $q_{p_a^*}^*$ which says that all the members of q/p_a^* are true. But now is $q_{p_a^*}^*$ a member of q/p_a^*? The members of q/p_a^* are those propositions which say of some matrix that all of its members are true, and which are not themselves members of the matrix of which they say this. $q_{p_a^*}^*$ satisfies the first of these conditions, so it is a member of q/p_a^* just in case it also satisfies the second condition by failing to be a member of the matrix all of whose members it asserts to be true. But since that matrix is q/p_a^* itself, we have a contradiction.

The semantic paradoxes are often taken as showing that the notion of truth should be excluded from logic. But in this case such a reaction would be inappropriate. First, the universality of logic means that we cannot exclude truth from our logic without rejecting the notion altogether, and this is something that Russell would certainly not have been prepared to do at this stage in his philosophical development. A second, more fundamental point, is that the substitutional theory demands that we employ the notion of truth. We cannot, for example, define membership in a matrix except by saying something equivalent to: 'b is a member of p/a' is to mean 'the q such that $p/a;b!q$ is true'. This use of the notion of truth is sometimes disguised by Russell's habit of using sentences ambiguously, sometimes as names of propositions and sometimes as assertions of them; but this ambiguity itself makes an essential, if tacit, use of the notion of truth.

The simple substitutional theory presented in 'On the Substitutional Theory of Classes and Relations' is thus vulnerable to paradox, and this presumably explains the odd history of this paper, which Russell read to the London Mathematical Society in May 1906, but withdrew from publication in October of the same year. In the intervening months he not only realised the problem, but also found a solution. On 'insolubilia' and their solution by symbolic logic (Russell, 'On "Insolubilia" ', first published in September 1906) directly addresses the semantic paradoxes (Russell speaks of the *Epimenides* or liar paradox, but his solution applies quite generally), and proposes to avoid them by distinguishing types of proposition. The distinction is effected according to the number and type of bound variables which they contain. The lowest level propositions contain no bound variables. Then we have propositions containing one variable ranging over individuals, propositions containing two variables ranging over individuals, and so on. Propositions containing variables ranging over propositions form a distinct and higher order, whose lowest level consists of propositions containing one variable ranging over propositions containing one variable ranging over individuals (propositions containing no variables seem to be counted among individuals), and so on. Whatever we may say about a proposition of one type cannot be said with sense about a proposition of any other type: words such as 'true' which appear to violate this requirement are deemed ambiguous (Russell, 'On "Insolubilia" ', 208). Thus the paradox which I explained above is blocked. Since p_a^* is $(\forall x)(p/a;x \supset x$ is true), p_a^* is of higher type than anything which can be substituted with sense for a in p, so $p_a^* \in p/a$ is nonsensical.

This version of the substitutional theory (ramified substitutional theory, as I shall call it) does not allow us to quantify over all propositions, but only over all propositions of a given type. As in the case of the analogous restriction on propositional functions in ramified type theory, this restriction threatens our ability to do mathematics. In particular, the law of mathematical induction becomes impossible to state (Russell, 'On "Insolubilia" ', 211). In ramified type theory the axiom of reducibility was introduced to avoid this difficulty, and here Russell makes an analogous move:

There is no objection, on the score of the *Epimenides* to the assumption that every statement containing x and a variable is *equivalent*, for all values of x, to some statement containing no apparent variable. (Russell, 'On "Insolubilia" ', 212)

This assumption makes the ramified substitutional theory as powerful as the simple version for all mathematical purposes, while still preserving its freedom from semantic paradoxes.

   To understand why Russell abandoned the ramified substitutional theory, we have to refer back to the reason which, I argued, explains why he first adopted the substitutional theory. If we make distinctions of type among the entities assumed by our logic, then we must be able to state the resulting type-restrictions. But such statements themselves violate type-restrictions. Thus any logic with the universality which Russell took as definitive of logic cannot be subject to type-restrictions. The substitutional theory seemed to be able to accommodate this argument without paradox, because there are no distinctions of type among the entities which it assumes (matrices are not entities). But this crucial virtue belongs only to the simple substitutional theory, for in the ramified version we have to acknowledge distinctions of type among the propositions which the theory assumes to exist. Statements of the restrictions upon meaningfulness which arise from these distinctions will be subject to the kind of difficulty which I discussed in the case of concepts or propositional functions: they cannot be reconciled with the universality of logic. If my account of the attraction which the simple substitutional theory had for Russell is correct, then the ramified version would have no such attraction for him. There would, in fact, be no reason for him to work within this theory rather than to assume propositional functions; he might well switch from one theory to the other for reasons of technical convenience.

IV

Whether the reduction of mathematics to logic is possible depends, of course, upon what one understands by logic; this will also determine the philosophical interest which a successful reduction would have. The essential feature of logic as Russell saw it was, I argued, its universality. If logic consists of the principles of correct reasoning, then all reasoning must be subject to logic. Logic will thus be all-pervasive and inescapable. It is only in terms of this conception of logic, I claimed, that we can understand the philosophical significance which Russell attributed to the logistic reduction.

It does not immediately follow from the universality of logic that the assumption of the existence of concepts or propositional functions is an extra-logical assumption. This assumption, unlike that of the existence of sets, does not appear to introduce any special subject-matter, for concepts are, arguably, involved in all propositions and thus in all reasoning. The difficulty comes from the fact that the indiscriminate assumption of concepts leads to paradox, and more discriminating assumptions require statements which are incompatible with the universality of logic. It was this problem which, I claimed, led Russell to develop the substitutional theory, for that theory appeared to be a consistent logic powerful enough to encode mathematics, but which did not violate the universality of logic. But this appearance, as we have seen, proved to be illusory. The notions of substitution and truth, which allowed Russell the hope of reducing mathematics to a theory which assumed neither classes nor concepts, also proved powerful enough to yield paradoxes. As in the case of the indiscriminate assumption of propositional functions, the restrictions which restored consistency were incompatible with the universality of logic.

The conflict between the universality of logic and the need to avoid the paradox thus remains, unresolved, in Russell's work. Not surprisingly, it tends to distort Russell's own account of that work. In *Principia* he sometimes writes as if neither propositions nor concepts had to be assumed outright:

. . . we will use such letters as *a, b, c, x, y, z, w,* to denote objects which are neither propositions nor functions. Such objects we shall call *individuals*. Such objects will be constituents of propositions or functions, and they will be *genuine* constituents, in the sense that they do not disappear on analysis as (for example) classes do. . . . (Whitehead and Russell, *Principia*, 51)

This seems to imply that only individuals (neither propositions nor propositional functions) are genuine constituents of propositions, constituents which do not 'disappear on analysis'. But this is wishful thinking on Russell's part. It is clear why Russell should want to think that his theory does not assume either propositions or concepts: what is at stake is not ontological economy for its own sake, but rather the coherence of the whole enterprise. It is equally clear, however, that *Principia* relies inescapably upon the assumption of the existence of propositional functions (and also, although less obtrusively, of propositions; see p. 103 above). This same unwillingness of Russell to acknowledge the implications of type theory shows up over the introduction and use of the circumflex notation, '^'. This is used as an abstraction operator: if '*Fx*' is an open sentence, then '$F\hat{x}$' is the name of an entity, a propositional function. It is never acknowledged as a piece of basic notation, however, and the first numbered sentence in which it appears—*9.131—is a definition of some other notion, as if the circumflex notation had already been defined.

In relating the curious history of Russell's substitutional theory I have articulated and insisted upon a tension in Russell's thought. *Principia Mathematica* is, notoriously, a technical achievement which is marred by apparent inconsistencies and incoherences, such as those I mentioned in the previous paragraph. What I wish to suggest is that many of the confusions in *Principia* are to be seen not as resulting from more or less trivial errors but from a fundamental tension in Russell's philosophy.

5

The Vicious Circle Principle[1]

The vicious-circle principle (hereafter, VCP) is, according to Russell, a central and unifying idea in the type theory which is the basis of *Principia Mathematica*.[2] Russell takes the principle from the work of the great French mathematician, Henri Poincaré. It is by no means obvious exactly how one should understand the principle. In the work of Poincaré and Russell there are a number of distinct formulations, and it is not clear which one should take as representing *the* VCP.

In what follows I shall focus on the issue of the formulation of the principle—or, in fact, on one aspect of this issue. I shall, however, seek to show how this relatively narrow issue leads to a general understanding of Russell's use of the VCP. The whole is perhaps best thought of as an attempt to understand the VCP from a Russellian point of view; our discussion, however, will invoke considerations which are by no means obviously to be found in Russell's work.

The VC principle can be formulated as follows:

No totality can contain members which are *defined in terms of* that totality.

Or we can replace the notion of definition, as it is used here, with the notion of presupposition, and formulate the principle like this:

No totality can contain members which *presuppose* that totality.

There are also formulations which use neither the notion of definition, nor the notion of presupposition, but which replace them with the idea of one entity 'involving' or 'concerning' another. I shall not discuss these formulations separately, as I take them to be more or less equivalent to the formulation which uses the notion of presupposition (or perhaps we should think of them as occupying more or less indeterminate points on the spectrum between the 'definition' formulation and the 'presupposition' formulation). I shall begin,

---

[1] This essay originated as a response to a presentation that Philippe de Rouilhan gave at the 1991 meeting of the Pacific division of the American Philosophical Association. (A version of de Rouilhan's talk is published under the title 'Russell's Vicious Circle Principle', in the same issue of *Philosophical Studies* as my essay.) My essay was originally published under the title: 'The Vicious Circle Principle: Comments on Philippe de Rouilhan'. In my presentation, I did not attempt to come to terms with the details of de Rouilhan's talk, but took advantage of the opportunity to present my own views about one issue raised in that talk. (This was perhaps rather unfair to de Rouilhan.) In reprinting the essay I have dropped the references to de Rouilhan's talk, including the subtitle of the essay.

[2] Whitehead and Russell, *Principia*, vol. i. I make the assumption that it is Russell, rather than Whitehead, who is responsible for the fundamental parts of the work which are my concern; see Whitehead, *Process and Reality* and Russell, *My Philosophical Development*.

then, by focussing on the difference between the formulation in terms of definition and the formulation in terms of presupposition.[3] The formulation in terms of definition is Poincaré's usual way of stating the principle, whereas Russell usually—though by no means always—formulates it in terms of presupposition, or of one entity 'involving' another.

Now my contention is that the formulation of the VCP in terms of definition, if taken as perfectly general and applicable to all sorts of objects and all sorts of definitions, cannot be correct. Whereas the formulation in terms of presupposition, taken equally generally, is plausible, but is too weak to give any results at all by itself. So neither formulation, by itself, seems entirely satisfactory. I shall claim, nevertheless, that the formulation in terms of presupposition is the more useful and, in particular, that it encompasses what is correct about the formulation in terms of definition.

To begin with, consider the formulation of the VCP in terms of definition. My contention was that, if taken as perfectly general, this cannot be correct. I take this to be shown by Ramsey's example:[4] we can pick out or define one person from among a particular group by speaking of 'the tallest man in the group'. (Perhaps this only succeeds if there is one man in the group taller than all the others in the group—but this is a point of detail that need not concern us.) Here we have a definition which makes reference to a certain totality, namely the members of some group, and picks out one object, where the object so defined is a member of the totality referred to by the definition. So the totality in question contains an object which is defined in terms of that totality. In short, if we take the formulation of the VCP in terms of definition, and understand it to be quite general, then Ramsey's example violates the VCP. Yet it is, I take it, clear that there is nothing vicious or in any way untoward about the sort of definition that Ramsey puts forward. So, as a perfectly general restriction on definitions, the VCP cannot be correct.

This is, of course, not the end of the story. Both Russell and Poincaré put forward versions of the VCP in terms of definition (though, as we have remarked, it is not Russell's usual way of formulating the principle), and clearly neither of them would make the obvious mistake of thinking that there is something illegitimate in the procedure of picking out one man as the tallest in a given group. So each of them, when putting forward this sort of formulation of the VCP, must have had in mind some restrictions. Before taking up this issue, however, let us move on to consider the second formulation of the VCP, in terms of presupposition.

What we have now to consider is a version of the VCP that says that no object can be member of a totality which it *presupposes*. What is problematic here is not

---

[3] This difference is also the one that Gödel emphasises in his criticism of Russell, in 'Russell's Mathematical Logic'.   [4] Ramsay, 'The Foundations of Mathematics'.

that this version of the principle is false, or false when taken with unrestricted generality, or anything of that sort. The problem, rather, is that the notion of presupposition is desperately obscure. To the extent to which we can make sense of that notion, however, the VCP formulated in terms of presupposition seems to me plausible—indeed one might almost take it as a partial definition of the notion of presupposition. In more detail, one might see this principle as following from two very general sub-principles: first, that to presuppose a totality is to presuppose each member of that totality; second, that nothing can presuppose itself. Each of these sub-principles seems plausible as a way of articulating the notion of presupposition. (As concerns the first of them, it is important to note that we should not identify a totality here with a set or a class, or with some object over and above the various members of the totality.) We do more to explain why our sub-principles are reasonable stipulations to make about the notion of presupposition by connecting each to the idea of priority (whether logical or temporal or of some third kind) which seems to be implicit in the notion of presupposition. In the case of the first sub-principle we may say that if the totality is prior to a given object, then each member of the totality is also prior to that object; the totality is, after all, nothing beyond its members. (Indeed we might say that they are prior to it, or that it presupposes them, in which case our sub-principle follows by the transitivity of presupposition.) In the case of the second sub-principle, we may say simply that nothing can be prior to itself, and hence nothing can presuppose itself.

The VCP formulated in terms of presupposition thus seems to be plausible as a general metaphysical principle—at least given that we are willing to accept the notion of presupposition at all. By itself, however, this formulation implies nothing. What it says is that *if* an object presupposes a given totality, then it cannot be a member of that totality. To apply this principle, or to infer any conclusions at all from it, we need further principles to tell us what entities should be thought of as presupposing what totalities. Given the difficulties and obscurities of the notion of presupposition, those principles are likely to be dubitable. So while the VCP, formulated in terms of presupposition, seems to be relatively uncontroversial, any particular use or application of that principle is likely to be controversial.

The situation is thus that neither of the two formulations of VCP that we are discussing is entirely satisfactory by itself. The formulation in terms of definition requires restriction as to subject, and perhaps also as to the means of definition to be included. The formulation in terms of presupposition requires supplementary principles to make any application of it possible. For each formulation, any given use will be controversial, but the controversy will be located in different places. In the case of the formulation in terms of definition, there will be room for argument as to whether any given set of restrictions which we may impose results in a correct restricted principle. Given that the unrestricted principle is not correct, the correctness of various restricted principles will need to be argued for case by case. What we call '*the* VCP' will thus only be a sort of heuristic guide as to what restricted principles may be useful and correct. In the case of the formulation in terms of presupposition, the controversies will be likely to occur at a different point. The VCP itself, in this formulation, seems relatively uncontentious. Any application of it, however will require a substantive principle about what presupposes what. Given the obscurity of the notion of presupposition, such principles are always likely to be controversial.

In either formulation, the VCP thus requires some supplementation, implicit or explicit, before it can be used. In spite of this similarity of the two versions, however, I shall argue that we have reason to prefer the formulation in terms of presupposition. One reason is that this formulation is a principle which is, at least arguably, literally true. While it may imply nothing by itself, we can still accept it as a principle. The formulation in terms of definition by contrast, is literally false, which is why it requires restriction. A second, and more significant, reason is that the formulation in terms of presupposition is more inclusive. It can achieve the effect of (a restricted version of) the formulation in terms of definition, if we supplement it with a principle to the effect that (a certain kind of) definition sets up relations of presupposition among the defined objects. This, indeed, seems to me to set out more perspicuously the working of the principle when formulated in terms of definition, for it brings into prominence precisely the interesting and controversial aspect of the definition version of the VCP, which is the claim that certain kinds of definitions set up presupposition relations. Yet taking the presupposition version as fundamental also leaves room for presupposition relations established in other kinds of ways. For these reasons, then, it seems better to formulate the VCP in terms of presupposition.

To this point I have argued, quite abstractly, that the VCP is ambiguous, because the formulation in terms of definition is, at least on the face of it, quite distinct from the formulation in terms of presupposition. And I have argued that the latter formulation is preferable. If this is correct, then the formulation in terms of presupposition should enable us to give a more perspicuous account of the historical situation, and of the respective views of Poincaré and Russell—including the fact that Poincaré typically (and Russell occasionally) formulated the VCP in terms of definition. It is to the historical situation, then, that I now turn.

Poincaré asserts the VCP, formulated in terms of definition, without any explicit qualification. In context, however, it is reasonable to see him as restricting the application of the principle to mathematical objects. We may therefore attribute to him some principle to the effect that mathematical objects are not wholly independent of their definitions, or of the acts whereby we specify them. (In other words, we attribute to Poincaré a principle to the effect that mathematical objects *presuppose* their definitions; this then allows the formulation of the VCP in terms of presupposition to take effect.) So Poincaré's use of the VCP must, I think, be taken as a sign of a fairly restrictive kind of constructivism about mathematics. Although nowhere fully articulated in his work, such a view is of a piece with his denial of the actual infinite. Even more strikingly, this kind of constructivism is suggested by his refusal to accept the independence of logic from psychology. In 'La Logique de l'infini' he concludes as follows:

M. Russell will doubtless tell me that these are not matters of psychology, but of logic and epistemology. I shall be driven to respond that there is no logic and epistemology independent of psychology. This profession of faith will probably close the discussion, since it will show an irremediable divergence of views. (p. 482)

The position of Russell may seem more puzzling. Constructivist tendencies in mathematics are quite alien to Russell's thought at this period; he is, to the contrary, an out-and-out realist. How then, is there room in his thought for the VCP? To answer this question we need to look at a baffling, yet also fundamental, concept of Russell's thought: the concept of a propositional function. Propositional functions are basic in *Principia Mathematica*; classes—or, strictly, symbols for classes—are defined in terms of them. And so, indirectly, all mathematical entities (or the corresponding symbols) are to be defined in terms of propositional functions. Russell is a realist about propositional functions: he does not think that the existence of a propositional function is dependent upon our ability to define it, or to construct it, or on any other features of the human mind. This realism seems to me sufficiently demonstrated by his willingness to assert the Axiom of Reducibility. This axiom asserts that for every propositional function whatsoever there is a co-extensive predicative propositional function. We cannot here go into the issue of how Russell understands predicativity.[5] The crucial point, for present purposes, is that the Axiom of Reducibility is in the highest degree implausible if we think of propositional functions in a constructivist fashion. This fact, together with the realist tendency of Russell's thought in general at this period, indicates that we should interpret Russell as a realist about propositional functions. Yet, in spite of this realism, Russell also accepts that there are presupposition relations among propositional functions, and between propositional functions and other entities. That is how Russell is able to use the VCP without any compromise—at least without any acknowledged compromise—of his realist principles: he accepts propositional functions as fully real, in a platonic sense, yet also maintains that they stand in relations of

---

[5] See the present author's *Russell, Idealism, and the Emergence of Analytic Philosophy*, ch. 7, especially pp. 307–8.

presupposition; it is these relations of presupposition that give rise to type restrictions. Let us consider this issue in a little more detail.

The fundamental fact about propositional functions, according to Russell, is what he calls their 'ambiguity'. A propositional function, say ϕx, he says in *Principia*, 'means one of the objects ϕa, ϕb, ϕc, etc. [these are the propositions that are the values of the propositional function, $\phi \hat{x}$], but an undetermined one. It follows that "$\phi \hat{x}$" only has a well-defined meaning . . . if the objects ϕa, ϕb, ϕc etc. are already well-defined. That is to say, a [propositional] function is not well-defined unless all its values are already well-defined' (*Principia*, vol I, p. 39). This, from our point of view, is the crucial principle. As is indicated by the word 'already', with its suggestion of some kind of priority, Russell is here laying down a presupposition principle: that a propositional function presupposes its values. It is this principle, together with VCP, that Russell uses to justify the distinctions which are the basis of his type theory.

In particular, the presupposition principle, together with the VCP, implies two less fundamental principles: First, that a propositional function is of a type different from that of any object which it can take as argument (this principle immediately blocks the Russell paradox, as stated for propositional functions). Second, a propositional function is of a type different from that of any object within the range of a quantifier contained in the propositional function. (Here it is crucial to note that on Russell's conception a propositional function itself, and not merely its linguistic expression, may contain a quantifier; and also that on his account a quantification contains a propositional function and therefore pre-supposes all the values of that propositional function, i.e., all the instances of the quantification. The upshot is the idea that a propositional function containing a quantifier presupposes all the objects which that quantifier ranges over.) Given Russell's other general assumptions, both of these less fundamental principles follow from the fundamental presupposition principle—that a propositional function presupposes all the propositions which are the values of that proposi-tional function—together with the VCP itself.

To this point we have considered Russell's use of the VCP as if he consistently formulated that principle in terms of presupposition. What, then, of the awkward fact that he sometimes puts forward a formulation in terms of definition? The answer must be that by a *definition* of a propositional function Russell does not mean simply any way of specifying it, or picking it out from among other entities (as we can pick out one man by speaking of him as 'the tallest man in the room'). Referring to a propositional function as, e.g., 'the first propositional function mentioned on p. 251 of vol III of *Principia*' would pick out a proposi-tional function, but would not be a definition in Russell's sense. When Russell formulates the VCP in terms of definition, what he means by the 'definition' of a propositional function is not merely a specification of this sort but is, rather, what

Goldfarb calls a *presentation* of it:[6] the propositional function, and its structure, are *given* by the presentation. The crucial point for our purposes is that the presentation of a propositional function will contain a quantifier (in, presumably, the linguistic sense) just in case the propositional function itself contains that quantifier (in the non-linguistic sense). In *this* sense of 'definition', it follows from views of Russell's which we have already mentioned that a propositional function defined in terms of (a quantifier ranging over) a particular totality therefore also presupposes that totality. (Formulating the VCP in terms of presupposition, however, is preferable as avoiding such potentially misleading uses of the word 'definition'.)

The basis for Russell's type theory, I have argued, is not only the VCP but also the view that a propositional function presupposes its values. Russell accepts a quite general version of the VCP, stated in terms of presupposition. On his view, at least, this is compatible with his general realism. For Russell, in other words, unlike Poincaré, the use of the VCP is not a sign of a general constructivist view. Russell remains as much of a platonic realist as ever. His use of the VCP is based, rather, on a particular doctrine about propositional functions, namely the presupposition principle that I have emphasised.

This fact explains something that ought to be quite puzzling, namely, that Russell frequently attributes the solution of the paradox to his 'no-classes theory', i.e., the view that expressions for classes can be given contextual definitions which mention only propositional functions. At first sight, it might seem that his move would help not at all with the paradox, for the paradox of the class of all classes which do not belong to themselves has an exact analogue in the propositional function which truly applies to all and only those propositional functions which do not truly apply to themselves. Russell was well aware of the danger of paradox from propositional functions, as well as from classes: so why did he think that eliminating classes in favour of propositional functions solved the paradox? The answer is that Russell thought that he could justify the presupposition principle for propositional functions, whereas if classes were assumed to be independently existing entities, no such principle could be justified for them. Hence, using the VCP, he thought, he could justify type distinctions for propositional functions. For classes assumed as independent objects, by contrast, he could see no basis for type distinctions. It is in this way—and, as far as I can see, *only* in this way—that we can understand Russell's repeated assertions that the elimination of classes was crucial in the solution to the paradoxes.

---

[6] Goldfarb, 'Russell's Reasons for Ramification'; see especially pp. 31–4.

6

Review of Dummett's *Origins of Analytical Philosophy*

The bulk of this book began life as a series of lectures that Michael Dummett gave at the University of Bologna in the spring of 1987. The lectures occupy 166 pages, to which I shall largely confine myself here. The remainder of the book consists of an interview with Dummett conducted by Joachim Schulte.

Dummett's view of the history of analytic philosophy is thoroughly imbued with his view as to what analytic philosophy is. On this matter, he is in no doubt: 'What distinguishes analytical philosophy . . . from other schools is the belief . . . that a philosophical account of thought can be attained through a philosophical account of language' and in no other way (p. 4). Elsewhere, he refers to this view as 'the fundamental axiom of analytical philosophy' (p. 128). Given this axiom, the issue of what constitutes a philosophical account of language becomes crucial. Hence Dummett's long-standing concern with the idea of a theory of meaning, for we can only settle the issue of what constitutes a philosophical account of language by 'an explicit enquiry into the correct form of a theory of meaning' (p. 166).

The starting point of analytic philosophy, on this view, is thus 'the linguistic turn,' which was decisively taken in Ludwig Wittgenstein's *Tractatus Logico-Philosophicus*. To see the significance of this turn, we must consider what Dummett—tendentiously, perhaps—calls *the philosophy of thought*. This he conceives of as a branch of philosophy concerned with such questions as: What is a thought? What is it to have a thought? What is the structure of a thought? What is it for a thought to be about an object? (See pp. 128–9.) This subject is crucial to the idea of analytic philosophy: what is definitive of analytic philosophy is the insistence that the philosophy of thought must be approached through the philosophy of language. It is this idea which makes the linguistic turn of such great importance. What made the linguistic turn possible—prepared the ground for it, to adapt Dummett's phrase (p. 127)—was the separation of thoughts from the mind, and thus of the philosophy of thought from the philosophy of mind. Only then could thought be treated in a nonpsychological

For discussion, and for comments on earlier versions, I am indebted to Sandra Bartky, Jim Conant, Burton Dreben, Warren Goldfarb, Bill Hart, and Joan Weiner.

fashion. Dummett refers to the crucial idea here as *the extrusion of thoughts from the mind.*

The extrusion of thoughts from the mind seems, on Dummett's account, to be not only a necessary condition of analytic philosophy proper but also, very nearly, a sufficient one. The extrusion first took the form of a 'third realm,' neither mental not physical, in which thoughts (in a nonpsychological sense) exist independently of our minds. The idea of such a third realm, however, was 'obviously very unsatisfactory' (p. 106; cf. also p. 25); the extrusion of thoughts from the mind thus makes 'virtually inevitable' (p. 26) the linguistic turn, whereby thoughts are located in language. (Dummett says of this move, indeed, that 'it is only puzzling why it took so long'; p. 26.)

Dummett's concern in this book is with the prehistory of analytic philosophy, and thus with the extrusion of thoughts from the mind. The hero of this moment of the dialectic is, as one would expect, Gottlob Frege. He took the decisive first step of extruding thoughts from the mind (though into the 'third realm,' which had to be *aufgehoben* before analytic philosophy proper could begin); he also anticipated the next step, the linguistic turn. Second billing, in Dummett's version of the story, however, is more surprising. It goes not to Bertrand Russell and G. E. Moore,[1] nor even to Alexius von Meinong, but rather to Edmund Husserl. Dummett is concerned to show that 'the roots of analytical philosophy . . . are the *same* roots as those of the phenomenological school' (p. ix); and to show also 'how close were the founders of the two schools [that is, Frege and Husserl] to each other at the beginning of this century' (p. xi). Much of the book consists, accordingly, of comparisons of Frege with Husserl. Since the book is written by an analytic philosopher, it is hardly surprising, as Dummett himself says, that Husserl almost invariably comes off second-best in these comparisons.

This is a stimulating book. In particular, it is likely to stimulate controversy on a number of topics, including the following: the characterization of analytic philosophy; the reading of Frege; the reading of Husserl; the claim that the extrusion of thoughts from the mind is the crucial idea which leads to analytic philosophy; and, finally, the methods to be used in thinking about the history of philosophy. In what follows, I shall try very briefly to indicate some of the ways in which one might differ from Dummett on each of these more or less closely connected subjects.

Let me begin with the view of Frege implicit in the book. The most striking fact here is that Frege's interest in logic and mathematics is almost completely ignored. (The words 'logic' and 'mathematics' do not appear in the index; the

---

[1] In the 'Preface,' Dummett totally dismisses the idea that Russell and Moore are among the precursors of analytic philosophy: 'neither was the, or even *a*, source of analytical philosophy' (p. ix). In the main text, however, he appears to withdraw this implausible claim (see pp. 1, 127).

index is not at fault here.) The closest we come to being told of Frege's concern with logic is the point at which Dummett says: 'We tend to think of Frege as a mathematical logician . . . who was gradually drawn into philosophy in the course of carrying out . . . his project of founding number theory and analysis upon pure logic' (p. 132). Dummett suggests, of course, that our usual way of thinking is misleading at this point.[2] Frege's interest in logic thus gets short shrift. By contrast, his views on perception, for example, receive a chapter to themselves—though, as Dummett himself remarks, we have only two brief and (as it seems to me) rather casual passages on this subject.

Now, Dummett's interest in Frege in this book is not an interest in Frege's thought for its own sake, but rather in his role as the crucial precursor of analytic philosophy. So the implicit claim here is perhaps not so much that logic is unimportant to Frege's thought in itself as that it is unimportant to his role as precursor of analytic philosophy. This latter claim is vital to Dummett's view that Husserl should also be considered as a precursor of analytic philosophy, for logic in the modern (that is, Fregean or post-Fregean) sense does not play a major role in *his* thought. So what is at stake here is not, or not only, the interpretation of Frege, but also the conception of analytic philosophy and of what leads to it.

It may help to focus our ideas in this regard if we consider Russell of the logical-atomism period (say, 1910–1918). The Russell of 1903 extruded thoughts from the mind by anyone's standards, into entities he called *propositions*; but by 1906 he was having doubts about the reality of propositions, and by 1910 he had definitely abandoned them. The multiple relation view of judgment, which was his replacement, does not extrude thoughts from the mind. When one understands (or, as Russell often says, judges) a proposition, there is no proposition that is the object of one's act (to speak of understanding a proposition thus becomes a mere *façon de parler*). In judgment, one is not related to some one proposition or proposition-like entity, for on the new view there are no such entities. Without the involvement of the mind, there is nothing proposition-like; in judging, the mind is related not to a proposition but to a number of entities, none of them proposition-like (it is for this reason that the view is known as 'the multiple relation' theory of judgment). Hence, crucially, the bearers of truth and

---

[2] As evidence for this, he cites brief unpublished remarks by Frege, 'Siebzehn Kernsätze zur Logik', in *Nachgelassene Schriften,* i. 189–90. These brief remarks do show a general interest in the nature of the contents of our judgments; in particular, Frege insists that a mere association of ideas cannot be true or false. Elsewhere, Dummett has argued that Frege's remarks are comments on the 'Introduction' to Lotze's *Logik,* and that the most probable date of composition of the remarks is 1876 or 1877; see 'Frege's "Kernsätze zur Logik" '. Even if this dating is correct, however, it does not seem to justify Dummett's statement that the remarks show that Frege 'was interested in general philosophical questions long before he attempted to build logical foundations for arithmetic' (p. 130). Frege's *Begriffsschrift* was published in 1879. Unless we are to suppose that that book was conceived and written with an astonishing rapidity, we can hardly think that 'Siebzehn Kernsätze zur Logik' precedes the main ideas of the book.

falsehood do not exist independently of minds that understand or judge. This is the theory advocated in the 'Introduction' to *Principia Mathematica, Volume I,*[3] and also in Russell's lectures on 'The Philosophy of Logical Atomism.'[4]

Now, according to Dummett's view of the matter, this change should make a world of difference: Russell gives up on the fundamental idea that leads to analytic philosophy; the *Principles of Mathematics* should perhaps be counted as among the precursors of analytic philosophy, but *Principia Mathematica* and the lectures on 'The Philosophy of Logical Atomism' should not. But surely this conclusion is unacceptable. *Principia Mathematica* and 'The Philosophy of Logical Atomism' are clearly paradigmatic works in analytic philosophy (or perhaps, if you make fine discriminations here, in its development). Russell's switch from the binary relation view of judgment (as we might call it) to the multiple relation view makes no difference to his status as analytic philosopher (or precursor). The reason that it makes no difference here is that on the new view, judgments, even though mind-dependent, nevertheless remain objective. The source of their objectivity is twofold. First, the constituents of the judgment are nonmental (sense data for Russell, it should be remembered, are not mental entities: even if in fact available only to one person, they are nonetheless objective). Second—and more important for our purposes—these constituents are combined into judgments in accordance with *logical forms*; the logical form of any given judgment here is identical with the logical form of the fact that obtains if and only if that judgment is true. What makes the idea of logical form here significant—what backs up the use of the words 'logical form'—is of course *logic*, that is, the account of the structure of correct inference due to Frege.

An idea emerging from this discussion is thus that what is central in Frege's work, and crucial to his role as precursor of analytic philosophy, is not simply the fact that he *says* that judgment has objects that are objective and nonmental. It is, rather, that his use of the notion of objectivity is backed up by a conception of logical form which is in turn backed up by logic—Fregean logic—itself. To put what may be the same point in a different way: what makes Frege's extrusion of thoughts from the mind significant, the reason that *that* seems like a plausible place to look for the origins of analytic philosophy, has to do with the fact that in his hands the extruded thoughts are the subject of logical analysis. What is crucial to the origins of analytic philosophy is not just that you say that thoughts are objective and nonmental; it is, equally, what you go on to do with thoughts. And for Frege, as for Russell, what you go on and do with them is to *analyze*

---

[3] Especially pp. 43–4. It is questionable whether this view is consistent with the logic put forward in the rest of the book. See also Russell, 'On the Nature of Truth and Falsehood'. Russell there says that 'there can be no truth or falsehood unless there are minds to judge' (p. 149; cf. also p. 158).

[4] A course of lectures given early in 1918, repr. in *Logic and Knowledge* and in *Collected Papers,* viii. 160–244.

them. The significance of the notion of analysis here depends on the idea that it consists in finding underlying logical forms, that is, forms that place the thought correctly in the inferential structure of (Fregean) logic.

The picture of analytic philosophy, and its origins, which I am suggesting still accords central place to Frege; but it emphasizes the importance of Frege's logic and of a conception of philosophical analysis which relies upon that logic. (For that reason, Husserl would not on this view merit much more than a footnote.[5]) A picture, of course, is not a definition. Any attempt to formulate a definition based on the picture I have suggested—a picture which gives an important place to logic—would be open to the immediate objection that it excludes such important figures as Moore and Gilbert Ryle and J. L. Austin. The most one could say about them, to fit them into such a picture, is that their work is importantly connected, perhaps by way of reaction, with a line of thought that was dependent upon the idea of logic and logical analysis. Dummett's definition does at least have the virtue of including them in a more direct fashion.[6] It is, however, questionable whether we ought to expect or even want a *definition* here. Indeed, one might think it puzzling that Dummett, who deplores the (alleged) fact that very little attention is paid to Wittgenstein in the United States (p. 170), should put forward a three-line definition of a phenomenon as complex and multi-faceted as analytic philosophy.

Dummett's definition seems to assume that 'the philosophy of thought' names a definite subject, which can be approached quite autonomously, with no presuppositions; accordingly, he assumes that questions about, for example, the structure of thought, taken all by themselves, are well defined and clear-cut. As against that, one might think that the notion of thought (as of understanding, or language, or communication) is too elusive to be taken for granted at the outset of philosophical inquiry. (One has only to think of what Wittgenstein would have made of the phrase 'a philosophical account of thought'—or, say, Austin, or W. V. Quine.) On this latter view, questions as to the nature and structure of thought, or the relation of a thought to an object, are too loose, too vague, to be well defined, unless we ask them within the context of a framework that lays down constraints on what is to count as an answer. In the hands of Frege, of

[5] It would indeed be a question why we should take Husserl's claims to be among the originators of analytic philosophy more seriously than those of, say, F. H. Bradley, who insisted that the constituents of judgment are not psychological entities; see his *Principles of Logic*, especially p. 7; or J. G. Hamann, who, we are authoritatively told, was 'quite clear that thought *is* the use of symbols, that nonsymbolic thought . . . is an unintelligible notion'—Berlin, *The Magus of the North,* 75.

[6] As footnote 5 suggests, however, Dummett's definition may be *too* inclusive; and our discussion of Russell's logical-atomist period—together with Dummett's own mention of Gareth Evans and Christopher Peacocke—suggests that in other ways in may not be sufficiently inclusive.

It is worth mentioning that what is under discussion here is theoretical, rather than practical, philosophy. The sense—if any—in which the work of John Rawls (to take an obvious example) is analytic philosophy is not illuminated either by Dummett's definition or by the picture I have sketched, at least as far as I have developed it.

Russell, of the young Wittgenstein, and of many who were influenced by them, logic was taken to provide just such a framework.

The fact that Dummett takes giving a 'philosophical account of thought' to be a well-defined task enables him to write as if Frege and Husserl, in their respective discussions of thoughts, were clearly concerned with the same question, and at least at one point gave similar answers. (One does not get the sense from this book that the identity conditions of a philosophical question or a philosophical idea might itself be a problematic philosophical issue.) Dummett says repeatedly that Husserl's conception of a *noema* was obtained by his *generalizing* on a notion of (linguistic) meaning, a notion which was closely analogous to Frege's *Sinn* (see pp. 26, 70, 112, etc.). He gives the impression that Husserl had a worked out theory analogous to Frege's theory of *Sinne;* rather than develop it in Fregean (or, more accurately, post-Fregean) directions, however, Husserl generalized it to cover all mental acts. It is for that reason that Husserl and his followers did not take the linguistic turn (see especially pp. 25–7). It may, however, be more plausible to think that Husserl's interest in what we might call 'linguistic meaning' was a specific case of a more general interest in the objects of mental acts of all sorts. And this position is in fact strongly suggested by the fact, which Dummett acknowledges, that Husserl was deeply influenced by Franz Brentano, and by the view that all mental acts must—in some sense—have objects. Dummett often makes it sound as if Husserl's work here was a less successful attempt to do what Frege did in his discussion of the *Sinn* and *Bedeutung* of linguistic expressions. For this reason, his Husserl frequently sounds like a third-rate Frege.[7] That this is so might in itself be taken to suggest that Husserl's thought has been distorted.

Finally, I shall briefly turn to Dummett's methodology, to which his methods largely conform. We have seen that Dummett abstracts philosophical ideas (such as the extrusion of thoughts from the mind) from the context of the wider views in which they occur. He also quite consciously abstracts from actual history and causality (see p. 2, for example). A central claim of the book, however, is that the extrusion of thoughts from the mind *led to* the linguistic turn, and thus to analytic philosophy (see p. 22, for example). If this is not a causal or historical claim, what is it? The answer seems to be that it is, roughly, the claim that there is correct or plausible argument from the one idea to the other. The argument goes like this (pp. 25–6). The extrusion of thoughts from the mind is liable to lead to a 'philosophical mythology'—Frege's 'third realm' and Husserl's 'ideal being.' But then 'one may feel unhappy with the ontological mythology' which is thereby generated. And then it is very natural to avoid this mythology

---

[7] For example, Dummett asks: 'can we not construe Husserl as having an account of the meaning of an expression in terms of the way its reference is given?' He answers: 'Doubtless we must so construe him; but we cannot derive from his work any serious rival to Frege's account' (p. 53).

by locating thoughts not in a third realm but in 'the institution of a common language.' It is, however, surely an important fact that this natural—indeed, 'virtually inevitable'—step did not occur to Frege or to Husserl, nor to Husserl's followers, nor to all of Frege's followers.[8] What Dummett's claim comes to is that to an analytic philosopher, such as himself, the step from the extrusion of thoughts from the mind to the linguistic turn seems natural, even inevitable. But now one might object that too little is required of a philosopher to count him as an originator of a given school of philosophy: all that seems to be required is that *we* can construct an argument (which seems to us correct, or at least plausible) from an idea we take to be represented in the given philosopher's writings to the main tenets of the school in question—regardless of whether that argument is in sympathy with the general tenor of the work of the philosopher under discussion. If *that* is all that it means for Husserl to be among the originators of analytic philosophy, however, then much of the apparent interest of the claim is dissipated.

---

[8] Dummett himself mentions Evans in this regard, and says of him—making a distinction that is not otherwise employed in the book—that he 'was squarely in the analytical tradition' though he was not himself an analytic philosopher (p. 4).

7

Functions and Propositional Functions in *Principia Mathematica*

Propositional functions, rather than sets or classes, are ontologically fundamental in *Principia Mathematica*. The actual work of defining the entities of mathematics, and proving the relevant theorems, is done in terms of classes, but the work makes no assumption of the existence of classes. Instead, classes, or more strictly symbols for classes, are introduced by definition at *20.01, which reads:

$$f\{\hat{z}(\psi z)\}. = : (\exists\phi) : \phi!x. \equiv_x \psi x : f\{\phi!\hat{z}\} \quad \text{Df.}$$

The symbol on the left following the 'f', '$\hat{z}(\psi z)$', is Russell's symbol for the class of objects z such that ψz. The whole of the left-hand side is his symbol for an assertion in which some property (that symbolized by 'f') is ascribed to that class. The definition shows that this assertion is to be understood simply as shorthand for the assertion on the right-hand side.[1] The right-hand side itself asserts that there is a propositional function which satisfies certain conditions. Since assertions of this latter kind are not themselves defined in other terms, it follows that propositional functions are ontologically fundamental.

This essay examines Russell's conception of a propositional function in the hope of shedding light on the fundamental portion of *Principia Mathematica*. We begin by focusing on the question of the relation of propositional functions to the general notion of a function. A natural assumption here is that propositional functions are a kind of function, a special case of a more general notion. The very name 'propositional function' seems to suggest this view. Thus, one might suppose that propositional functions should be thought of as those functions which, for suitable arguments, have propositions as values. If this were Russell's understanding of propositional functions, then his procedure would be analogous to Frege's: for Frege the general notion of a function, explicitly taken

A talk, on the basis of which this paper was written, was delivered to the Philosophy Department of the University of Illinois, Chicago, as well as to the University of British Columbia conference on Russell's early work. I thank both audiences. For their comments on an earlier draft of this paper I should also like to thank Andrew Irvine, Gary Kemp, Tom Patton, and Thomas G. Ricketts.

[1] *Cf.* Whitehead and Russell, *Principia*, 11: 'A definition is a declaration that a certain newly introduced symbol or combination of symbols is to mean the same as a certain other combination of symbols of which the meaning is already known'.

over and adapted from mathematics, is fundamental, and concepts (*Begriffe*) are explicitly introduced as a special case of functions.[2]

In fact, however, the natural assumption is wrong. Russell does not take the general notion of a function as fundamental and pick out propositional functions as a special case. He proceeds, rather, in the opposite direction: he takes propositional functions for granted, and uses them to define particular (non-propositional) functions as needed. Thus, in section *30 *Principia*, he says:

The functions hitherto considered . . . have been propositional . . . But the ordinary functions of mathematics . . . are not propositional. Functions of this kind always mean 'the term having such and such a relation to x'. For this reason they may be called *descriptive* functions . . .

 The general definition of a descriptive function is:
$$R'y = (\imath x)(xRy)$$
 All functions that occur in ordinary mathematics are instances of the above definition . . .

Take as an example the successor function. Russell does not assume that there is such an entity—an entity which takes a number as argument and yields its successor as value. What he assumes is, rather, that there is the two-place propositional function, $\hat{x} = \hat{y} + 1$. In accordance with the general definition above, the successor function can then be introduced by definition:

$$S'y = (\imath x)(x = y + 1)$$

i.e. the successor of y is the x such that x equals y plus one. (Note that here, as in *30.01 above, the inverted iota, '$\imath$', is the definite description operator, which is in turn introduced by contextual definition in the familiar Russellian fashion at *14.01. No doubt part of the reason for Russell's emphasis on definite descriptions is that he uses them in this way to define the ordinary functions of mathematics.)

 So for Russell propositional functions are not a species of the genus function. Rather it is propositional functions that are primitive; non-propositional functions are introduced by definition as needed. Technically this procedure is unproblematic. It is, none the less, likely to strike one as unnatural, for it seems as if Russell takes for granted a special case of functions, rather than taking for granted the general notion and introducing various special cases as needed. Why, then, does Russell proceed by assuming propositional functions, rather than the general notion of a function? What is the significance of the fact that he proceeds in this way?—It is, of course, always possible in such a case that there is no significance to be attached to a philosopher's proceeding in one way rather than

---

[2] See Frege, *Funktion und Begriff*. If Russell took functions for granted, and defined propositional functions as those functions which have propositions as values, his procedure would still not be exactly the same as Frege's. Fregean concepts are functions that have *truth-values* as values for any argument.

in another that strikes us as more natural. It is, that is to say, always possible that such a fact is simply an accident relative to other significant aspects of the philosopher's overall view. But such is not the case here, as we shall see in the remainder of this essay. On the contrary: the minor technical difference that we have uncovered between Russell and Frege issues from philosophical differences which are fundamental and quite general. Understanding why Russell proceeds as he does in this apparently quite minor matter will also shed light on the notion of a propositional function, and thence on the structure of *Principia* as a whole— in particular, on the fact that that it puts forward a *ramified* type theory.

1. DIRECT REALISM

Let us begin our discussion of the relevant aspects of Russell's philosophy[3] by drawing a crude distinction. On almost any account of language there are, on the one hand, the words or thoughts that we have and, on the other hand, the things that our words or thoughts are about. On many views there are also entities of a third kind, intermediate between the words and the things. Let us call a view that accepts the existence of such intermediate entities a three-stage analysis of language. Frege's view may be taken as a paradigmatic example of such a three-stage analysis. Frege distinguishes the *Sinn* of an expression from its *Bedeutung*. The *Bedeutung* of an expression, on this view, is naturally thought of as what the expression refers to or is about. The *Sinn* of an expression is what I have called an intermediate entity: it mediates between the words and their subject-matter. In particular, *Sinn* is what the mind grasps when one understands some expression. Thus, in the case of a simple sentence such as 'Mary loves John,' the *Bedeutung* of 'Mary' is Mary, that of 'John' is John, and that of 'loves' is (presumably) the relation of loving. The *Bedeutung* of the sentence as a whole, however, is, on Frege's account, its truth-value, true or false. Each expression in the sentence has a *Sinn* as well as a *Bedeutung*. Frege speaks of the *Sinn* of an expression as the 'mode of presentation' of its *Bedeutung*.[4] The *Sinn* of a word is also what one understands who understands the word. Thus, the *Sinn* of the word 'Mary', in our example, is what one understands who understands [that utterance of] the word.[5] An important point is that the *Sinn* of the whole sentence is made up of the *Sinne* of the various words that make up the sentence (clearly the same is

---

[3] Russell held a great variety of philosophical views in the course of his long life. Our concern here is with the period during which the work leading up *Principia* was done, and with the immediate aftermath of that period—say, 1900 to 1918. [4] See, for example, Frege, *Collected Papers*, 158.

[5] Proper names are likely to pose special problems for Frege's account. We can distinguish two reasons for this. First, a number of people may share a single proper name; many people, for example, are called 'Mary'. Second, even if two people both use a name to talk about the same person, they may understand the name in different ways if, for example, each knows the person in a context quite different

not true of *Bedeutungen*). Quite generally, the *Sinn* of a semantically complex expression is itself complex, and made up of the *Sinne* of the semantically simple expressions that make up the complex expression.

I rehearse these well-known points about Frege's three-stage analysis of language for the sake of the contrast with Russell's view. For Russell a two-stage analysis is paradigmatic: an analysis which accepts only the words or thoughts, on the one hand, and the entities which form their subject-matter, on the other hand. For Russell, in other words, the paradigmatic kind of analysis rejects any intermediate entities analogous to Fregean *Sinne*. A sentence such as 'Mary loves John' is taken to express a proposition. The proposition here is not an intermediary between the words and their subject-matter, for the proposition *contains* the entities which the sentence is about: the actual woman, Mary, and the actual man, John, are among the constituents of the proposition. Along the same lines, if Mary does indeed love John, then the fact that Mary loves John is not a further thing over and above the proposition: facts, for Russell, just are true propositions.[6]

We have explained Russell's two-stage analysis in a way that presupposes that there are propositions. After 1910 Russell no longer accepts the existence of propositions (not, at least, in the earlier sense—as objective non-linguistic entities). The two-stage analysis, however, continues. Now a sentence is said to express a judgment, which is the subjective act of a mind. In judgment the judging mind is in direct contact with the entities which are the subject-matter of the corresponding sentence; if the sentence is true then there is a corresponding fact, but the fact is made up of the entities with which the judging mind is in direct contact.[7] Again, there is no room for intermediate entities of any sort.

The point of the two-stage analysis, for Russell, is indicated by the idea which emerged in the previous paragraph: that the mind is in direct contact with the entities that it thinks or speaks about. Intermediate entities, whether Fregean *Sinne* or any other sort, would be a denial of this direct contact; for Russell, however, it is only our being in direct contact with entities outside the mind that makes it possible to speak or think of them at all. This point is clear from an exchange between Russell and Frege.[8] Frege, agreeing with Russell that truth is

from that in which the other knows him or her. For these reasons it is much less plausible in the case of names than in the case of other words that what two people understand who understand a word is the same. Yet Frege tends, in general to assume this—*i.e.* to assume that a word has a *Sinn*, not that it has many different *Sinne* corresponding to its different users.

[6] For further discussion of this aspect of Russell's metaphysics, and of its Moorean antecedents, see Hylton, *Russell, Idealism, and the Emergence of Analytic Philosophy*, chs. 4 and 5, esp. pp. 134–43 and 171–4. [7] For further discussion, see again ibid., ch. 8 § 1.

[8] Frege, *Nachgelassene Schriften*, ii. 250–1. I have followed the translation of Frege, *Philosophical and Mathematical Correspondence*, except for leaving 'Satz' and 'objectiver Satz' untranslated (Russell wrote to Frege in German). In the first case, one might translate as 'sentence' or 'statement'. In the second case, I think Russell uses '*objectiver Satz*' in German as he uses 'proposition' in English. His claim is that propositions, the objects of thought, are objective, and can have things as concrete as mountains among their constituents.

not itself a part of a thought, illustrated this idea by what he took to be an uncontroversial analogy: truth is not a part of the thought, 'just as Mont Blanc with its snowfields is not itself a component part of the thought that Mont Blanc is more than 4,000 metres high.' Russell replies, not to the point being illustrated, but rather to the analogy, in a way that makes clear his insistence on the mind's being in direct contact with the entities it thinks about:

I believe that in spite of all its snowfields Mont Blanc itself is a component part of what is actually asserted in the *Satz* 'Mont Blanc is more than 4,000 metres high'. We do not assert the thought, for this is a private psychological matter: we assert the object of the thought, and this is, to my mind, a certain complex (an *objectiver Satz*, one might say), in which Mont Blanc is itself a component part. *If we do not admit this, then we get the conclusion that we know nothing at all about Mont Blanc.* (emphasis added)

A rather different passage from the essay 'Knowledge by Acquaintance and Knowledge by Description' illustrates the same underlying point:

. . . it is necessary to examine the view that judgments are composed of something called 'ideas'. . . The view seems to be that there is some mental existent which may be called the 'idea' of something outside the mind of the person who has the idea, and that, since judgment is a mental event, its constituents must be constituents of the mind of the person judging. *But in this view ideas become a veil between us and outside things—we never-really, in knowledge, attain to the things we are supposed to be judging about, but only to ideas of those things* . . . On the contrary, I hold that acquaintance is . . . a relation, not demanding any such constituent of the mind as is supposed by advocates of 'ideas'. . . [and that] in judging, the actual objects concerning which we judge . . . are constituents of the complex which is the judgment. ('Knowledge by Acquaintance', 221–2; emphasis added)

Let us call the view that these two passages illustrate *direct realism*. The crucial feature of the view is that all knowledge depends upon our being in direct and unmediated contact with objects, and that in paradigm cases of knowledge we have this sort of contact with the objects which we know. (I allow here for the possibility of non-paradigmatic knowledge. This sort of knowledge still requires direct and unmediated contact with objects, but the objects that we know are not the objects with which we are in direct contact. Before 'On Denoting' Russell refers to this indirect knowledge as 'denotative knowledge'.[9] After 'On Denoting' he refers to it as 'knowledge by description', and it comes to assume a significant place in his thought.) No doubt Russell's emphasis on direct and unmediated contact with objects is to be explained in part by his reaction to Kant and to post-Kantian Idealism; those views emphasize the mediation of all knowledge by necessary structures which impose form on the known

---

[9] See Russell, *Collected Papers*, iv. 369.

object (see Hylton, *Russell, Idealism, and the Emergence of Analytic Philosophy*). Whatever be the basis for Russell's direct realism, however, the important point for our purposes is that it underlies all of his thought in the relevant period. One sign of this is his use of the notion of *acquaintance*, which is important throughout the relevant period (before 1905 the notion is used casually, as something that can simply be taken for granted; after 1905 it comes increasingly under explicit examination; but its role in Russell's thought is crucial throughout). To be *acquainted* with an object, as Russell uses the word, is precisely to be in direct and unmediated contact with it.[10]

The issue of direct realism is closely related to our earlier distinction between a two-stage analysis of language and a three-stage analysis. To invoke intermediate entities, as in a three-stage analysis of language, would violate direct realism, at least as Russell understands it. Paradigmatically, on his view, the entities that the mind grasps or is in contact with are not intermediate between the mind and the objects that it thinks about; rather they are those very objects. For a brief period, however, Russell departs from this paradigm. In *The Principles of Mathematics*, Russell introduces the theory of denoting concepts. According to this theory, a description, such as 'anyone who loves John' or 'all prime numbers less than seventeen', most immediately stands for a denoting concept. The denoting concept is in turn related to (denotes) the objects that the phrase is used to talk about. On this theory, then, denoting concepts are intermediate entities of just the kind envisaged by a three-stage analysis of language; if a sentence is expressed using a description, then the corresponding proposition contains not the described entity or entities but rather a denoting concept which denotes them. In such a case it is thus denoting concepts with which the mind is in direct contact; its contact with the described entities, which are the subject-matter of the sentence, is indirect, being mediated by the denoting concept. The theory of denoting concepts is thus a three-stage analysis of language, or rather of some parts of the language, for it is only descriptions that are treated in this way.

The theory of denoting concepts is thus a departure from the paradigm of the two-stage analysis of language; but it is a short-lived departure. 'On Denoting' is Russell's rejection of the theory of denoting concepts for descriptions, and his adoption of an alternative analysis. We shall not go into this matter here, as the

---

[10] Russell's views on what objects we are acquainted with shift considerably during the relevant time period. The general trend is that, as he examines the notion of acquaintance, he narrows the range of objects with which he thinks we are acquainted. Throughout the relevant period, however, he continues to think that we are acquainted with many objects, both concrete objects (in sense perception) and abstract objects (in what can only be described as non-sensory perception).

These facts bear on the sense in which Russell was, and the sense in which he was not, an empiricist. In the clearest sense he is not an empiricist: he continues to think not only that there are abstract objects but also that our non-sensory 'perception' of them is a source of knowledge. His emphasis on direct contact with objects, however, gives his view a structure which is in important ways like that of empiricism.

main points are well known. It is worth emphasizing, however, that from the present point of view the achievement of 'On Denoting' is that it enables Russell to dispense with intermediate entities in his analysis of language. He is thus able to retain the two-stage analysis throughout, as is required by his direct realism.[11]

2. COMPLEX REFERRING EXPRESSIONS

The relevance of Russell's direct realism, and his use of a two-stage analysis of language, to the issue of functions and propositional functions can be seen if we raise another issue: that of complex referring expressions. By a (putative) complex referring expression I mean a complex expression that appears to refer, or to purport to refer, to an object. It is crucial here that a simple object may none the less be singled out by a complex referring expression. 'The centre of gravity of the Solar System' is an example of Russell's. The centre of gravity of the Solar System (at a given moment) is a point, and therefore, presumably, simple; yet the phrase referring to it (if it does indeed refer to it) is complex. More generally: even when the object is not simple, still there need be no complexity in the object that corresponds to the complexity of the expression. Thus, the expression 'the teacher of the teacher of Alexander' refers (perhaps) to Plato, yet it would be unnatural to think of Plato as containing a complexity corresponding to that of the phrase. Similarly, 'the positive square root of nine' is a complex expression referring to the number three, which is not naturally thought of as having a complexity corresponding to that of the phrase.

The existence of complex referring expressions (if indeed they do exist) thus makes it clear that our ways of talking about objects often have a complexity which is not reflected in the objects themselves. Furthermore, it is almost irresistible to accept that the complexity of our ways of talking here is not just a matter of the *words*, but has semantic significance. What is in common to the expressions 'the teacher of the teacher of Alexander' and 'the teacher of the teacher of Aristotle' is not just a matter of their using some of the same letters

---

[11] This point suggests, correctly, I think, that the rejection of the theory of denoting concepts in Russell, 'On Denoting', is motivated not only by the detailed arguments set out there but also by very general philosophical considerations. These considerations make Russell inclined to reject the theory of denoting concepts as soon as he can see how to do so. The decisive breakthrough is that he sees how to analyse definite descriptions without appeal to denoting concepts, or other kinds of intermediate entities. Definite descriptions are crucial here only because Russell had seen the same point about indefinite descriptions some years earlier.

Some qualification should be made to the claim that Russell, 'On Denoting', enables him to dispense entirely with denoting concepts. In order to avoid assuming the existence of denoting concepts, Russell has to take the notion of generality for granted. Yet the theory of denoting concepts was introduced, in Russell, *Principles*, primarily to account for generality (although the theory also lent itself to other uses). Some of Russell's remarks about generality after 1905 suggest that he continues to think of generality as explicable by something like the theory of denoting concepts. See Hylton, *Russell, Idealism, and the Emergence of Analytic Philosophy*, ch. 6, esp. pp. 254–6.

(sounds); the situation here is not as it is in the case of, say, the expressions 'cattle' and 'catalogue', or 'Canada Goose' and 'canned goods'. Nor does this point have to rest purely on appeals to what is called the 'intuition' of various philosophers; rather it rests on the behaviour of the phrases in the inferences which are recognized as valid. For example, 'The teacher of the teacher of Alexander is wise' and 'The teacher of the teacher of Aristotle is wise' both follow from 'All teachers of teachers are wise' (together with the relevant existence and uniqueness clauses). The phrases are systematically related in this and countless other ways.

The point of the above is that complex referring expressions have semantic properties which are not exhausted by their reference. There is more to say about the semantics of 'the teacher of the teacher of Alexander' than that this phrase refers to Plato. We have been dwelling on this perhaps rather obvious point because it is in *prima facie* conflict with the two-stage analysis of language which we have attributed (with some qualifications) to Russell. According to the two-stage analysis, there are the words (or thoughts) and there are the objects that they are about. At neither stage, however, can we do justice to the semantic complexity of complex referring expressions. That complexity, we saw, is not merely a matter of the words; nor is it in general reflected in the objects that the expressions are about. Since the relevant complexity must be accounted for in some way, and cannot be accounted for at either of the two stages acknowledged by the two-stage analysis, we seem bound to invoke a third stage of analysis, *i.e.* to invoke intermediate entities, such as Fregean *Sinne*, to account for the relevant semantic complexity. Thus, while Plato is not easily thought of as containing a complexity corresponding to that of the phrase 'the teacher of the teacher of Alexander', one might think that the phrase refers to Plato *via* a *Sinn* which does contain exactly that sort of complexity. (Here we see that it is crucial that intermediate entities have a complexity, or structure, of the right sort.)

There thus appears to be an argument from the existence of complex referring expressions to the need for a three-stage, rather than two-stage, analysis of language.[12] What then of Russell, whose direct realism gives him reason to reject the three-stage analysis? From a Russellian perspective the argument for a

---

[12] I say that there *appears* to be such an argument because, as so often in philosophy, a simple argument relies upon background assumptions which are difficult even to articulate. Thus, the conclusion of the argument might seem to be contradicted by Davidson's example of a theory which gives the reference of all expressions of the form 'the father of . . . the father of Annette' while making no mention of meaning, or of any entity corresponding to 'father of'. (See Davidson, *Inquiries into Truth and Interpretation*, 17 f.) The example appears to show that it is possible to explain complex referring expressions without appeal to intermediate entities. A Russellian response would, I think, be to say that Davidson's theory does this only by assuming that we understand a metalanguage which contains functional expressions. If these functional expressions are taken to give rise to complex referring expressions then we shall require intermediate entities to explain their semantic properties (unless we appeal to a meta-metalanguage, *etc.*). If there is a disagreement here between Russell and Davidson it is a complex one, and probably has much to do with the purposes of a philosophical discussion of language.

three-stage analysis is, I think, strong—given the existence of complex referring expressions. And one might think the existence of such expression undeniable. Yet Russell *does* deny the existence of complex referring expressions in 'On Denoting'. His repeated insistence, in that work and later, that descriptions 'have no meaning in isolation' is precisely a denial that such phrases are complex referring expressions. It is this denial that enables him to escape the force of the argument for the three-stage analysis, and to accept the two-stage analysis universally. (As we saw, before 'On Denoting' he accepts intermediate entities for some parts of language; the present suggestion is that he is forced to do so precisely because he accepts that those parts of language are complex referring expressions. When he denies that there are any complex referring expressions he is then free to deny intermediate entities quite generally.)

From the present perspective, then, the point of 'On Denoting' is to analyse phrases which appear to be complex referring expressions in a way that makes them out not to be.[13] Thus, Russell does not deny the claim that if there are complex referring expressions then there must be a third stage in the analysis of language. Instead, he evades the force of this claim by denying its antecedent. This position is a peculiar one. A phrase such as 'the younger author of *Principia Mathematica*' looks for all the world like a complex referring expression. But Russell's claim is that it is not, that the superficial appearance is quite misleading. Hence Russell's direct realism, and his concomitant rejection of intermediate entities in the analysis of language, leads him to claim that the overt structure of language is quite misleading. A paradigmatic philosophical task thus becomes that of finding words which are *not* misleading, which reflect how language really operates. This task is philosophical analysis, in the important and influential sense in which it emerges from 'On Denoting'. The criterion of success in this task is that we end up with a sentence that *is* susceptible of a two-stage analysis, *i.e.* a sentence in which all of the referring expressions can be understood as having no semantic properties except that of standing for those objects which they stand for. This implies, as we have seen, that all referring expressions are simple. Thus, phrases which appear to be complex referring expressions will be shown not to be referring expressions at all; many phrases which might appear to be referring expressions will thus be shown not to be. In a complete and successful analysis, the only apparent referring expressions which occur will be simple.[14] This criterion of success, and thus also this conception of analysis, is

---

[13] The analysis is as follows: a sentence of the apparent form 'The *F* is *G*' is correctly understood if thought of as being of the form 'There is one, and only one, thing which has the property *F*; and that thing has the property *G*' or, in quantificational notation '$(\exists x)[Fx \ \& \ (\forall y)(Fy \equiv y = x) \ \& \ Gx]$'. As is evident, this analysis takes for granted the notion of generality; see n. 11, above.

[14] They will also be referring expressions which, at least in normal use, cannot fail to refer (*e.g.* 'I' or 'my current visual sense-datum' and expressions which purport to refer to abstract objects whose existence is a matter of 'direct inspection', and thus equally certain). This is because a view which makes

bound up with metaphysical and epistemological issues. What is at stake is not just finding, for a given sentence, a reformulation which may be convenient for this or that purpose. The reformulation is, rather, supposed to make clear what is really going on in language (and thought), *i.e.* to expose the structure that makes representation possible at all.

3. FUNCTIONS AND PROPOSITIONAL FUNCTIONS

The issues we have been discussing so far may appear to be far removed from our original question about functions and propositional functions. But in fact there is a clear connection: if we accept functions as primitive and undefined then it follows straightaway that there are complex referring expressions. The application of a functional expression to the name of an object immediately produces such an expression. Thus, if we accept the successor function, $s(x)$, as primitive, it is apparent that '$s(17)$', say, is a complex referring expression referring to the number eighteen. Similarly (to give a non-mathematical example), if we take $f(x)$ as an undefined function which maps each person onto his or her father, then '$f(Alexander)$' is a complex referring expression which refers to Philip of Macedonia. Any way of analysing away these complex referring expressions will have the result that they no longer use the functions $s(x)$ or $f(x)$ (respectively).

Thus, if we accept functions as primitive, then we have to accept that there are complex referring expressions; hence, by the argument given in § 2 we have to accept that the two-stage analysis of language is inadequate.[15] Russell's direct realism, however, gives him reason to want to stick to the two-stage analysis. It is, therefore, unsurprising that he should not accept that there are functions (as primitive, undefined, entities). To recapitulate: Russell's direct realism leads him to insist that we are in direct contact with the entities that we think and talk about, not merely with intermediate entities. This rejection of intermediate entities in turn leads to a rejection of complex referring expressions, and to maintain this one has to reject functions.

The crucial question at this stage is why this argument, to the effect that Russell cannot accept the existence of functions, does not apply also to

no room for a third stage in the analysis of language has no easy and straightforward way of handling reference failure. In this essay, however, our focus is not on this issue but rather on the issues arising from the complexity of many (putative) referring expressions.

[15] It follows that *Sinn*, or at any rate the acceptance of some kind of intermediate entity, is implicit in Frege's thought from the outset. Frege begins by taking functions in more or less the mathematical sense as primitive, and so is bound to acknowledge the existence of complex referring expressions. So he is bound to find a two-stage analysis inadequate.

Here I disagree with a suggestion made by T. G. Ricketts, that the notion of *Sinn* is forced on Frege by the existence of names that name nothing. See Ricketts, 'Generality, Meaning and Sense'.

propositional functions. If it did it would simply show that Russell's two-stage analysis of language is untenable, for he cannot proceed with the analysis of language at all if he accepts neither functions nor propositional functions.[16] Yet the mere fact that Russell does not define propositional functions as a special case of functions in general will not show that the argument against functions does not apply to propositional functions. It is not enough merely to *say* that propositional functions are not a kind of function. To show that propositional functions are not vulnerable to the argument against functions one needs to show that they do not have those features which make functions in general vulnerable to that argument. So we need to see exactly why functions in general are problematic on a two-stage analysis, and to show that those reasons do not apply to propositional functions.

Functional expressions have a semantically significant complexity which is not (in general) reflected in the object to which they refer. The complexity is therefore lost if we have only the object referred to, on the one hand, and, on the other hand, the expression, which is thought of as simple, *i.e.* as not possessing a significant structure. So the complexity of functional expressions is of a kind that the two-stage analysis cannot account for, or even acknowledge. If one accepts the two-stage analysis, indeed, it is hard even to make sense of the idea of a function. If the *whole* semantic story about 'the teacher of Plato' is that it refers to Socrates, and the *whole* semantic story about 'the teacher of Alexander' is that it refers to Aristotle, then the two phrases have nothing semantically significant in common (any more than 'cattle' has something semantically significant in common with 'catalogue'). So functions are problematic for the two-stage analysis because they give rise to expressions that have a semantic complexity that is not reflected in the objects to which those expressions refer.

These reasons for the incompatibility of the two-stage analysis with functions in general, however, do not apply to propositional functions. If a propositional function is applied to an object to yield a proposition, then the proposition preserves the relevant complexity. For example, the propositional function $\hat{x}$ *is wise* applied to Socrates yields the proposition that Socrates is wise, which contains Socrates. This is true quite generally: if a proposition is the value of a propositional function for a given argument then the proposition will *contain* that argument. (Whereas the same is not true for functions in general: Socrates is the value of the *teacher of* function with Plato as argument, but it does not follow that Socrates contains Plato.) The point applies not only to the argument of the function but also, though a little less straightforwardly, to the

---

[16] Here I ignore an idea that Russell attempted to implement in 1905 and 1906, namely that we might take as fundamental the notions of a proposition and of substitution of one entity for another within a proposition. See ch. 4, above. Russell's use of the notion of substitution is in effect equivalent to the assumption of the existence of propositional functions.

function itself. We cannot find in, say, Philip of Macedonia and W. V. Quine any common element which indicates that they are both values of one and the same function for different arguments, or what that function might be. (Both are values of the *father of* function, for appropriate arguments; no doubt there are countless other functions of which the same is true.) For functions in general there is no backward route, from the object which is the value to the function. For propositional functions, however, there is. The two propositions, that Socrates is wise and that Plato is wise, *do* have something in common that shows that both are values of the propositional function $\hat{x}$ *is wise*. Propositions, on Russell's account, are complex structured entities. Two propositions which have some part of their structure in common are both values of one and the same propositional function, which also shares that structure (one might almost say, which *is* that structure). Contrariwise, if two propositions are both values of one propositional function, then they will have a structure in common with it, and with one another. So while a proposition does not actually *contain* a propositional function,[17] it is nevertheless clear from a proposition that it is or is not the value of a given propositional function for some argument. Both the propositional function and the argument, we might say, are *recoverable* from the proposition; clearly the same is not in general true of a function and an object which is the value of that function for some argument.

There is thus a crucial disanalogy between propositional functions and ordinary functions such as the successor function. Both propositions and propositional functions are complex structured entities. A proposition which is the value of a given propositional function for a given argument will, first, *contain* the object which is the argument, and, second, have the same structure as the propositional function. Thus, the object which is the value of a given propositional function for a given argument has a structure which reflects this fact, and hence also reflects the semantic complexity of the phrase. Thus, the reasons that lead to the incompatibility of functions with the two-stage analysis of language do not apply to the particular case of propositional functions.

Let us put these points in a somewhat larger perspective. In talking about the argument from the existence of functions (of the ordinary sort) to the existence of intermediate entities, such as *Sinne*, we saw that it is essential that *Sinne* (or other intermediate entities) be entities with a certain definite structure. The role of such entities, at least as it emerged from that argument, was to reflect the complexity and structure of complex referring expressions. One way to make the point about propositional functions would be to say that there is no need for intermediate entities, between us and them, precisely because they themselves

---

[17] See *Principia*, 54 f.; for discussion see Hylton, *Russell, Idealism, and the Emergence of Analytic Philosophy*, 289 n. 7.

have the essential feature: they are structured entities, with a structure that reflects the semantic complexity of the corresponding phrases. More generally we can say, albeit somewhat vaguely, that propositions and propositional functions themselves have the 'intensional' features which are usually associated with intermediate entities.[18]

4. RAMIFIED TYPE THEORY

We began with the point that propositional functions are ontologically fundamental in *Principia Mathematica*. Our subsequent discussion showed that propositional functions are complex, structured entities; and that this fact is not adventitious but is, rather, intimately bound up with Russell's adherence to direct realism. Propositional functions are in this way quite different from ordinary functions, which are not conceived of as having any significant structure at all. (It is for this reason that an ordinary function can be represented set-theoretically, simply as a set of ordered pairs. All that matters is what value is produced by each argument. To represent a propositional function in this way would leave out something crucial: the structure of the propositional function.)

  This difference between propositional functions and ordinary functions is crucial for the possibility of ramified type theory. The distinction between ramified type theory and simple type theory is that in ramified type theory two propositional functions which are applicable (truly or falsely) to arguments of the same type may nevertheless themselves be of different types, whereas in simple type theory this is not possible. If one assimilates propositional functions to ordinary functions, and adopts the 'extensional' viewpoint,[19] then the crucial fact about ramified type theory becomes incomprehensible. For under those assumptions two propositional functions which apply truly to the same objects and falsely to the same objects (*i.e.* which are materially equivalent) must be identical, and two propositional functions which apply truly to objects of the same type must themselves be of the same type. On the Russellian conception of propositional functions, however, there is also another crucial aspect to a propositional function: its structure.

---

  [18] The point is expressed vaguely here because the notion of intensionality has clear application only within the context of a three-stage analysis of language, such as Frege's, where we distinguish between *Sinn* (or its analogue) and *Bedeutung* (or its analogue). In that context, the intensional is that which has to do not with *Bedeutung* but rather with *Sinn*. Strictly speaking, this notion does not apply at all within a Russellian context, where we have only the words and their subject-matter. The above point might be made less vaguely by saying that for Russell some entities at the level of subject-matter (propositions and propositional functions) have the sort of properties which in a Fregean context are characteristic of intermediate entities.

  [19] See previous footnote for qualifications surrounding the use of the contrast between intensional and extensional.

To illustrate this point, let us adapt one of Russell's own examples.[20] Consider the two propositions expressed by the sentences 'Napoleon was a soldier' and 'Napoleon had all the properties that make a great general', where the latter may be represented as

($\forall F$) [F is a property that makes a great general $\supset$ F(Napoleon)].

Let us assume that each of these propositions is true. Each of them can be obtained by the application of a propositional function to Napoleon. In the first case, the propositional function is: $\hat{x}$ *is a soldier*. In the second case, it is

($\forall F$) [F is a property that makes a great general $\supset$ $F(\hat{x})$].

These two propositional functions are both truly applicable to Napoleon. More generally, each is applicable (truly or falsely) to objects of the same type (to human beings). Yet for Russell the two propositional functions are of different types, because their internal structures differ. In particular, one contains a quantifier over properties, whereas the other does not. If we do not conceive of propositional functions as having a structure, as well as having arguments and values, then this difference cannot be understood at all.

A common charge against Russell's ramified type theory is that while the *definition* of a certain propositional function may use quantification, this fact does not make the propositional function itself intrinsically different from one whose definition does not use quantification. In particular, this sort of objection has been made to Russell's use of the Vicious Circle Principle, to which he appeals for the justification of type distinctions. The principle states that an object may not involve or presuppose a totality of which it is a member, or, in Russell's words: 'whatever involves *all* of a collection must not be one of the collection' (*Principia*, 37). Ramsey argues that it is in fact perfectly legitimate to pick out an object by reference to a collection or totality of which it is a member.[21] His example, which seems to make the point convincingly, is that of picking out a man by means of the phrase 'the tallest man in the room'. Here we mention a totality or collection— that of men in the room—in order to pick out one member of it, namely the tallest. Yet clearly there is nothing illegitimate about that way of referring to someone. Gödel insists that this sort of method of defining or specifying an object must be legitimate unless we take an idealist or constructivist view of the objects, and see them as somehow brought into being by our acts of definition.[22]

These objections are correct, if Russell's use of the Vicious Circle Principle is seen as limiting ways of picking out or specifying objects. But for Russell the Vicious Circle Principle is not about definition, in that sense. To say in the relevant

---

20 Whitehead and Russell, *Principia*, 56.   21 See Ramsey, 'The Foundations of Mathematics'.
22 See Gödel, 'Russell's Mathematical Logic'.

sense that an object *involves* a certain totality or collection is not merely to say that the object can be picked out in a way that makes use of generalization over that totality. That would be true of every object. Even the simplest propositional function, for example, can be picked out by a method that involves generalization over all propositional functions. (Indeed, referring to one propositional function as the simplest, if legitimate, is such a method.) Nor is it to say that the object can only be picked out by a method which makes use of generalization over the given totality. That would be true of no objects. One can always find some method of picking out an object while avoiding reference to any given totality. Thus, I can always pick out an object, *e.g.* as the object referred to on such and such a line of such and such a page of a given book. The point of saying that a propositional function involves a certain totality (or, as Russell does say, that it is defined in terms of a certain totality) is that the propositional function itself *contains* the generality.[23]

What is essential to Russell's use of the Vicious Circle Principle, and to ramified type theory, is thus a conception of propositional functions as the sorts of entities that can, for example, contain generality. In short, what is required is that propositional functions be understood as entities with a certain structure. This conception of propositional functions, however, is not simply a response to the exigencies of a ramified type theory created more or less *ad hoc* to solve a bunch of only dubiously related paradoxes. Russell's conception of propositional functions stems, as we have indicated, from his most general and fundamental philosophical concerns: in particular, from what we have called his direct realism. This conception in turn makes ramified type theory not inevitable but at least a natural enough idea.

5. CONCLUSION

Finally, by way of conclusion, let us use the perspective established above to comment on one further issue. *Principia Mathematica* looks in many ways like a system of intensional logic, *i.e.* a logic designed to be suitable for formalizing what Russell calls the 'propositional attitudes'.[24] Russell himself, however, shows relatively little interest in the characteristic problems which lead to intensional logic. His concern, in developing a system of logic, is an interest in reducing mathematics to logic. So it is natural to ask: why does Russell produce a system which looks so like an intensional logic, if in fact he has little or no interest in intensional logic?

---

[23] See Goldfarb, 'Russell's Reasons for Ramification', and ch. 5, above.

[24] Thus Church says: 'If, following the early Russell, we hold that the object of an assertion or a belief is a proposition and then impose on propositions the strong conditions of identity which this requires, while at the same time undertaking to formulate a logic that will suffice for classical mathematics, we find no alternative except ramified type theory, with axioms of reducibility' (Church, 'Russell's Theory of Identity of Propositions', 521).

The answer, as our earlier discussion indicates, is that the features of *Principia* which make it appear suitable as a system of intensional logic are not, so to speak, added extras, built onto a superstructure of non-intensional logic to enable it to cope with certain particular issues arising from intensionality. The 'intensionality' of *Principia* is, rather, built into it from the start, because it is a feature of the propositions and propositional functions which are fundamental to Russell's philosophy and therefore to his logic. The question, indeed, betrays a modern assumption that is quite inappropriate when thinking about Russell. The assumption is that logic is naturally thought of as extensional, *i.e.* as dealing with truth-values and sets (extensions) and other aspects of Frege's *Bedeutungen*, rather than with aspects of Frege's *Sinne*. The problem with importing this assumption into a discussion of Russell is not so much that it is false (although certainly it is not true) as that even stating it begs the question. The assumption, that is to say, presupposes in its turn that logic is either extensional, and concerned with *Bedeutungen*, or intensional, and concerned with *Sinne*. But this distinction relies on just that three-stage analysis of language which, as we have seen, Russell rejects.

From this perspective, we can reach a new appreciation of the differences between Frege and Russell. Frege's great achievement was not simply to logicize mathematics but also, or rather, to mathematize logic.[25] This he does, above all, by importing into logic a clarified and extended version of the mathematical notion of a function. It is the logic which is constructed on the basis of this notion which is then used to logicize arithmetic. The use of the notion of a function as primitive requires, as we have seen, a three-stage analysis of language, and thus also requires a distinction such as that between *Sinn* and *Bedeutung*. This distinction enables us to ask which sort of entities should be of primary importance to logic—*i.e.* whether logic should be intensional or extensional. Frege's answer to that question is clear: since logic is to be based on the notion of a function, it is extensional. Although Russell shares with Frege a concern to logicize mathematics, he does not share with him the step of first mathematizing logic. The logic which Russell develops thus has a quite different basis from that of Frege, or indeed of most modern logicians. The superstructure of Russell's logic is familiar. Its foundations, however, are not. What we have attempted in this essay is to show that these foundations are connected with, and can be understood by reference to, Russell's most general philosophical concerns.

---

[25] I owe this way of putting the point to Burton Dreben. It should be noted that strictly speaking it is not all of mathematics that Frege attempts to logicize, for he excludes geometry from this project.

8

Functions, Operations, and Sense in Wittgenstein's *Tractatus*

The notion of an *operation* plays a crucial role in the *Tractatus*.[1] The account of representation which that book gives—the so-called 'Picture Theory of meaning'—applies directly only to what Wittgenstein calls elementary propositions.[2] It is clear, however, that none or almost none of the propositions which we utter or write or enquire about satisfy the conditions for being an elementary proposition. We therefore need an explanation of non-elementary propositions, and of their relation to elementary propositions. Such an explanation must have the consequence that the fundamental account of representation which does not apply directly to non-elementary propositions nonetheless does apply to them indirectly—so the explanation must show that all the real work of representation is done at the level of elementary propositions, and that what goes on in non-elementary propositions requires nothing new in principle. Wittgenstein's explanation is, as is well known, that all propositions are truth-functions of elementary propositions (5). So for Wittgenstein an explanation of the truth-functional compounding of simpler propositions into more complex propositions is required not simply for an account of logic but rather for an account of the possibility of representing the world (indeed it is a crucial doctrine of the *Tractatus* that in a sense *nothing* is required for logic—nothing, that is, that is not already implicit in any kind of method of representing the world in any way at all). To say that non-elementary propositions are truth-functions of elementary propositions is not enough. On a Fregean or Russellian account of truth-functional compounding, it introduces new elements—the truth-functions—which are not

---

[1] Ludwig Wittgenstein, *Tractatus Logico-Philosophicus*. References and citations to this work are made by section numbers standing alone. I have generally followed the Pears and McGuiness translation, but have occasionally made minor changes.

[2] It might be said, further, that the account applies directly only to *fully analysed* elementary propositions. I think this is correct, and I take it to be Wittgenstein's view that thought is, so to speak, a fully analysed language. Note that the notion of a thought is introduced before that of a proposition (at 3), and the notion of a proposition introduced in terms of a thought and its expression (at 3.1). Wittgenstein, I think, does not attribute 'magical' properties to thought—does not make it do what could not be done by any language; but I think he does take it to be a fully analysed language. Since we are clearly not aware of the complete analysis of the things we say, this position commits Wittgenstein to the view that we are in some sense not fully aware of our thoughts—that the mind is not transparent to itself. But this is a view that he explicitly accepts; see n. 17 below.

required for elementary (i.e. non-compound) propositions. (It is for this reason that logic, on the accounts of Frege and Russell, sometimes seems to be a subject with a distinct subject-matter of its own—as opposed to Wittgenstein's account of logic as made up of tautologies.) As I hope our quick sketch indicates, Wittgenstein must avoid any such new elements; he must, therefore, give an explanation of truth-functional compounding which does not, in the relevant sense, require new elements. The notion of an operation is central to this explanation.[3]

There is, however, a major interpretive problem surrounding the passages in which the notion of an operation is introduced and explained (the 5.2s, i.e. 5.2–5.254). The problem, moreover, comes at a crucial juncture, for it arises from Wittgenstein's insistence, in 5.25, that 'Operation and function must not be confused with each another'. Here, it seems plausible to suppose, Wittgenstein is recording his disagreement with the Fregean and Russellian treatments of truth-functional compounding, and is claiming that his account is crucially different. Let us look briefly at the Fregean and Russellian accounts. Frege's account of negation and the conditional—which he takes as primitive in the *Grundgesetze*—is that they are functions. He introduces the notion of a function by mathematical examples (section 1). He introduces truth-values as the denotations (*Bedeutungen*) of indicative sentences (section 2). This then enables him to give an account of predicates as a special case of functional expressions: they denote a special case of functions, called *concepts* (*Begriffe*), defined as those functions whose values for any argument are always truth-values (section 3). This in turn enables Frege to introduce negation as a concept, in this sense. It is, he says, 'a function whose value is always a truth-value; it is a concept under which falls every object with the sole exception of the True' (section 6). The conditional is introduced in similar fashion, as a two-place function whose values are always truth-values (section 12; note that here, as in the case of negation, Frege does not stipulate that the *arguments* of such functions are always truth-values: it is his consistent view that any function must be defined for all arguments). Russell introduces his primitives, negation and disjunction, very sketchily in the main body of the text of *Principia Mathematica* (see p. 93).[4] The Introduction contains a somewhat more discursive, though perhaps confusing, discussion. Russell first introduces the general notion of a function of propositions (meaning a function which takes propositions as arguments and as values), by saying: 'An aggregation of propositions . . . into a single proposition more complex than its constituents, is a function *with propositions as arguments*' (p. 6; emphasis in the

[3] This is not to say that this is the only role that the notion of an operation plays in the *Tractatus*. It is crucial also for the notion of a formal series, and hence for Wittgenstein's account of mathematics. But the role that I have emphasised—as part of the account of truth-functional compounding—is, I think, the central one.

[4] All my references are to the first volume. I take Russell alone to be responsible for the more fundamental parts of the work, which are my concern in what follows.

original). He then introduces four special cases of such functions, negation, disjunction, conjunction, and material implication, and says that only two of these need be taken as primitive. (We shall return to Russell's confusing statement.)

For both Frege and Russell, then, it might seem that ways of truth-functionally compounding sentences are functions. So, it is natural to assume, in insisting that operations are not functions, Wittgenstein is insisting that his treatment of such ways of compounding is different from theirs. But what are the differences? It appears, as Max Black points out,[5] that everything, or almost everything, that Wittgenstein says about operations could with equal correctness be said about functions. Thus, for example, the statement that function and operation must not be confused is immediately preceded by the statement that 'an operation does not assert anything; only its result does, and this depends on the bases of the operation' (5.25). But, as Black says, what is said here of operations could equally be said of a function, such as the function 'x^2'; it too does not assert anything or say anything. Again, Wittgenstein says: 'A function cannot be its own argument, whereas the result of an operation can be its own basis.' (5.251). Here too it seems that Wittgenstein takes himself to be marking a difference between functions and operations, but it is quite unclear that he has in fact done so, for what he says would seem also to be true of operations. An operation itself (as opposed to the result of an operation) cannot be the argument or basis of an operation; and surely the *result* of applying a function to an argument can, at least in some cases, in turn be an argument for that function (as Black says: 'a *value* of a function can sometimes be an argument of that function—3^2 can itself be squared', p. 261).

The interpretive difficulty is thus that, on the one hand, Wittgenstein is clearly concerned to emphasise the difference between functions and operations; yet, on the other hand, what he says about operations does not seem in fact to introduce a notion which is significantly different from that of a function. Now a first step towards resolving this difficulty is to reconsider exactly what Wittgenstein's target is. When he insists that the truth-operations—such as negation, or disjunction, or his own symbol 'N', a generalised version of the Sheffer stroke—are not functions, what is he primarily concerned to deny? Black assumes that his target is the idea that such operations can be assimilated to mathematical functions, such as 'square of'.[6] This idea, it might be assumed, is

---

[5] Black, *Companion to Wittgenstein's 'Tractatus'*, 258. I discuss Max Black's view because it does, I think, represent a natural response to the passages I am chiefly concerned with. Most subsequent commentators do not consider the issues I am concerned with in any detail.

[6] There is a question here about how we are to understand ordinary mathematical functions. I shall assume that they are to be understood extensionally—i.e. that functions which for every argument have the same value (i.e. are co-extensive) are not distinct. This is the sort of view of functions that leads some to identify them with sets of ordered pairs. Although Frege does not adopt a set-theoretic account, I think that he presupposes an extensional view of functions. The question of Frege's views here is complicated by the fact that he does not think that the notion of identity applies to functions; he does, however, take co-extensiveness to play the same role among functions as identity does among objects.

common to Frege and Russell, and is thus a natural target for Wittgenstein. I shall argue, however, that these natural assumptions about Wittgenstein's target are mistaken. As I see the matter, Russell employs a notion of a propositional function which is in fact quite distinct from that of an ordinary mathematical function (whereas Frege explicitly employs a generalised and clarified version of the mathematical notion). And we can make clear sense of Wittgenstein's remarks in the 5.2s if we see them as directed in the first instance against Russell's view that the truth-operations are propositional functions in something like Russell's sense of that expression. (I say that we should see Wittgenstein's remarks as directed *in the first instance* against Russell, but I take them to be anti-Fregean as well as anti-Russellian. Our discussion will put us in a position to return to the idea of truth-operations as functions in the Fregean sense.)

It is crucial to our discussion of this issue that what Wittgenstein is opposing is the idea that truth-functional compounding takes place by means of propositional functions *in Russell's sense*, and that that sense is not Frege's. Before we examine that issue, however, it is worth noting that if there is such a difference between Russellian propositional functions on the one hand and Fregean (or mathematical) functions on the other hand, then it is plausible that Wittgenstein is discussing propositional functions, rather than functions in the mathematical sense. We know that Wittgenstein studied the fundamental portions of *Principia Mathematica*,[7] and in that book Russell uses 'function' always to mean 'propositional function', referring to non-propositional functions as 'descriptive functions',[8] and it is not unreasonable to suppose that Wittgenstein would have followed him in this usage. At least some of the uses of the word 'function' (*funktion*) in the *Tractatus*, moreover, *must* be taken to mean 'propositional function', if we are to make even *prima facie* sense of them. Thus 5.501 states, as a method of describing a number of propositions, the following: 'Giving a function *fx*, whose values for all values of *x* are the propositions to be described.' And, again, 5.5301 speaks of an object as *satisfying* a function (the German is *genügen*), which hardly makes sense unless it is a propositional function that Wittgenstein has in mind.

If propositional functions are, as is perhaps natural to assume, simply a kind of function, then it can make little difference whether Wittgenstein is speaking, in the 5.2s and elsewhere, about functions or about propositional functions. If propositional functions are simply a special case of functions—those functions

---

[7] Apart from the external evidence, which is clear, Wittgenstein twice refers to 'Russell and Whitehead'—at 5.252 and 5.452. Along with Frege, Mauthner, and Russell standing by himself, they are the only authors explicitly referred to in the *Tractatus*.

[8] Thus the footnote to p. 39 of *Principia Mathematica* says: 'When the word "function" is used in the sequel, "propositional function" is always meant.' Russell first introduces non-propositional functions in § 30, which is entitled 'Descriptive Functions': unlike propositional functions, descriptive or non-propositional functions thus play no part in the fundamental portions of the work.

whose values happen to be propositions—then to interpret Wittgenstein as speaking about propositional functions, rather than about functions *tout court* is simply to interpret him as speaking about the special case rather than the more general notion. In some cases this might seem to be an unduly restrictive interpretation. In the present case, however, it seems as if it could make no difference at all. If ways of compounding propositions truth-functionally are to be thought of as functions at all, then surely they should be thought of as propositional functions,[9] for the upshot of any such compounding is always a proposition, never a number, say, or some other object. So one might think: perhaps in denying that operations are functions Wittgenstein is to be construed, if we are really concerned with accuracy, as denying that they are *propositional* functions—but what difference does it make? The answer is that it makes a great deal of difference, because propositional functions, as Russell conceives of them, are *not* special cases of a more general notion of a function, but have some crucial features which distinguish them from functions in the general sense. This matter is crucial for our purposes, and must be explained at some length.[10]

In *Principia Mathematica*, as already noted, Russell does not take the general notion of a function for granted and introduce propositional functions as a special case, picked out by the fact that propositional functions have propositions as values (as Frege does take the general notion of a function for granted, and picks out concepts as a special case of functions, namely those whose values for any argument are truth-values). Rather he takes propositional functions for granted, and defines other functions (descriptive functions) as needed. By means of the definite description operator (which is, of course, defined in its turn) we may define a one-place function $f(x)$ from a two-place propositional function, xRy, by saying that $f(x)$ = the object y such that xRy (this only succeeds in defining a function if R obeys the right uniqueness conditions: for any given object a, there must be at most one object y such that xRy). Russell gives the general form of this kind of definition at § 30.01 of *Principia Mathematica*. Obviously the technique can be generalised: from any $n + 1$ place propositional function (which satisfies the relevant uniqueness condition) we can define an n-place function.

So far the point is merely technical: rather than taking for granted the general notion of function, as Frege does, and distinguishing propositional functions as special cases, Russell rather takes the notion of a propositional function as fundamental, and introduces descriptive (i.e. non-propositional) functions as needed. Lying behind the technique is the fact that for Russell propositional

---

[9] Here I am, of course, thinking of matters in Russellian rather than Fregean terms. For Frege such a function is a concept (*Begriff*), i.e. a function whose value for any argument is a truth-value. For the moment I shall continue to take this Russellian framework for granted; we shall return to the contrast between Wittgenstein's view and Frege's.

[10] The next three paragraphs draw heavily on my essay 'Functions and Propositional Functions in *Principia Mathematica*' (Ch. 7 above).

functions have characteristics which one cannot suppose functions (if taken as primitive, rather than defined) to have. Both propositions and propositional functions, on Russell's account, are structured entities, which contain parts. Propositional functions bear a particular structural relation to the propositions which are their values: a proposition shares the structure of any propositional function of which it is the value. (Similarly, a proposition which is the value of a given propositional function for a given object as argument *contains* that object.) Two propositions which are both values of a given propositional function, for different arguments, have some aspect of their structure in common, and that structure is also shared by the propositional function. (Conversely, I think it is also true that if two propositions have some aspect of their structure in common, then they are values, for different arguments, of some one propositional function.) It is worth emphasising the contrast that this makes between propositional functions and functions in the ordinary sense, mathematical functions, for example. A mathematical function is not naturally thought of as a structured entity (if it were, then the set-theoretic representation of a function as a set of ordered pairs would be grossly inadequate). And there is no plausible sense of 'structure' in which a mathematical function, and an object which is the value of that function for some argument, shares a structure.

On Russell's conception of propositional functions, however, the propositional function *x is wise* does share a structure with the proposition that Socrates is wise: the propositional function is not mere mapping of objects onto propositions. Thus it makes sense to say of a propositional function—and not merely of the words which express a propositional function—that it contains a variable ranging over certain entities—e.g. over all propositional functions of a certain type.[11] This point also enables us to make sense of the curious way in which Russell introduced the idea of a function whose arguments are propositions. He describes such a function, as we saw, as 'An aggregation of propositions . . . into a single proposition more complex than its constituents' (see p. 139 above, where this phrase is quoted in context). Now this would be a very puzzling description if he had in mind the notion of a function in something like the mathematical sense. No one would describe a mathematical function, say, as being or resulting in 'an aggregation of numbers into a single number more complex than its constituents'. On the contrary, it is characteristic of a function in the ordinary sense that the result of applying a function to an object or to a number of objects is in no sense an 'aggregation' of those objects, or more complex than they. Thus twelve results from applying the two-place plus function to five and seven, but it is in no clear sense an aggregation of them, or more complex than either.

---

[11] This point is crucial to an understanding of the fact that *Principia Mathematica* puts forward a *ramified* theory of types. Besides the essay referred to in the previous note, see also Goldfarb, 'Russell's Reasons for Ramification'.

Even more clearly, if we take a non-mathematical function such as 'father of,' there is no sense at all in which Philip of Macedonia is an aggregation of his son Alexander, and no relevant sense in which the former is more complex than the latter. But Russell's phrase is not simply a piece of nonsense: it is, rather, a reflection of the fact that he is presupposing a notion of a propositional function which cannot be assimilated to the ordinary or mathematical notion of a function. The value of a propositional function for a number of arguments can be described as an aggregation of them, and more complex than them, for it contains them. It is this Russellian notion of a propositional function, I wish to claim, that is Wittgenstein's immediate target in the 5.2s.

Let us, then, return to the vexed passages in the 5.2s and see how we can interpret them if we take Wittgenstein to be arguing against Russell's view that truth-functional ways of compounding propositions are propositional functions in the sense indicated. Wittgenstein insists in 5.25 that 'The occurrence of an operation does not characterize the sense of a proposition.' This seems to me the crucial point. The remarks of the previous paragraph indicate that it *is* a characteristic of a proposition, in Russell's sense, that it can be obtained as the value of a certain propositional function: two propositions which are values of some one propositional function have something in common with each other (and indeed with the propositional function).[12] Thus on Russell's account a proposition which is obtained by application of the propositional function *disjunction* to two propositions p and q is a disjunctive proposition—it contains a constituent corresponding to disjunction. It must thus be a different proposition from that which we obtain if we first apply to each of p and q the propositional function corresponding to negation, then take the resulting propositions as arguments to the propositional function corresponding to conjunction, and then take the resulting proposition as argument to the propositional function corresponding to negation. In short: for Russell 'p v q' must represent a different proposition from that represented by '$\sim(\sim p \, . \, \sim q)$'. But this is precisely the result that Wittgenstein wants to avoid. His view is that the above sentences express the same proposition, and hence that the occurrence of e.g. disjunction does not characterise the sense of a proposition.[13]

5.25 continues: 'Indeed, no statement is made by an operation (*Die Operation sagt ja nichts aus*), only by its result, and this depends on the bases of the

---

[12] I do not speak here of a propositional function *occurring* in a proposition, for it is Russell's view in *Principia Mathematica* that propositional functions are not themselves constituents of propositions, i.e. do not occur in propositions. See pp. 54–5 of *Principia Mathematica*. The reasons for this view have to do with the theory of types; see Hylton, *Russell, Idealism, and the Emergence of Analytic Philosophy*, 300–1.

[13] Robert J. Fogelin speaks of Wittgenstein's '*disappearance* theory of logical constants', and compares it with Russell's analysis of the apparent referring expressions which are definite descriptions (see Fogelin, *Wittgenstein*, 36). This comparison, however, seriously understates the point. On Russell's theory of descriptions, two propositions each of which is naturally expressed by a sentence containing the phrase 'the King of France' have something in common—the result of the theory is that

operation.' Here again there is a contrast with Russellian propositional functions. A propositional function, such as *x is wise*, it might be said, *does* make a statement, in a loose sense—only as yet an incomplete statement: it says of some as yet unspecified object that it is wise. For Russell, it is worth noting, this idea that we can think of a propositional function as making a statement, in a certain sense, is elevated to an important point of doctrine. He speaks of asserting a propositional function, as distinct both from asserting a particular value of the propositional function, and from asserting all values of the propositional function. This is at the basis of his idea of typical ambiguity, by which he hopes to resolve some of the problems created by the restrictions of type theory. Thus he says: 'When we assert something containing a real [i.e. free] variable, we cannot strictly be said to be asserting a *proposition*, for we only obtain a definite proposition by assigning a value to the variable, and then our assertion only applies to one definite case, so that it has not at all the same force as before. When what we assert contains a real variable, we are asserting a wholly undetermined one of all the propositions that result from giving various values to the variable. It will be convenient to speak of such assertions as *asserting a propositional function*,' (*Principia*, 18; emphasis in the original).[14] The point of the sentence from 5.25 which we are discussing is surely that even in the loose sense in which a propositional function can be thought of as saying something—as making at least an incomplete statement—an operation does not say anything. This point is very closely connected with the idea that operations, unlike Russellian propositional functions, do not characterise the sense of a proposition. In a loose or incomplete sense a propositional function can be said to say something, and the value of that propositional function is a proposition that says the same thing about a particular object. That, of course, is why two propositions that are values of the same propositional function have an aspect of their sense in common: although they may be about different objects, what the one says about the one object is the same thing that the other says about the other object. Whatever else operations are, Wittgenstein is here saying that they are not like *that*.

The final article in which Wittgenstein makes the contrast between functions and operations is 5.251: 'A function cannot be its own argument, whereas the result of an operation can be its own basis.' The interpretive difficulty which this poses is, as we saw, that Wittgenstein seems to be marking a difference between objects and functions, yet if we take 'function' in the Fregean or mathematical

what they have in common is not the occurrence of a certain object, referred to by that phrase, but is rather that they share a certain structural property, and that each contains certain predicates. Wittgenstein's view, however, is that two propositions each of which is expressed using disjunction, say, have *nothing* in common in virtue of that fact: the occurrence of the operation does not characterise the sense of the proposition.

[14] It is perhaps this that Wittgenstein is criticising when he insists, as early as 1912, that the propositions of logic contain only apparent, i.e. bound, variables. See the letter to Russell, dated 22/6/12, in *Letters to Russell, Keynes and Moore*, 10.

sense, then what he says would seem to hold equally if we interchange the words 'operation' and 'function'. If, on the other hand, we take 'function' in the first half of this sentence to be referring to propositional functions, then the difficulty is at least partly solved. The result of applying a propositional function to an object is, of course, a proposition. And this proposition cannot in turn be taken as an argument for that propositional function. Where F(a) is a proposition which is the value of the propositional function F($\hat{x}$) for the argument a, F(F(a)) is nonsense. Such an expression is banned by Russell's theory of types, and it is clear that while Wittgenstein rejected the idea of theory of types; he largely accepted the restrictions that Russell imposed.[15] This appears to be only a partial solution to the interpretive problem, for it does not seem to explain the first half of the sentence: 'A function cannot be its own argument'. While this is clearly something that Wittgenstein believed, for it is stated also at 3.333, it cannot be taken as marking a difference between propositional functions and operations, for an operation (as distinct from the result of an operation) is surely also something that cannot be taken as its own argument. The solution here, I think, is that for Wittgenstein the point that a propositional function cannot be its own argument, and the point that it cannot be applied to one of its own values, are very similar. The reason that Wittgenstein gives for the former point is 'because the function sign already contains the prototype of its own argument, and it cannot contain itself' (3.333). Whether we attempt to apply a propositional function to itself, or to one of its values, the fundamental point is the same: we are giving the propositional function arguments which presuppose, or contain, the propositional function itself. I take it that Wittgenstein is here relying on his earlier discussion of these matters, in the 3.33s; the first half of the sentence serves to remind us of that discussion.

To this point I have argued that the contrast that Wittgenstein draws in the 5.2s is between operations and *propositional* functions in Russell's sense, and that this enables us to make clear sense of passages which are other wise quite baffling. The crucial point of this contrast, as we have seen, is that the occurrence of an operation does not characterise the sense of a proposition. Hence, as Wittgenstein says in 5.254, 'Operations can vanish [*verschwinden*] (e.g. negation in "~~p" . ~~p = p).' This point is of course directly connected with what Wittgenstein himself calls his 'fundamental thought': that the logical constants do not name anything, are not the representatives of entities (4.0312; see also 5.4). Put a little differently, the point is that the logical constants do not introduce new

---

[15] Wittgenstein's objection to the theory of types is that the restrictions cannot be stated, and that a correct understanding of language would make it clear that there is nothing that needs to be stated: 'The rules of logical syntax must go without saying, once we know how each individual sign signifies,' (3.334). The discussion of the theory of types, especially in 3.333, suggests that Wittgenstein thought that all of Russell's restrictions were correct—only their status was misunderstood.

elements into the senses of the sentences in which they occur. The fundamental connection between language and the world is set up simply at the level of elementary propositions, and our ways of compounding elementary propositions into non-elementary propositions do not require any further connections of this sort.

At this point it may seem as if the point that Wittgenstein makes by means of the notion of an operation could have been made more simply and perspicuously if he had said: truth-functional symbols do not stand for Russellian propositional functions; rather they stand for Fregean functions. Many of the points that we have made about operations *do* seem to apply equally to functions in the ordinary mathematical sense, which Frege generalises. So what is the point of the notion of an operation? This sort of criticism of Wittgenstein seems to overlook the most fundamental element in Frege's view of language. For Frege all linguistic expressions—including, in particular, functional expressions, and expressions containing them—have two aspects: *Sinn* and *Bedeutung*. It is only if we focus on functions themselves—i.e. on the *Bedeutungen* of functional expressions— that we have something which appears to play the same role as Wittgenstein's operations. In particular, functions do *vanish* in the sense that Wittgenstein requires of operations: three squared divided by three, say, is just three over again—the number bears no trace of the fact that it is obtained by the application of two functions. But the 'vanishing' of functions in this sense is just a special case of a more general phenomenon, which makes it clear that a Fregean account which deals only with Fregean *Bedeutungen* will not be adequate for Wittgenstein's purposes. At the level of Fregean *Bedeutungen* too much vanishes. Wittgenstein's concern here is with propositions, sentences. And for Frege the *Bedeutungen* of a sentence is simply its truth-value—*everything* vanishes, everything, that is, that distinguishes one sentence from another with the same truth-value.

The issue, let us remember, is what explanation we can give of non-elementary propositions, i.e. to put the matter roughly in Fregean terms, of the senses of compound sentences. Wittgenstein has (we are assuming) an account of how elementary propositions represent atomic facts; the explanation of non-elementary propositions is then supposed to show, or to have as a consequence, that no new elements are required to extend this account to propositions which are truth-functions of elementary propositions. Clearly, it will not do simply to equate such propositions with what Frege called the *Bedeutungen* of the corresponding sentences. That has the consequence that there are only two non-elementary propositions—clearly not a view that Wittgenstein can accept. Nor, on the other hand, will it do to equate non-elementary propositions with what Frege called the senses (*Sinne*) of the corresponding sentences. There is at least a strong strain in Frege's thought which suggests that the sense of a complex expression is made up of the senses of the parts of that expression.[16] The *Sinn* of the double negation of a sentence is thus different from the *Sinn* of the sentence itself, because the first does, as the second does not, contain the *Sinn* of the negation symbol. Therefore, Frege's account has the same drawback as Russell's, from Wittgenstein's point of view: the (*Sinne* of the) logical constants do *not* vanish.

At this point one might think that Wittgenstein's view can be described as a sort of hybrid. Elementary propositions are to be treated as Russell treated them, or to be thought of as having senses like Frege's *Sinne*. Logical constants, on the other hand, are to be thought of as Fregean functions, only without *Sinne*. This idea has the merit of capturing a crucial point of Wittgenstein's view: that the logical constants are not like ordinary, fully meaningful, words—that they do not contribute to the senses of sentences in which they occur in anything like the same way as other expressions. But what account is there, on this view, of the sense of the non-elementary sentence? On Frege's own account, the sense of the non-elementary sentence is presumably that of the sense of the elementary sentence[s] combined with the sense of the logical constant. But if the logical constant has no sense, what then? A logical constant, on this account, is presumably a function which maps one or more senses (those of elementary, or relatively simple sentences) onto other senses—but there is not, in this account, any suggestion that there must be an internal relation between the argument sense and the value sense, still less that the latter contain the former. An object which is the value of a function for a given argument does not, except in odd cases, contain the object which is the argument. But it is crucial to Wittgenstein's account that the sense of a proposition which is a truth-function of a number of other propositions is made up out of the senses of those other propositions. In other words, it is characteristic of a function, in the Fregean sense, that not only does it vanish but also its arguments vanish: there is no internal connection that two entities must have if the first is the value for some function with the second as argument. But this is not so in the case of Wittgenstein's operations: the operations themselves vanish, but the propositions which are their arguments do not.

I go into the relation between Wittgenstein's operations and Frege's functions because it indicates how hard it is to make sense of what Wittgenstein says from within a Fregean framework, and it suggests why this should be so: because Wittgenstein's notion of an operation is integral to a re-conceiving of the idea of the sense of a sentence. Wittgenstein's conception of an operation cannot easily be captured in Fregean or Russellian terms because it is part of a conception of the sense of a sentence—i.e. a conception of a proposition—which also cannot easily

---

[16] Thus Frege says, for example, 'thoughts have parts out of which they are built up . . . as we take a thought to be the sense of a sentence, so we may call a part of a thought the sense of that part of the sentence which corresponds to it' (Frege, *Posthumous Writings*, 225). For some qualifications to the attribution of this view to Frege, see (Baker and Hacker, *Frege: Logical Excavations*, 325, 380–5).

be captured in those terms. To go further into these matters we need to go beyond the distinctness of the notion of an operation from that of a function, and consider more positively the role that operations play for Wittgenstein. And here there are two points, each of which is crucial, and which may seem to contradict one another. On the one hand, as we have seen, an operation does not characterise the sense of a proposition. No proposition is intrinsically disjunctive rather than conjunctive or negative: any proposition can be expressed in a way that uses any one of these operations (even an elementary proposition—see e.g. 5.441). This is fundamental to Wittgenstein's conception of sense, which individuates senses or propositions far more coarsely than does that of Frege or of Russell: any two logically equivalent sentences, for Wittgenstein, have the same sense, or express the same proposition.[17] On the other hand, clearly the occurrence of an operation in a sentence contributes to its sense. The disjunction of two sentences yields a sentence with a sense different from that obtained if we conjoin those same sentences. So although operations vanish—they do not occur as part of the proposition—still they do affect which proposition it is that a given sentence expresses.

How is it possible that both of these things can be true of operations?—It seems almost to demand that operations be something and yet nothing!—In a way this is right. An operation is not itself part of, or an element in, the sense of a proposition. It is, rather, the expression of a relation (an internal relation, in Wittgenstein's sense) between one proposition and another. As Wittgenstein says at 5.22: 'An operation is the expression of a relation between the structures of its results and of its bases.' (The relation is internal precisely because it concerns the structures of propositions in this way.) Similarly, perhaps more explicitly, at 5.241 we have: 'An operation is not the mark of a form, but only of a difference in forms.' Conjunction expresses a different difference, so to speak, from that expressed by disjunction: hence the proposition which is a conjunction of two others is not the same as that which is a disjunction of those same two others. Given two sentences, conjoining them expresses a proposition that differs from them in a determinate way—by being their conjunction. But this proposition is not intrinsically conjunctive: it is, for example, also expressed by a sentence which negates the disjunction of the negations of two propositions, or by one that uses only the Sheffer stroke. The conjunction symbol serves only to express

---

[17] Such a conception of sense is possible because Wittgenstein does not accept that our thoughts are, so to speak, transparent to us. He does not accept, that is to say, that if I have a thought I must know what thought it is, that if I have two thoughts I must know whether they are the same, and so on. This is, I think, implicit almost from the start. It becomes explicit at such moments as these: 'every possible proposition is legitimately constructed, and if it has no sense this can only be because we have given no meaning to some of its constituent parts. (Even if we believe that we have done so.)' (5.4733). This view is, I think, crucial for the doctrine of the *Tractatus* as a whole.

the difference between the propositions that you start with and the proposition that you end with: it does not also characterise the proposition that you end with.

All of this may, however, seem simply to assert that both of the two apparently conflicting points apply to operations, without doing anything to dispel the apparent conflict. But I think there is progress. The crucial point of the above discussion is this: that an operation may express the difference between two senses, without at the same time characterising either sense. Why should these two points be thought to conflict? Surely because we assume that the only way to express the difference between two senses is by being part of one of them (and, presumably, by *not* being part of the other, or at least not being part of it in quite the same way). If this seems to be an obvious principle, it is perhaps because we think of senses of sentences, or of propositions, in a Fregean way. We assume a principle of compositionality about sense: that the sense of the sentence (or indeed of any complex piece of language) is made up of the senses of its parts—and made up of them almost in the way that a wall is made of bricks (I call this way of thinking of sense *Fregean*; as we have seen, however, some qualifications may be necessary in ascribing this view to Frege himself. See n. 16 above). Now Wittgenstein does not simply reject this view, he rejects the assumptions implicit in it. For Wittgenstein the constituent parts of a fully analysed sentence—*names*, in his sense—do not have *Sinn* at all: this is implicit in various remarks in the 3.1s and 3.2s, and is made explicit at 3.3, which says 'Only propositions have sense'. Names have *Bedeutung* (3.203), a name stands for (*vertritt*) an object (3.22), but only propositions have sense. Thus on Wittgenstein's view there is not even a sensible question to be asked, whether the sense of a sentence is made up of the senses of the parts of the sentence. A fully analysed sentence is made up of names (3.2), and names have no senses. Sense, for Wittgenstein, is not an attribute of the simplest linguistic expressions, and we cannot see the senses of sentences as made up from the senses of their simpler parts. Sense is, rather, a phenomenon that first arises when names are combined into meaningful sentences. Although Wittgenstein uses the Fregean terminology of *Sinn* and *Bedeutung*, he is clearly putting forward a radically different conception from that of Frege.

The fact that only propositions have *Sinn*—that Wittgenstein does not use the expression at all in connection with sub-sentential units of language—may make it seem all the more mysterious that the logical constants have no *Bedeutung*. If logical constants have neither *Sinn* nor *Bedeutung*, does it not follow that they are simply meaningless marks, marks which play no role at all in the language? But that conclusion is intolerable: the negation of a proposition has a different sense from that proposition itself, and the conjunction of two propositions has a sense different from the disjunction of the same two propositions. The force of these can perhaps be diffused by a comparison which

Wittgenstein himself makes in the 5.46s. Parentheses, or other ways of marking distinctions of scope, are crucial to the sense of logical schemata in many systems. A string of symbols such as '$p \supset q \mathbin{\&} r$' can be punctuated in either one of two ways, as '$p \supset (q \mathbin{\&} r)$' or as '$(p \supset q) \mathbin{\&} r$'.[18] In some systems, that is to say, parentheses or brackets or some other explicit sign of grouping are essential to the sense of what is expressed. Yet, as Wittgenstein himself says, 'surely no one is going to believe that brackets have an independent meaning' (5.461). Yet the same questions that we asked about logical constants can be asked about brackets: if they have neither a *Sinn* nor a *Bedeutung*, how can they be more then meaningless marks? How can they be crucial for the sense of what is expressed? This question does not seem pressing. In some cases, at least, we seem to have no trouble accepting that symbols may affect the sense of what is expressed without themselves having sense.[19] But if we can accept this of brackets, parentheses, and other signs of punctuation, why not of logical constants? This, I take it, is the point that Wittgenstein is making at 5.4611 where he says: 'Signs for logical operations are punctuation-marks.'

Now an example of a phenomenon is, of course, not an explanation of that phenomenon. If we wished to know how logical constants can affect the sense of a proposition without themselves having sense, it is not an answer to be told: in the same way that brackets do. What the example may do, however, is to lead us to see that the question is based on certain assumptions about sense, assumptions that are not inevitable. In particular, it comes naturally to us to think of the sense of a sentence as a sort of entity (subject, as noted above, to a principle of compositionality), and to think that this entity has a structure or complexity which corresponds to that of the sentence itself (or would do so if the sentence were in ideal form—a fully analysed sentence of a logically perfect language). Both Frege's conception of the *Sinn* of a sentence, and Russell's conception of a proposition, at least approximate this view, and it has great appeal for those who have followed Frege and Russell. Thus Carnap, for example, in *Meaning and Necessity*, introduces a distinction between intension and extension as a modification of Frege's distinction between *Sinn* and *Bedeutung*. He introduces the term 'proposition' to mean the intension of a sentence (p. 27), which he takes to be a

---

[18] Rather than parentheses, or other explicit signs of grouping, and conventions governing their use, we can, of course, adopt conventions which make such use of parentheses unnecessary—e.g. that '$\supset$' is always to mark a larger break than '$\&$'. Or we may adopt Polish notation, which removes such ambiguities with no conventions beyond those of the basic semantics. But these alternative possibilities are not to the present point.

[19] Church classifies brackets among what he calls 'improper symbols': 'in addition to proper symbols there must also occur symbols which are *improper* . . . i.e. which [have] no meaning in isolation but which combine with proper symbols (one or more) to form expressions that do have meaning in isolation' (Church, *Introduction to Mathematical Logic*, 32). (I owe this reference to Leonard Linsky.) Carnap, however, takes the distinction to be a matter of degree, and also to be 'highly subjective'. See Carnap, *Meaning and Necessity*, 7. Neither author says anything about the present issue, however.

complex entity: 'Any proposition must be regarded as a complex entity, consisting of component entities, which, in their turn, may be simple or again complex . . .' (p. 30). This Fregean conception of sense leads inevitably to the problematic questions about the logical constants (and, indeed, about parentheses): how can they affect the senses of the sentences in which they occur if they do not themselves have sense?

Wittgenstein, however, opposes this Fregean conception of sense in the *Tractatus*. The sense of a proposition is simply that things are a certain way: 'A proposition *shows* its sense. It *shows* how things stand *if* it is true. And it *says that* they do so stand,' (4.022; emphasis in the original). The sense of a non-elementary proposition, in particular, is that one of a number of combinations of elementary propositions obtains, while all of the other combinations do not obtain. 'The sense of a proposition is its agreement and disagreement with possibilities of holding and non-holding of atomic facts' (4.2), where we are immediately told that an elementary proposition asserts that an atomic fact obtains (4.21). To revert to the case of parentheses: one might wish to say that parentheses function not by having a sense themselves, but rather by indicating how other senses should be combined. In Wittgenstein's view, I think, something similar can be said of operations. An operation, as its name perhaps suggests, is less like an entity, that might be a constituent of more complex entity, than it is like something we *do*. We can use the senses of one or more elementary propositions to say that such-and-such a sense does *not* obtain—this is how things are: *not* like this; or that one or other of these senses obtains—this is how things are: either like this or like that. To reify the notion of sense and then inquire into the composition of the sense of this or that sentence, as if we were chemists enquiring into the composition of some substance—that, I take it, is exactly the view that Wittgenstein opposes.[20]

[20] The volume in which this essay first appeared was a tribute to Leonard Linsky, and based on a conference given in April 1992 to mark Leonard's retirement from the University of Chicago. The essay that I read at that conference was not this one but rather a version of ch. 7, above. But this essay is, I hope, a fitting tribute to Leonard for another reason. It arises out of a seminar on Wittgenstein's *Tractatus* that I gave in the spring of 1993; Leonard was an active participant (to put it mildly) in that seminar. As well as Leonard, I thank the other members of that seminar. Jim Harrington, in particular, may recognize some ideas from an interchange between us.

9
Frege and Russell

Frege and Russell are often linked, as the founders of twentieth-century analytic philosophy. Besides this historical, retrospective, connection, there are also important similarities in doctrine between them.[1] Each was a logician, whose work in logic was closely integrated with his work in philosophy; each held that philosophical problems can be clarified and, in some cases, solved, by means of logic. (This view that the technical and the philosophical are not distinct is characteristic of one clear line of thought in twentieth-century analytic philosophy.) Each argued for, and tried to prove, logicism, the thesis that arithmetic can be reduced to logic, and is thus no more than logic in disguise.[2] Each was strongly opposed to psychologism; each believed in a 'third realm', neither physical nor mental, which provides the subject matter for objective judgments about abstract matters. (In Frege's case, however, it is perhaps unclear just what this belief comes to.) In particular, each believed that our declarative sentences have an objective content, independent of human action—that, as Frege puts it, there is not *my* Pythagorean theorem and *your* Pythagorean theorem but *the* Pythagorean theorem, independent of both of us, and timelessly true.[3] (Russell to some extent backs away from this view after 1906, as we shall see; the shift, however, has relatively little effect on the issues I shall be discussing in this essay. See pp. 175–6, below.)

The primary focus of this essay, however, is not on the similarities between the views of Frege and of Russell but on their differences. It is no part of my

---

[1] I speak, here and throughout this essay, of Russell's views after his break with Idealism, around 1900, and before his shift towards pragmatism and behaviourism, around 1920. All of his works which played a foundational role for 20th-century analytic philosophy were written in these two decades. Frege's views change much less markedly. I do attribute logicism to Frege, although he abandoned that view towards the end of his life. I also attribute to him a view of functions as non-linguistic entities, in spite of some remarks to the contrary in the early sections of *Begriffsschrift*. Finally, I attribute to him some version of the distinction between *Sinn* and *Bedeutung* that he puts forward in the 1892 essay 'Sense and Meaning'; although not articulated clearly until that essay, the distinction seems to me present, although in nascent form, as early as *Begriffsschrift*.

[2] Russell accepted, as Frege did not, that geometry can be reduced to arithmetic, and thus, via logicism, to logic. Frege's view here reveals something important about his inchoate epistemological views; I shall not go further into this matter here, however.

[3] See 'Der Gedanke', p.68 of the original printing; pp. 362–3 of Frege's *Collected Papers*. The expression 'third realm' is in this same passage.

concern to deny the similarities indicated above; they are real, and central to the thought of each of our philosophers. Nor do I mean to cast in doubt the natural pairing of Frege with Russell. On the contrary: it is because their views are in some ways so similar, and the pairing so natural, that differences between them are of great interest. Let me briefly outline my discussion of some of these differences.

I begin, in section II, with a rather well-known difference. Frege distinguishes the *Sinn* of an expression from its *Bedeutung*,[4] whereas Russell denies that any such distinction is fundamental. I connect this difference with aspects of Russell's epistemology; in particular, with the fact that he takes acquaintance— a direct and unmediated relation between the mind and a known object—to be the foundation of all our knowledge. These views of Russell's pose significant difficulties. In the period before 'On Denoting' he attempted one kind of resolution of these difficulties, putting forward what I shall call 'the theory of denoting concepts'. This theory accepts a distinction, for some expressions, which is in some ways akin to Frege's distinction between *Sinn* and *Bedeutung*; it is the subject of section III. The next section deals with the theory of descriptions, which Russell put forward in 'On Denoting' and held thereafter. Section V elaborates on the way in which that theory enables Russell to avoid any analogue of the Fregean distinction. Central to Russell's answer is the idea that most apparent referring expressions are not genuine referring expressions; in particular, that there are no *complex* referring expressions. Functional expressions, such as '2 + 3' or 'the father of Alexander the Great', are, on the face of it, complex referring expressions. In accordance with what we have just said, Russell's new (post-1905) view cannot accept these expressions as primitive; they must, rather, be defined as needed. This point leads in turn to a further issue. For Frege, the function-argument method of analysis is fundamental. Since Russell does not take functions as primitive, he cannot agree with Frege on this central point. Section VI concerns this difference, and the conception of the world that underlies Russell's idea of analysis. It also takes up the question of how, consistent with this conception, Russell can define functions. Finally, in section VII, I discuss ways in which the metaphysical differences which have occupied us in earlier sections make a difference to the logics of Frege and of Russell. Throughout these discussions I devote more space to Russell than to Frege.

Before beginning the comparison and contrast outlined above, I shall very briefly discuss the question of the influence of Frege on Russell. Russell's work

---

[4] I leave these German terms, and a few others, untranslated, as in n. 1, above, so as to avoid confusion between Frege's terminology and Russell's. In particular, '*Bedeutung*' is standardly translated as 'meaning', but Russell sometimes uses the word 'meaning' for something akin to Fregean *Sinn*.

in the philosophy of mathematics does not begin until the mid-1890s; his anti-psychologism, his development of a system of logic, and his logicism, all post-date his rejection of Idealism in 1899. By this time most of Frege's works were already in print. (Volume ii of *Grundgesetze*, and the three late essays 'Thoughts', 'Negation', and 'Compound Thoughts', form the main exceptions, together, of course, with those of his works which were not published at all in his lifetime.) In view of this chronology, and of the doctrinal overlap indicated in the first paragraph of this essay, one might be inclined to think that Russell learned a great deal from Frege. Further plausibility accrues to this idea from similarities in the techniques used at certain points in the attempt to reduce mathematics to logic, including the technique for the definition of number, the so-called Frege–Russell definition of number.

According to Russell, however, the main lines of his philosophical views, his logic, and his attempt to reduce mathematics to that logic, were all laid down before he studied Frege's work. He completed the main text of *The Principles of Mathematics* on the last day of December 1901. By his own account he had looked at some of Frege's work before that date, but had not studied it with the care needed to understand it. In June 1902 he wrote his famous letter to Frege, announcing the discovery of the contradiction in Frege's logic (i.e. of what is now known as 'Russell's Paradox'). That letter makes it sound as if his close study of Frege's work is just beginning: 'I have known of your Basic Laws of Arithmetic for a year and a half, but only now have I been able to find the time for the thorough study I intend to devote to your writings'.[5] Similarly, in the Preface to *The Principles of Mathematics*, dated December 1902, he says: 'Professor Frege's work, which largely anticipates my own, was for the most part unknown to me when the printing of the present work began' (p. xvi). For this reason, he says, he discusses Frege's work in detail in an appendix, written while the main body of the work was at press. Later in the Preface, he acknowledges the influence of Cantor and of Peano and says: 'If I had become acquainted sooner with the work of Professor Frege, I should have owed a great deal to him, but as it is I arrived independently at many results which he had already established' (p. xviii). In later works, looking back on this period, he tells the same story.[6]

It would be easy to be sceptical, even cynical, about Russell's account of what he learned from Frege. What evidence there is, however, seems to favour it. Without pretending to have a definitive view, I am inclined to take Russell's

---

[5] Russell to Frege, 16 June 1902. The correspondence is published in Frege, *Nachgelassene Schriften*, vol. ii. The passage quoted here is at p. 213. I largely follow the English translation by Hans Kaal in Frege, *Philosophical and Mathematical Correspondence*, except that I leave certain crucial terms untranslated, as indicated. (The entire correspondence is in German.) The passage quoted here is at p. 130 of this work.
[6] See 'My Mental Development' in Schilpp (ed.), *The Philosophy of Bertrand Russell*, especially p. 13; and *My Philosophical Development*, 66.

account at face value, and to think that the decisive influences on Russell, from his rejection of Idealism to the writing of *The Principles of Mathematics*, were G. E. Moore, in metaphysics; Peano, in logic: and Cantor and Weierstrass in mathematics. To begin with, Russell was always generous in his acknowledgements; there is no reason at all to think he would make an exception in this one case. More important, perhaps, the internal evidence strongly suggests that Russell first developed his logic by building on what he learned from Peano, rather than by following Frege. The logic of *The Principles of Mathematics* strikes anyone who has studied Frege with care as clumsy, or perhaps even confused. The idea that this logic was developed by beginning with Peano, by contrast, seems entirely plausible.

Taking Russell's account at face value, however, does not mean that we should conclude that he owes nothing at all to Frege. Frege, Russell, and Peano did not live in separate intellectual worlds. There is some reason to believe that Russell may have first come across the idea for his definition of number (which is also Frege's) in a 1901 essay by Peano (who discusses the idea, but rejects it). And Peano, presumably, had read Frege's *Grundgesetze*, since he wrote a review of it in 1895.[7] Russell's logic, moreover, developed significantly after he wrote *The Principles of Mathematics*, and there is every reason to think that Frege's influence, along with the continuing influence of Peano, was important in this development. This influence is, indeed, explicitly acknowledged; on p. vii of the Preface to *Principia Mathematica*, Whitehead and Russell say: 'In all questions of logical analysis, our chief debt is to Frege.'

II

Let us begin our main discussion with a disagreement between Frege and Russell that occurs in their correspondence. The issue arose from a discussion of truth. In a letter dated November 1904, Frege had said: 'Truth is not a component part of a thought, just as Mont Blanc with its snowfields is not itself a component part of the thought that Mont Blanc is more than 4,000 metres high'.[8] Russell's reply ignored the issue about truth, which was the point of Frege's remark (and with which he agreed), and seized on the incidental illustration to articulate his objections to Frege's distinction between *Sinn* and *Bedeutung*:

I believe that in spite of all its snowfields Mont Blanc itself is a component part of what is actually asserted in the *Satz* 'Mont Blanc is more than 4,000 metres high'. We do not

---

[7] See the editor's Introduction to Russell, *Collected Papers*, vol. iii, by Gregory H. Moore, especially p. xxvii.

[8] This passage is on p. 245 of the German edition of the correspondence, p. 163 of the English edition. See n.5, above.

assert the thought, for this is a private psychological matter: we assert the object of the thought, and this is, to my mind, a certain complex (*objectiver Satz*, one might say) in which Mont Blanc is itself a component part. *If we do not admit this, then we get the conclusion that we know nothing at all about Mont Blanc.* . . . In the case of a simple proper name like 'Socrates', I cannot distinguish between *Sinn* and *Bedeutung*; I see only the idea, which is psychological, and the object. Or better: I do not admit the *Sinn* at all, but only the idea and the *Bedeutung*.[9]

This passage indicates very general differences in the underlying philosophical views of Frege and of Russell.

Consider the judgment expressed by the sentence 'Mont Blanc is over 4,000 metres high.' Each of Frege and Russell holds that in making this judgment we are somehow related to an objective non-linguistic entity—we 'grasp' it (*fassen* is Frege's word). Frege calls this entity a 'thought' (*Gedanke*). Russell speaks of such an entity as a 'proposition' (*objectiver Satz*, in the letter to Frege); for him a thought is 'a private psychological matter'. Thus far the differences are perhaps only terminological, but the next point is substantial. For Russell, a proposition, what we are most directly related to in making judgments, will in paradigmatic cases *contain* the entity we are talking about. It is explicit in the above passage that Mont Blanc is a constituent—a 'component part'—of the proposition expressed in the judgment. For Frege, by contrast, thoughts do not contain the entities themselves, the subjects of our judgment. The constituents of Fregean *Gedanke* are the *Sinne* of expressions that refer to the entities we mean to be talking about—not those entities themselves.[10]

Russell's view can be elaborated and illustrated by briefly considering his attitude towards truth and facts. Truth, for him, is an indefinable property of propositions (as, of course, is falsehood); a fact is simply a proposition which is true. In this view, he retains something like the ordinary notion of a fact, as consisting perhaps in an object's having a certain property, or standing in certain relations to one or more other objects. These 'objective complexes', as Russell calls them, are made up of one or more objects, together with some of their properties or relations.[11] And true propositions are identified with such entities.

---

[9] This passage is on pp. 250–1 of the German edition of the correspondence, p. 169 of the English edition. Again, see n. 5, above. The emphasis here is added.

Russell makes a very similar point in the 1911 essay 'Knowledge by Acquaintance and Knowledge by Description'. He discusses 'the view that judgments are composed of something called "ideas" ', and says: 'in this view ideas become a veil between us and outside things—we never really, in knowledge, attain to the things we are supposed to be knowing about, but only to the ideas of those things' (*Collected Papers*, vi. 155).

[10] There are some reasons to be hesitant in attributing to Frege the idea that *Gedanke* have constituents at all. The attribution is supported by some of Frege's texts, however, and certainly facilitates the comparison between Russell and Frege that is my concern here.

[11] The phrase 'objective complex' occurs, for example, in an essay dated June 1905 called 'The Nature of Truth', first published in *Collected Papers*, iv, 492–506. See p. 495.

Thus Russell says:

People imagine that if *A* exists, *A* is a fact; but really the fact is '*A*'s existence' or 'that *A* exists'. Things of this sort, *i.e.* 'that *A* exists' . . . I call *propositions*, and it is things of this sort that are called *facts* when they happen to be true.[12]

Here again we see, in a slightly different context, the view that a proposition about a particular object will, paradigmatically at least, contain that object, just as one might naturally think of a fact as containing, or made up of, an object (together perhaps with a property of the object). If the proposition is true, then it simply *is* the fact; if the proposition is false, then it is, so to speak, just like a fact except that it happens not to be true. The proposition is equally real in either case.

So far we have elaborated a little on Russell's opposition to Frege about the way that names function: for Russell, the presence of a name in a sentence implies, at least in paradigmatic cases, that the sentence expresses a proposition which contains the named object. We have as yet, however, seen no reasons for this opposition. The vital clue here, I think, is given by the sentence emphasized in the passage quoted above: 'If we do not admit this, then we get the conclusion that we know nothing at all about Mont Blanc . . .'. The emphasis here should be on the 'about' rather than on the 'know'. The issue is not one of our having *correct* beliefs about Mont Blanc, but rather one of our having beliefs which are genuinely *about* that mountain at all. (I shall speak of this sort of issue as epistemological, since it is not merely about how things are but also about our relation to them. This is perhaps an extension of the usual sense of the word.) Let us suppose, with Frege and Russell, that the sentence 'Mont Blanc is over 4,000 metres high' expresses an objective entity, and that we do indeed 'grasp' that entity. How does that grasping enable us to believe something about the actual snowy mountain itself? For Russell, it does so because the entity that we grasp *contains* that mountain as a constituent. Frege's view, if we express it in these alien terms, must be quite different: that what we most directly or imme-diately know or grasp has as a constituent (perhaps) the *Sinn* of the expression 'Mont Blanc'. But how, in virtue of grasping that entity, do we know something about the mountain, which is altogether distinct from it? From Russell's point of view this question—'the *in-virtue-of* problem', we might call it—presents a severe difficulty; his view attempts to avoid that difficulty by insisting that, at least in paradigmatic cases, we grasp propositions which contain the very entities which they are about.

These issues must be seen in the context of epistemology. Throughout the period which is our concern, Russell takes it that knowledge is at bottom a matter of a direct and unmediated relation between the mind and the known object.

---

[12] 'The Nature of Truth' (see previous footnote), 492.

(Clearly nothing of the sort holds for Frege.) Russell insists that there is such a relation, and that it plays the fundamental role in knowledge. It is only by being in direct contact with some external object that the mind is able to know anything at all outside itself. 'External' here does not carry its usual spatio-temporal implications: it means only non-mental, or outside the mind. Russell has no qualms at all about assuming that we also have this kind of knowledge of purely abstract entities. On the contrary: he applies his basic picture of knowledge both to abstract objects and to concrete. That distinction, indeed, is relatively unimportant to his thought during the time with which we are concerned. For the first few years of that period he holds that all entities *subsist* or have being; some have the additional property of *existing* (i.e., roughly, being in space and time). Our being in a direct epistemic relation to an entity does not, in this view, require that it should exist, in this sense.

Russell thus postulates a fundamental epistemic relation holding between a mind, on the one hand, and an object—existing or merely subsisting—on the other hand. After 1905 Russell calls this relation *acquaintance*, and it comes to play an increasingly explicit role in his thought. But even before 1905, from his rejection of Idealism onwards, it is an essential element in his philosophy. In the Preface to the *Principles of Mathematics*, for example, he says:

> The discussion of indefinables—which forms the chief part of philosophical logic—is the endeavour to see clearly, and to make others see clearly, the entities concerned, in order that the mind may have that kind of acquaintance with them which it has with redness or with the taste of a pineapple. (p. xv)

Russell speaks here of our knowledge of simple sensory qualities to suggest the directness and immediacy which are characteristic of his notion of acquaintance. There have, of course, been philosophers—including his Idealist opponents— who thought that not even simple sensory qualities are in fact known in the direct and immediate way that Russell wants to convey. Such qualities, however, may at least *seem* to be known in that sort of way, and this may be enough to achieve his rhetorical purposes here.

I shall speak of Russell's insistence on a direct and unmediated relation between the mind and the known object as his *direct realism*; I shall include under this head the idea that propositions paradigmatically contain the entities they are about.[13] This view, or nexus of views, must, I think, be traced to Russell's

---

[13] It might be said that the term 'direct realism' is inappropriate, because Russell comes to believe that we do *not* have direct knowledge of ordinary objects—tables and chairs and other people, and the like. By 1912, his view is that our knowledge of these things is indirect, mediated by our knowledge of sense-data and universals (which are known directly). I use the term 'direct realism' because it emphasizes the fact that his view is always that *some* entities must be known directly and immediately, even though his view about *which* entities are known directly changes over time. Still, there are no doubt uses of the term according to which Russell's view, at least in the second half of the period we are concerned with, would not count as direct realism.

rejection of Idealism. The Idealists had insisted that knowledge is mediated by a complex structure, which is also (or therefore) the structure of the world; our knowledge of this structure thus gives us knowledge of the world which is purely rational in its basis. Russell, following G. E. Moore, had cut through all such considerations by insisting, to the contrary, that the most basic sort of knowledge is direct and unmediated. The presence of an intervening structure would, from that point of view, simply mean that our knowledge failed to attain its desired object. We would end up knowing not the object itself but rather only the intervening structure. There is, of course, much more to be said about the origin of this view of Russell's, but that would take us aside from the comparison of Frege with Russell. We shall therefore treat Russell's direct realism, in the sense indicated, as more or less an axiom of his thought.[14]

III

Russell's direct realism seems to give a clear and straightforward answer to the question how the propositions we express manage to be about the entities they are about: they are about them in virtue of containing them. Presumably our 'grasping' a proposition implies our 'grasping' its constituents; presumably it is this that allows our thought to get right through to those objects, which are the things that we mean to be talking about. This picture was, I think, his underlying instinctive view throughout the period which is our concern—the view towards which he was always attracted, and which he tended to assume. It faces, however, great difficulties. Russell attempted to resolve those difficulties in one way in the period from 1901 until June 1905, when he came across the fundamental idea of 'On Denoting';[15] thereafter he resolved them in a quite different way. These two different ways of responding to difficulties in the underlying picture go along with differences in the view that Russell takes of analysis, and related matters, and are therefore of quite general significance. In this section I shall briefly discuss the first method of resolution and its concomitants; in the next section I shall turn to the second.

Let us begin with the difficulties facing the underlying picture. It is undeniable, one might suppose, that I understand propositions about Socrates; but it may appear as quite implausible that I stand in some direct epistemological relation to him, for he no longer exists. The case of Pegasus or the present

---

[14] For a much more detailed discussion of this and of related issues, see the present author's *Russell, Idealism, and the Emergence of Analytic Philosophy*, especially ch. 4.

The fact that Russell is reacting against neo-Hegelian Idealism, whereas Frege is not, is itself an important point of contrast between the two, and connected with others. I shall not, however, go into this matter further in this essay.

[15] The first statement of the new view is in a manuscript entitled 'On Fundamentals', published for the first time in *Collected Papers*, iv. 360–413; the manuscript is dated '1905', and the words 'begun June 7' are on the first folio.

King of France, who have never existed, may seem to be worse. So Russell must accept that I can be in direct epistemological contact with what we might call non-existent *concreta*—entities which are of the right kind to exist, but happen not to. This consequence is something that Russell was for a time willing to accept, making heavy use of the distinction, to which we have already alluded, between existence and subsistence. Pegasus, though he does not exist (roughly, is not in space and time), does, Russell thinks, *subsist* (is nonetheless real). And Russell was, as we have said, willing to accept that we can stand in direct epistemological relations to non-existent *concreta* (as well as to other non-existent objects, those that we would call abstract objects). So he was, for a time, willing to accept this sort of apparently implausible consequence of his direct realism. (As we shall see, however, this is a point on which he changed his mind, even before 'On Denoting'.)

There is, however, another sort of difficulty which he never accepted. Suppose I say, for example, 'Every natural number is either odd or even'. The underlying picture of direct realism might suggest that I am expressing (and grasping) a proposition which contains all of the infinitely many natural numbers. Russell was willing to be agnostic about whether there in fact *are* any such infinitely complex concepts. But he denied that we can grasp propositions that have this sort of infinite complexity (see *Principles*, section 72). That we grasp infinitely complex propositions was too implausible for Russell to accept, even in the most extreme and unrestrained phase of his realism. So the issue of *generality*—how we can, for example, grasp a proposition about all the natural numbers—is one which does not fit neatly into his direct realism. It is this issue which first forces upon Russell some modification of his direct realism.[16]

An unqualified version of direct realism thus serves as a paradigm for Russell. He relies on it and presupposes it at many points, and makes statements which seem to imply this unqualified view. The passage we saw in the letter to Frege is an example. But it is always a modified or qualified version which he explicitly advocates. He takes it that the most direct way in which a proposition can be about an object is simply by containing it; but he recognizes that we must have some way of making sense of cases in which a proposition is about an entity or entities which it does *not* contain; in such cases we might speak of the proposition's being *indirectly* about the entity. (In these terms we can say that Frege's view is one in which there is only indirect aboutness: a thought is about an object in virtue of containing the relevant *Sinn*. But of course these terms of description are Russell's, and quite foreign to Frege's thought.)

---

[16] In the Preface to *Principles* he speaks of his work on the philosophy of dynamics, and says: 'I was led to a re-examination of the principles of Geometry, thence to the philosophy of continuity and infinity, and thence, with a view to discovering the meaning of the word *any*, to Symbolic Logic' (p. xvii). The question of 'the meaning of the word *any*' is exactly what I am calling the issue of generality.

From 1900 or 1901 until June 1905 the modification to the underlying picture—Russell's way of accommodating indirect aboutness—is what I shall call the theory of denoting concepts. This doctrine simply accepts that direct realism does not hold in all cases; it allows a large class of exceptions to the general rule that the entity which a proposition is about is contained in the proposition; the general rule functions as a paradigm in Russell's thought, but certain cases are allowed to violate it. For certain kinds of phrases Russell accepts a distinction in some ways analogous to Frege's distinction between *Sinn* and *Bedeutung*. The analogue of the *Sinn* of an expression is what he calls the *denoting concept* which it expresses, or as he later comes to say, its meaning; the analogue of the *Bedeutung* is denotation of the expression, or object, it denotes—if it does in fact succeed in denoting something.[17] The phrases to which Russell initially applies this distinction are descriptions, both definite descriptions such as 'the President of the USA in 2000' and indefinite descriptions, such as 'any prime number'. Where such a phrase occurs in a sentence, that sentence is taken to express a proposition which contains not the corresponding object or objects but rather a concept which *denotes* that object or those objects; the proposition contains a denoting concept but is about—indirectly about—the denoted object or objects. Here there is an in-virtue-of problem. How, in virtue of containing a denoting concept, is the proposition *about* an entity wholly distinct from it, an entity which we do not in any sense 'grasp'? To this question Russell has no answer: the relation of denoting is simply asserted to have that effect.[18]

Using this theory, Russell hopes to account for generality by (roughly speaking) treating a phrase such as 'any natural number'—or 'any object'—as representing a denoting concept. In this attempt he is unsuccessful; the theory proves unable to give a coherent account of multiple generality.[19] The theory was, however, more successful in resolving other difficulties. Russell uses it, for example, to explain how true identity statements can be informative: at least

[17] Here there is a point which, though more or less incidental to our discussion, is in other contexts quite crucial. It is not implied by Russell's other views about denoting that a denoting concept must always succeed in denoting; it is entirely consistent with his view that such a concept should not in fact denote anything. At some moments he recognizes and accepts this point quite explicitly; see, for example, *Principles*, section 73. (At other moments, however, he seems to imply the opposite; see section 427 of the same work.) For further discussion, see the work cited in n. 14, above, especially ch. 5 and 6; also pp. 95–6 of ch. 4, above, and pp. 198–9 of ch. 10, below. The point made in passing here undermines one still very common account of Russell's motivation for adopting the theory of descriptions.

[18] There are, passages in Russell's writings, not written for publication, which suggest that he was attempting to find an explanation of denoting in terms of propositional functions. There is, however, no sign that he ever found a way of doing this which satisfied him—unless, indeed, one thinks of the theory of descriptions as being such an explanation. See especially *Collected Papers*, iv. 340, 342. (In this essay I have not attempted to do justice to all the intricacies of Russell's thought suggested by his unpublished work.) In this note I am indebted to correspondence with Russell Wahl.

[19] He says: 'Thus *x* is, in some sense, the object denoted by *any term*; yet this can hardly be strictly maintained, for different variables may occur in a proposition, yet the object denoted by *any term* is, one would suppose, unique.' *Principles*, section 93, p. 94. I am here attempting to do no more than indicate the difficulties which Russell encounters.

one of the expressions flanking the identity symbol must be a denoting phrase (see *Principles*, section 64, pp. 63–4). And Russell came to see that the theory could be extended to cover proper names (ordinary proper names, as opposed to what Russell later called 'logically proper names') quite generally. This extension resolves the issue of names which appear to name concrete existing objects, but where in fact there is no such object ('Pegasus' or 'Vulcan', for example). In *The Principles of Mathematics* Russell had denied that there are any such names: names which seemed to name nothing were said to name non-existent but still subsistent (and thus real) entities. But in fact the theory of denoting concepts has the resources to avoid that conclusion; it can thus avoid non-existent *concreta*, and the idea that we can be acquainted with such things.[20]

Russell himself, in Appendix A of the *Principles of Mathematics*, says that Frege's distinction between *Sinn* and *Bedeutung* is 'roughly, though not exactly, equivalent' to his own distinction between a denoting concept and the denoted object (see section 476, p. 502). The most obvious difference is that Frege applied the distinction very widely, whereas for Russell it was far more restricted. The clear point of similarity is that in each case we have what we might speak of as a *representational* element in the object of judgment (Frege's *Gedanke*, Russell's proposition). A paradigmatic subject-predicate proposition for Russell, one *not* containing a denoting concept, does not contain something which *represents* its subject; rather the subject itself is contained in the proposition. But when we employ a description we express a proposition which contains an element which does in this sense *represent* the subject; this element is of course the denoting concept corresponding to the description, for that denoting concept is not itself the subject of the proposition, not what the proposition is about.[21] Frege's *Sinne*, if we think in such terms about them, are clearly representational in the same sort of way: a *Gedanke* is not about the *Sinne* which (perhaps) make it up, but rather about the *Bedeutungen* (if any) of the expressions whose *Sinne* they are.[22]

The theory of denoting concepts strongly suggests a picture according to which the structure of a proposition is, in general, quite closely related to the structure of a sentence which expresses it. (It may be that Russell was in part led to the theory because he already held the general picture.) The proposition expressed by the sentence 'Every natural number is either odd or even', according to the theory of denoting concepts, expresses a proposition which contains a component corresponding to the words 'every natural number'. This component

[20] For Russell's acknowledgement of these points, see, in particular, his 'The Existential Import of Propositions'.

[21] Of course there can be propositions which have denoting concepts as their subjects, but such a proposition must contain not that denoting concept which it is about, but rather some other denoting concept which denotes it.

[22] This rather cumbersome way of speaking is necessary because for Frege it is an *expression* which has a *Sinn* and (in the usual case) a *Bedeutung*. For Russell, by contrast, it is the denoting concept, not a linguistic item, which denotes the object.

is of course a denoting concept, and for further progress in analysing the sentence we need to consider that denoting concept and its function. When we analyse the sentence, to gain insight into the structure of the proposition which it expresses, we retain its grammatical structure. The point is quite general: grammatical structure is taken as a good, though not infallible, guide to the structure of the underlying proposition; each word or semantic unit is assumed to correspond to an element in the proposition. Thus Russell says:

The study of grammar . . . is capable of throwing far more light on philosophical questions than is commonly supposed by philosophers. Although a grammatical difference cannot be uncritically assumed to correspond to a genuine philosophical difference, yet the one is *primâ facie* evidence of the other. . . . Moreover it must be admitted, I think, that every word occurring in a sentence must have *some* meaning . . . . The correctness of our philosophical analysis of a proposition may therefore be usefully checked by the exercise of assigning the meaning of each word in the sentence expressing the proposition. On the whole, grammar seems to me to bring us much nearer to a correct logic than the current opinions of philosophers. . . . (*Principles*, section 46, p. 42)

The picture of analysis which this suggests is one which will go word by word, or phrase by phrase, rather than sentence by sentence. For the most part it will be taken for granted that a word or phrase in a sentence corresponds to some element in the proposition expressed by the sentence; the interesting question will then be as to the nature of that element. (Is it, for example, a denoting concept, and if so of what kind?) There is here no general contrast between grammatical structure, or surface structure, and underlying or logical structure. On the contrary: we can, for the most part, read off the underlying structure from the structure of the sentence. To put essentially the same point a different way: language is conceived as a largely transparent medium, through which propositions may be perceived without systematic distortion; the transparency of the medium makes it possible largely to ignore it.

These ideas, like Russell's reliance on the notion of acquaintance, can be put in the context of his opposition to Idealism, and especially to the monism which he attributed to F. H. Bradley. Pluralism, the existence of many distinct things which (at least sometimes) stand in relations to one another, is immediately suggested by our ordinary discourse, by the surface of our language. If the surface of language is a generally reliable guide to the underlying structure, then propositions will indeed contain a plurality of objects in relation to one another. So Russell's opposition to Idealism gives him reason to hold that there is no systematic distortion here, that the grammatical structure of a sentence is in general a good guide to the underlying structure of the proposition which it expresses. This is an idea which, as we shall see, is in very marked contrast to the view he held after June 1905.

IV

Russell's famous essay 'On Denoting' rejects the theory of denoting concepts, and argues for the theory of descriptions. The essay contains detailed arguments against the theory of denoting, arguments which we shall not examine here.[23] The crucial thing to note about them is that they all operate within the context of Russell's direct realism. Within that context the theory of denoting concepts is an anomaly from the outset; once Russell sees how to avoid that theory he is very ready to do so. A crucial shift from the earlier view is that now Russell takes the idea of generality—'the variable', as he says—as primitive and unexplained. The major motive for the theory of denoting was to explain generality—roughly, by treating the phrase 'any object' as expressing a denoting concept. But, as we have seen, the theory of denoting did not in fact succeed in this task; Russell now abandons the goal entirely, and simply takes generality for granted, as primitive and unexplained. (But see n. 25, below, for a qualification to this statement.)

Presupposing generality, Russell is then able to explain indefinite descriptions in the familiar manner: 'Every prime number is odd' is explained as 'For any object x, if x is a prime number then x is odd', and so on. He had seen the possibility of doing this as early as 1902, but at that stage it had not influenced his philosophical views. Definite descriptions presented more of a challenge; it was Russell's seeing how to treat them in the analogous way that made it possible for him to develop the new view. The analogous treatment of 'The President of the USA in 2000 was a Democrat' is to explain it as 'There is an object x such that x served as President of the USA in 2000 and x was a Democrat, and for every object y, if y served as President of the USA in 2000 then y is identical to x.' More briefly and idiomatically: 'There is one and only one thing which served as President of the USA in 2000, and it was a Democrat.'

The sentence we started with above is certainly about President Clinton. As analysed, however, it expresses a proposition which does not contain that man; it is *indirectly* about him. So one might think that here too, as in the theory of denoting, there is a violation of Russell's direct realism. But in fact this is not so: here there is no in-virtue-of problem. Here the idea of indirect aboutness does not rely on a mysterious relation of denoting, introduced only for this purpose. It relies, rather, on familiar ideas. The sentence is about Clinton because it contains a predicate, '. . . served as President of the USA in 2000' which holds of him and of no one else. This explanation uses the idea of a predicate's holding of,

---

[23] The interpretation of these arguments is very controversial. For a general account, see again, ch. 6 of the work cited in n. 14. For an attempt to come to terms with the text in detail see Pakaluk, 'The Interpretation of Russell's "Gray's *Elegy*" Argument'. See also Noonan, 'The "Gray's Elegy" Argument—and Others', and Kremer, 'The Argument of "On Denoting" '.

or being true of, an object; this is not an idea which is mysterious or objectionable in the same way that the idea of denoting is. In particular, it is not an idea introduced *ad hoc* to solve—or to label—this particular problem; it is, rather, an idea which is needed for quite general purposes in almost any account of language.

So one way of putting the point of the theory of descriptions is that it is to explain in a transparent and wholly unmysterious way what the theory of denoting 'explains' in a mysterious and *ad hoc* fashion: how a proposition succeeds in being about entities which it does not contain. Since the entities contained in a proposition that I understand must be entities with which I am acquainted, the theory equally explains, in non-mysterious fashion, how I can understand propositions about entities with which I am not acquainted. Russell says, for example: 'All thinking has to start from acquaintance; but it succeeds in thinking *about* many things with which we have no acquaintance.'[24] This idea is not new in Russell's thought in 1905. What is new is that he now has an explanation of indirect aboutness which does not appeal to an unexplained representational element. The explanation is not question-begging or *ad hoc*, and does not raise an in-virtue-of problem.[25]

Russell now has no hesitation in extending this analysis to many phrases which grammatically are proper names, and treating them as if they were disguised or truncated definite descriptions.[26] He is thus left with a very small category of genuine (or logically) proper names; for those names, unlike others, their occurrence in a sentence does indicate that the sentence expresses a proposition in which the corresponding object occurs. Logically proper names can only be used to name objects with which the speaker is acquainted, and from 1905 on Russell holds that each person is acquainted only with a limited range of entities. (The range gets more limited as time goes by; this trend started before 'On Denoting', and is to some extent independent of it.) So philosophical analysis is required to show that sentences about other entities are only indirectly about them, and to work out what such sentences are directly about. Only entities with which we

---

[24] 'On Denoting', *Mind* (1905), p. 480; *Collected Papers*, iv. 415.

[25] It might be thought that, by doing this, 'On Denoting' vindicates direct realism. Certainly this is one of the aims of that work, but we should not exaggerate the extent to which it succeeds. The crucial qualification here is one which we have already mentioned: the theory leaves Russell wholly without an explanation of generality. According to the new theory, generality is involved in almost everything we say, yet it is entirely unclear how it fits into the picture of direct realism. It is all the more important to stress this point, in view of the fact that generality was the strongest of Russell's original motives for introducing the theory of denoting. In some writings after 'On Denoting', which were not intended for publication, Russell speaks of 'On Denoting' not as eliminating denoting but rather as reducing it all to a single case, that of the variable. See pp. 255f. of the work cited in n. 14, above.

[26] Russell speaks of the name 'Romulus' as 'a sort of truncated description' in the sixth of his 'Lectures on the Philosophy of Logical Atomism'; *Collected Papers*, viii. 213. In *The Problems of Philosophy* he says: 'Common words, even proper names, are usually really descriptions. That is to say, the thought in the mind of a person using a proper name correctly can generally only be expressed explicitly if we replace the proper name by a description.' (p. 54).

are acquainted can occur in propositions we can grasp. Almost all of our knowledge appears to violate this dictum, and so must be analysed to show that it does not in fact do so. Russell's position thus commits him to an extensive programme of analysis which is, in the broad sense, epistemologically driven: by the need to show how we are able to think about various entities with which we are not acquainted. It is this programme which issues in such works as *Our Knowledge of the External World.* (Such a programme of analysis, it need hardly be said, has no analogue in Frege's work; Frege's general philosophical views simply do not give rise to a need for anything of the sort.)

The theory of descriptions assumes enormous importance for Russell. He quickly comes to hold that we are acquainted with almost none of the concrete objects that we take ourselves to know about. (His reasons essentially have to do with the possibility of error and illusion. In the case of abstract objects he is more willing to accept that we are acquainted with the things we appear to know about.) So most of what we take to be our knowledge about things is descriptive knowledge, not acquaintance by acquaintance. And all such knowledge, so he holds from 1905, is to be explained along the lines laid down by the theory of descriptions. The theory of descriptions is *the* method of analysis, and hence of the first importance for Russell's epistemology.

One immediate consequence of the developments we have been discussing is a complete repudiation of the idea that (surface) grammar is, in general, a good guide to the form of the underlying proposition. We briefly examined this idea, as it occurs in the *Principles of Mathematics*, and saw that it is a natural concomitant of the theory of denoting concepts. In that theory, a subject-predicate sentence, with a description (definite or indefinite) for the subject, is taken to express a proposition with subject-predicate form, with a denoting concept taking the place of the subject. In the new theory, however, from 1905 onwards, such a sentence is taken to represent a proposition with a wholly different form. (A sentence containing a definite description expresses an existentially quantified proposition.) From 1905 on, Russell's work is full of warnings that the structure of a sentence, its surface grammar, is almost always misleading as to the form of the underlying proposition. The goal of analysis remains, as before, the production of a sentence which accurately reflects the proposition expressed by the original sentence. But now the emphasis is very much on the *form* of the proposition (and, hence, of the sentence produced by the process of analysis). This form will not in general be the same as that of the sentence being analysed; this will, indeed, hardly ever happen. Logical forms become the focus of analysis.

This change in turn has a consequence which may at first sight appear paradoxical. Precisely because it is misleading, language, which Russell had previously more or less ignored, becomes an increasing concern. When he thought of language as a more or less transparent medium, through which the proposition could be readily perceived, Russell could afford to pay it no special attention; he proceeded at once to talk of the underlying proposition, his true concern. But after 1905 he has to be self-conscious about language, if only to avoid being misled by it.[27] Before 1905 all of Russell's remarks about language (in the sense of the actual words) are casual and superficial, not in any sense part of a theory of language. After 1905 this begins to change. With the notion of an *incomplete symbol* we have, for the first time in Russell's work, a technical term which is quite explicitly and exclusively linguistic: some symbols are incomplete, but no constituents of propositions are (in anything like the same sense) incomplete. Russell is driven to pay attention to language precisely because of its misleadingness; one might say that it is here that 'Philosophy of Language', in something approximating its modern sense, comes into being.

Another consequence of the new paradigm of philosophical analysis is a shift in the role played by the idea of acquaintance, or rather the reinforcement of a shift which was already under way. This is a complex and subtle matter, and concerns shifts in Russell's attitude as much as real changes in doctrine. In the *Principles of Mathematics* the notion of acquaintance had functioned, more or less, as a 'dependent variable': if Russell's philosophical analyses made it expedient for him to claim that we are acquainted with a certain entity, then he would make the claim.[28] After that work the notion of acquaintance comes increasingly to impose independent constraints upon analysis; the results of a preliminary philosophical analysis are to be checked by seeing whether we are in fact acquainted with the entities which, according to the analysis, we must be. The results of this checking were not wholly independent of the exigencies of the analysis; still Russell is increasingly restrictive in his view of what entities we are acquainted with. It is for this reason that one finds, in Russell's work after the *Principles of Mathematics*, appeals to 'inspection', which is meant to remind us with which entities we are actually acquainted; these facts are supposed to constrain philosophical theorizing.

This trend towards greater psychological realism about acquaintance begins before 'On Denoting', but the new view greatly encourages the trend. Before 1905, analysis takes the form of a sentence for granted, and aims to clarify our understanding of the parts; the analysis is complete, presumably, when we have

---

[27] Thus: 'There is a good deal of importance to philosophy in the theory of symbolism, a good deal more than at one time I thought. I think the importance is almost entirely negative, i.e., the importance lies in the fact that unless you are fairly self-conscious about symbols, unless you are fairly aware of the relation of the symbol to what it symbolizes, you will find yourself attributing to the thing properties which only belong to the symbol.' Russell's 'Lectures on the Philosophy of Logical Atomism', *Collected Papers*, viii. 166. Later in the paragraph Russell says that good philosophers think about the real philosophical concerns, as opposed to symbols, for a minute every six months, whereas bad philosophers never do.

[28] This may overstate the matter to some extent, but not by much. I owe the comparison with the idea of 'dependent variable' to Andrew Lugg.

a clear understanding of each of the parts of the sentence. It may not always be evident how we are to know when the analysis is complete, but at least it makes sense to think that each step is bringing us closer to the fully analysed sentence, and thus to the form of the proposition itself. But after 1905 the process of analysis may at any step reveal a wholly new logical form. There is no particular reason to think that the seventeenth step in the progressive analysis of a sentence is closer to the real form of the proposition than is the thirteenth. How are we to know that we have reached the terminus of analysis, if we cannot easily think of ourselves as getting closer and closer to it? The notion of acquaintance comes to provide an answer to this question: the terminus of analysis is reached when we have a sentence where each term refers to an object with which we are acquainted. But of course this answer presupposes that acquaintance functions, at least to some extent, as an 'independent variable', and is not simply answerable to the needs of the analysis.

Over the last few paragraphs we have been emphasizing the difference that the theory of descriptions makes to Russell's view of how analysis proceeds, and something of the wider significance of this shift. But it is also important to stress that there is an underlying continuity in Russell's conception of analysis. It is, one might say, the same sort of question he is trying to answer before 1905 and after, even though the answers he gives are not the same. The question is: what are the constituents of this proposition? Russell continues, that is to say, to conceive of a proposition as a complex entity made up of simpler entities, in something like the way a wall is made up of bricks. This general conception largely survives even Russell's adoption of the so-called 'multiple relation theory of judgment', which involves his abandoning the idea that propositions exist as objective entities independent of us (we shall discuss the new theory at more length shortly). The question of the constituents of a proposition is simply reframed, to ask about the constituents involved in a judgment; the underlying conception does not seem to change. We shall return to these matters in section VI.

V

As we have seen, the theory of descriptions was, for Russell, a way of defending his direct realism (at least if one does not focus on the issue of generality). Let us come at this from a different angle, by seeing exactly how the theory of descriptions enables Russell to avoid any version of the distinction between *Sinn* and *Bedeutung* for singular referring expressions. In the next section we shall draw on these ideas to articulate a further consequence of Russell's position, concerning the notion of a function; this is, again, directly relevant to the contrast between Frege and Russell.

I shall consider two kinds of reason for holding that there must be a distinction analogous to Frege's distinction of *Sinn* from *Bedeutung*, and argue that in each case the theory of descriptions enables Russell to avoid that reason. The first kind of reason is straightforward: there are empty names, names which name nothing, such as 'Vulcan' and 'Pegasus'. If understanding a name consists in being related to an object, then it would seem that one cannot understand an empty name. Yet we do seem to understand sentences containing such names. Frege accounted for this by saying that in such a case the name has a *Sinn*, and hence it is possible to understand it even though it lacks a *Bedeutung*. He takes it to be a consequence of this view that a sentence containing such a name will also have a *Sinn*, and hence be capable of significant use, but lack a *Bedeutung*, i.e. lack a truth-value.

Russell's approach is quite different. He claims that (apparent) names are of two wholly different kinds.[29] On the one hand there are logically proper names, which function simply as labels which the speaker affixes to objects with which he or she is acquainted. These names function in accordance with Russell's paradigm; they are, however, very rare, at least in our ordinary language. On the other hand there are all the other (apparent) names. These are not, by Russell's standards, genuine names at all. Sentences in which they appear are to be analysed in accordance with the theory of descriptions, and in the analysed sentences the apparent names do not appear. (I shall sometimes call these apparent names 'descriptive names', just to have a label for them.)

Now it is Russell's view that logically proper names *cannot* be empty: If I can use a word as such a name then I am acquainted with its bearer, and this is not possible unless there is such an entity. I thus have an epistemological guarantee that the name is not empty. Names which lack this guarantee are not logically proper names, but merely descriptive names. When a sentence containing an (apparent) name of this latter sort is analysed we obtain a sentence in which the given name does not appear at all. (Hence Russell's view that these names are not genuine names at all: they do not survive analysis.) So for Russell there is no problem of empty names. Genuine names, logically proper names, cannot be empty. Other apparent names are not really names at all, and hence cannot be empty names. (Russell's approach also has the advantage that a sentence containing an empty descriptive name will have a truth-value; avoiding truth-valueless sentences in this way will make for a smoother logic. Frege achieves the same end by stipulating a referent for any singular referring expression which would otherwise be empty.)

There is also a second sort of reason for introducing some version of distinction between *Sinn* and *Bedeutung* which is rather more complex, and shows up

---

[29] Note that this kind of contrast can be drawn, to much the same effect, within the theory of denoting concepts. I am here not concerned to contrast that theory with the theory of descriptions, but rather to contrast the latter with Frege's view.

in various ways. The underlying point could be put like this: two singular referring expressions with the same referents, such as 'Socrates' and 'the teacher of Plato', may nonetheless have different semantic roles. So saying that it refers to a certain object cannot be the whole story about the semantic role of such an expression, and understanding such an expression cannot consist simply in being in some relation to its referent. Therefore the semantics of such an expression must take account not only of what Frege calls the *Bedeutung* of the expression but also of something else, and this something else will be at least analogous to what Frege calls the *Sinn* of the expression. Let us flesh out this argument by seeing why we cannot take a singular referring term's referring to the object that it refers to as the whole story about its semantic role. (Our doing this will also indicate what the idea of 'semantic role' comes to here, for we should not take that idea to be self-evident in this context.)

Consider a true statement of identity, such as 'Socrates is the teacher of Plato'. It is clear that someone may understand the sentence without knowing whether it is true—or while being convinced that it is false.[30] This possibility seems to be straightforward, and to arise in quite ordinary cases. But if the two expressions flanking the identity symbol have the same semantic role, then such a case would appear to be impossible, or at least quite anomalous. The sentence seems to convey information, whereas the sentence 'Socrates is Socrates' does not. If the two (apparent) singular referring expressions, 'Socrates' and 'the teacher of Plato', have the same semantic role, then it is hard to see how this can be so. Similarly, there is the phenomenon now known as 'referential opacity'.[31] John may believe that Socrates died from drinking hemlock, while not believing that the teacher of Plato died from drinking hemlock. So John's understanding of each expression must involve more than simply a relation to object to which it refers; the word 'Socrates' must have a different semantic role from that of the phrase 'the teacher of Plato'. Yet another way of getting at what is, I think, the same underlying issue has to do with inference. From 'All teachers are wise' and 'Plato had exactly one teacher' we may immediately infer 'The teacher of Plato is wise'. But we cannot, from the same premises, infer 'Socrates is wise'. If the two expressions had the same semantic role, however, then we should be able to do so.

These considerations may be put in more Russellian terms by speaking of objects occurring in propositions, rather than of semantic roles. It is highly implausible to think of our sentence, 'Socrates is the teacher of Plato', as expressing a proposition which simply contains the same object twice over, along with the notion of identity. The two expressions function differently for us: we understand

---

[30] Frege begins 'Sense and Meaning' by talking about cases of this sort.
[31] The term is Quine's; see *From a Logical Point of View*, 142. As he acknowledges, he draws on Russell's use of the term 'transparent' in Appendix C of the second edition of *Principia Mathematica* (i. 665). The underlying point is, again, made by Frege in the first few pages of 'Sense and Meaning'.

them differently, they may play different roles in our expression of belief, and in the inferences we recognize as valid. So we cannot happily think of them as indicating the presence of the same object in a proposition, unless we think of our grasp of propositions and their constituents as itself mediated. But that would undercut Russell's direct realism, the aim of which is precisely to avoid the idea that there is anything mediating between us and the objects that we hope to think about.

On a straightforward, or superficial, view of what things count as singular referring expressions, then, we cannot think of co-referential singular expressions as always playing the same semantic role. In Russellian terms, such expressions cannot be thought of as always merely indicating the presence of the corresponding object in the proposition. Frege deploys the distinction between *Sinn* and *Bedeutung* to resolve all of these problems. How is Russell to resolve them, without resorting to any analogous distinction? As in the case of empty names, the distinction between logically proper names and merely apparent names (descriptive names) is crucial. In a fully analysed sentence, he holds, no descriptive names occur; hence the question of the semantics of such names does not arise. And for real names, logically proper names, Russell simply denies the applicability of the pressures which might lead one to make some version of the distinction between *Sinn* and *Bedeutung*. If a given speaker has two logically proper names for a given object, then that speaker will be aware that the two names name the same object. Acquaintance gives us complete and unmediated knowledge: you cannot be acquainted with the same object twice over and not know it, for there are no *ways* of being acquainted with an object. Again, a logically proper name lacks any semantically significant structure, and gets its meaning, for a given speaker, simply by being a label for an object with which that speaker is acquainted. A logically proper name thus has no semantic structure which can be exploited in inference; it is in this sense a simple referring expression, not a complex referring expression.

Let us put these points another way. The considerations we examined seem to show that there must be more to the semantics of a singular referring expression than the fact that it picks out a certain object. Russell's logically proper names form an exception, but in general there is a need for an account at the level of *Sinn* as well as for an account at the level of *Bedeutung*.[32] One way to understand this is in terms of semantic complexity. In the case of definite descriptions this complexity is right on the surface, for they are made up of semantically significant parts. Russell assimilates descriptive names to definite descriptions, treating them as covertly complex in the same way. On his account, then, the apparent need for *Sinn* arises from the semantic complexity of most singular referring

---

[32] For an elaboration of this point, see Ch. 7, above, especially section 2.

expressions. The semantics of a complex referring expression cannot be understood simply in terms of what it refers to; its semantic complexity must also be taken into account.

Now Russell's theory of descriptions avoids this argument by simply denying that there are any complex referring expressions. This, I think, is in part what he means by saying that descriptions have no meaning in isolation:[33] what is being denied is that such phrases are referring expressions. Definite descriptions look for all the world like complex referring expressions, but it is not hard to see how the theory of descriptions avoids treating them as such. A phrase of the form 'The F' is accorded a meaning only in the context of a sentence, in which we say something of the form 'The F is G'. And this sentence is analysed as having the underlying structure: there is an object which is F, that object is also G, and no other object is F. Here, in the analysed form, we have occurrences of the predicate '. . . is F' but not of the (apparent) complex referring expression 'the F'. For Russell, complex referring expressions are merely apparent, misleading superficial features of language which do not correspond to anything in the underlying structure.

In Russell's view, then, the only genuine referring expressions (for a given speaker) are those which are simple, i.e. lacking semantically significant structure, and which get their significance by referring to entities which are objects of acquaintance (for that speaker). These features ensure that for those expressions no analogue of the distinction between *Sinn* and *Bedeutung* is called for in the case of such expressions. Apparent referring expressions which do not meet these criteria are to be analysed away—to be shown to be merely apparent. The theory of descriptions supplies the means of analysis here.

VI

To this point we have discussed Russell's direct realism, his consequent rejection of any analogue of Frege's distinction between *Sinn* and *Bedeutung*, and his use of the theory of descriptions to mitigate what would otherwise be the implausibilities of this view. This nexus of Russellian views is closely connected with sharp differences from Frege on fundamental metaphysical issues.

Let us begin with conceptions of philosophical analysis, for this is of the first importance. 'Analysis' here is no mere convenience, not a merely pragmatic point of philosophical method. The correct method of analysis is the correct way

---

[33] In Lecture VI of the 'Lectures on the Philosophy of Logical Atomism' Russell says that incomplete symbols, by which he means to include descriptions, 'have absolutely no meaning in isolation, but merely acquire a meaning in context', *Collected Papers*, viii. 221. In 'On Denoting' he says that such phrases 'never have any meaning in themselves' , *Collected Papers*, iv. 416.

to understand the world; this corresponds to—and reveals—the fundamental nature of the world. For Frege, the method of analysis is function and argument. His notion of a function is essentially a clarified and extended version of the familiar mathematical notion, and he takes it as philosophically primitive. Concepts are treated as special cases of functions: they are those functions whose values are always truth-values. So a predicate such as '. . . is prime' is taken to stand for a function. Applied to some objects this function yields the truth-value *True* as its value; applied to others it yields the truth-value *False*. The idea of a function's taking one object as argument, and yielding another as value, is simply taken for granted here. There is no sensible question as to why a certain function applied to a given argument yields the value it does: that it does so is the unexplained fact in terms of which other things are to be explained.

These general Fregean views are sharply opposed to Russell's; the issues which we examined in the last section are directly relevant to this opposition. Functional expressions, if taken as primitive, give rise to complex referring expressions. The expression '2 + 3', if taken at face value, picks out the number five, and does so in a complex way. Saying what the expression picks out is clearly very far from being a full and adequate account of its semantic function. To understand the functioning of the phrase we need a distinction between *Sinn* and *Bedeutung*. So if the general notion of a function is fundamental, a semantic account must deal with (something analogous to) *Sinn* as well as *Bedeutung*. Since Russell rejects any such idea, he also denies that functional expressions in general are primitive. Hence nothing like Frege's function-argument analysis is available to him as a fundamental way of understanding the world. (We shall see at the end of this section that Russell does take as primitive the notion of a *propositional* function, and we shall consider why the reasons he has against taking functions in general as primitive do not apply to this special case.)

The contrast that I am drawing between Russell and Frege, then, is this. Frege takes the notion of a function as primitive; his doing so commits him to a distinction between *Sinn* and *Bedeutung*. But Russell denies that there is such a distinction. He therefore cannot accept the general notion of a function as primitive, and cannot accept Frege's fundamental mode of analysis. This leaves us with two questions. First, what is Russell's fundamental method of analysis? The answer takes us immediately to his ontological views, especially about the nature of complexity. Second, if Russell does not take functions as primitive, how does he account for them? The two questions are connected: the first provides the constraints within which the second must be answered. Russell must have an understanding of functions which is compatible with his general view of the nature of the world. I shall consider the two questions in turn.

Russell's view of analysis is based on his atomistic conception of the world. He sees it as made up of simple objects standing in relations to one another. What appear to be complex objects are to be understood as simpler objects standing in certain relations to one another. The complex object is made up of simpler objects as a whole is made up of its parts. (This relationship sometimes seems to be understood in something like the way in which a wall is made up of bricks.) Propositions provide a crucial example. A proposition, for Russell, paradigmatically *contains* the objects which it is about; they are the parts, and the proposition is the whole. Propositions here, however, are more than an example. That certain objects stand in certain relations is itself a proposition. So by treating all complexity as the complexity of relations and relata Russell is implying that all complexity is propositional complexity. (We shall enter a partial qualification to this point shortly.)

The theory of descriptions, seen from this perspective, eliminates an apparent exception to the idea that all complexity is propositional complexity, namely complex denoting concepts. It is for this reason, I think that Russell throughout 'On Denoting' speaks of 'denoting *complexes*'; it is the complexity, as well as the denoting, that he is concerned to eliminate. This terminology may also reflect the idea that denoting is not wholly eliminated, but rather reduced to one simple case, that of the variable. (See n. 25, above.) A phrase such as 'the present King of France' is not explained by saying that it indicates the presence in the proposition of a complex object, a denoting concept. Rather, it is explained in terms of the logical form of the whole proposition: there is one and only one object such that it currently reigns over France, and that object has whatever property the sentence ascribes. The semantic complexity of a definite description is thus accounted for in terms of the complexity of the complete proposition, not in terms of the complexity of any constituent part of it.

I have been speaking here of 'propositional complexity', the kind of complexity that is characteristic of a proposition. A change in Russell's views is relevant here. Sometime between 1906 and 1909 he comes to adopt what he calls 'the multiple relation theory of judgment'.[34] According to this theory, the notion of a proposition is not fundamental; it is replaced as the fundamental metaphysical idea by the notion of a fact. Propositions are explained in terms of facts, rather than vice versa. Russell continues, however, to think of all complexity as arising from simple objects standing in relations to one another. Under both the old view and the new view, this is the kind of complexity which

---

[34] Russell first adumbrates, but does not endorse, this view in the 1906 essay 'The Nature of Truth'; the introduction to the first edition of *Principia Mathematica,* however, explicitly advocates the new view. It is perhaps worth adding that this view does not seem to fit with the logic of *Principia Mathematica,* which quantifies over propositions; also that Russell never found a version of the view that satisfied him for very long.

typifies propositions. The difference is that, according to the new view, this sort of complexity is to be understood as being, at bottom, the complexity of a fact. For our general comparison between Russell and Frege this change is, I think, of relatively little importance. It does, however, make Russell's view in two significant ways less like Frege's. First, Russell now abandons the idea that the bearers of truth and falsehood are objective and mind-independent entities. Second, Russell had earlier held, with Frege, that truth is indefinable; with the new view, he advocates a version of the correspondence theory of truth.

Russell thus conceives the world as consisting of complex objects made up of simpler objects and, ultimately, presumably, of absolutely simple objects.[35] His dominant mode of analysis is, accordingly, the decomposition of a whole into its parts. Frege sees the world as divided into functions and objects. One consequence of this difference concerns the stratification of the universe into ontological categories. Functions and objects are naturally conceived of as being of distinct ontological kinds, with functions themselves coming in various levels which are similarly distinct: first-level functions apply to objects, second-level functions to first-level functions, and so on. Russell's fundamental metaphysical instincts are to deny any such distinctions; a whole is not naturally thought of as being of a different ontological kind from its parts—a wall is not of an ontologically distinct category from the bricks which compose it. The dominance of the part–whole metaphor suggests that there are no fundamental ontological distinctions, that all entities are of the same general kind. In the *Principles of Mathematics*, indeed, Russell argues that no fundamental ontological distinctions are tenable: everything is, in Russellian jargon, a term, that is, very roughly, capable of being a logical subject in the simplest kind of subject-predicate proposition. To deny that something is a term is, he claims, logically self-refuting, since *a* appears as a term in the proposition expressed by '*a* is not a term'.[36] I speak here of Russell's metaphysical instincts because he is forced, by the need to escape the paradox which bears his name, to acknowledge fundamental distinctions, in the form of the theory of types. Those distinctions, however, always seem to be imposed, for the purpose of avoiding the paradox, upon a structure in which no such distinctions exist. For Frege, by contrast, the distinctions between function and object, and among functions of various levels, are built in to his thought from the outset. (We shall return to these points in the

---

[35] 'Presumably' because Russell does, at least at one point, suggest that it would be possible to maintain that analysis is infinite, 'that complex things are capable of analysis *ad infinitum*', though he does not accept this view. See the discussion at the end of the second of the 'Lectures on the Philosophy of Logical Atomism', *Collected Papers*, viii. 180.

[36] We might phrase this by saying that Russell takes very seriously the concept horse problem, whereas Frege wants to dismiss it as due to a mere awkwardness of language. See Appendix A of *Principles*, especially sections 481–3.

next section, putting them in the context of the logics developed by Frege and by Russell.)

An illustration of Russell's view, and an important fact in its own right, is the difficulty that he faces in accounting for the unity of the proposition. The constituents of a proposition, 'placed side by side', Russell says, 'do not reconstitute the proposition' (*Principle*, section 54). 'A proposition is essentially a unity, and when analysis has destroyed the unity, no enumeration of constituents will restore the proposition.' (loc. cit.). How is this unity to be understood? From within Russell's early post-Idealist metaphysics the unity of the proposition can be neither avoided nor explained.[37] Frege, by contrast, is not troubled by any analogous problem. For him there is no issue about how judgments are possible, about how concepts and objects unite. From a Russellian perspective, it might appear that he is simply ducking a problem, but in fact I think we have here an indication of how different his presuppositions are from Russell's. Let us focus on Frege's context-principle: 'it is only in the context of a *Satzes* that words have any meaning'.[38] This principle, as I understand it, implies that the notions of an object, and of a concept, are not to be understood independently of one other, and of the role that concept-expressions and object-expressions have in forming complete sentences.[39] On this kind of reading, Frege presupposes the notion of judgment as fundamental, and understands both concepts and objects in terms of it. For him there thus can be no question as to how these separate and independent entities can form a unity, since they are not correctly thought of as separate and independent at all.

A page or two back, we saw that there is a clear ontological difference between Frege and Russell: Frege sees the world as divided into functions (of various levels) and objects; Russell, with a view dominated by the part–whole metaphor, rejects functions, and cannot easily adopt any such distinctions at a fundamental level. Our recent discussion, however, suggests that as well as this ontological difference there is also a difference in the very notion of ontology that is at issue here. Russell holds what one might call an object-based metaphysics: for him the existence of an object is a fundamental and independent fact, the idea of an object's existing or not existing makes sense by itself, in isolation from other ideas.[40] For Frege, by contrast, the fundamental ideas are those of truth and falsity, and of a judgment as that to which truth and falsity can be

---

[37] It may have been the ramifications of this issue that were responsible for the major change in Russell's metaphysics that took place when he adopted the multiple relation theory of judgment. See Ricketts, 'Truth and Propositional Unity in Early Russell'.

[38] Frege, *Die Grundlagen der Arithmetik*, section 62; cf. also p. x and sections 60, 106.

[39] For this line of interpretation see, for example, Ricketts, 'Objectivity and Objecthood: Frege's Metaphysics of Judgment'.

[40] As we saw, Russell distinguishes existence from subsistence in his early post-Idealist work (even as late as the 1912 *Problems of Philosophy*; see p. 100). Here, however, I use the word 'existence' broadly, to encompass both ways of being.

ascribed.[41] Here ontology is derivative: questions of existence are to be settled primarily by seeing what is required for the judgments that we make, and to account for the way those judgments behave in inferences that we make.

These metaphysical differences are connected with differences in epistemology—not just in the answers to epistemological questions, but also in the questions themselves. For Russell, as we have emphasized, the notion of acquaintance is crucial. The idea of an object's existing or not existing draws on our (supposed) capacity for acquaintance, our ability to stand in a direct cognitive relation to an object. Our knowledge and understanding must all ultimately be explained in terms of this relation. This imperative defines a philosophical task: since most of our knowledge and understanding seems to concern things which are not objects of acquaintance, we need to show how it can be explained in terms of acquaintance.

A foundationalist epistemology is thus implicit in Russell's general view. He assumes that all knowledge is based on our acquaintance with certain objects, some of them abstract (he is somewhat open-minded about exactly which objects, and changes his mind about this over time). So he then needs to show how, and to what extent, the knowledge and understanding which we take ourselves to have can be explained on this basis, and thereby justified. Here there is a very sharp contrast with Frege. Frege does not seem to be at all concerned to raise questions about the basis of our knowledge, how it is acquired, and what ultimately justifies it. Nor does his fundamental view seem naturally to generate such questions. (Unless, of course, such questions are inevitable and thus naturally generated by any serious thought; the point is that nothing peculiar to *Frege's* thought naturally generates such questions.) Frege seems, rather, to think of the philosophical task as primarily one of systematizing knowledge, setting out the relations of justification which hold among the various items we know. Axiomatization, of Euclidean geometry, for example, serves as a partial paradigm here, but in the ideal this model would be extended both deeper, to include the underlying logic, and wider, to include all systematic knowledge. In this way the body of our knowledge will be given greater clarity, and our understanding of exactly what it is that we know may be modified in the process. Russellian foundationalist questions, however, have no place in Frege's work; nor does scepticism play any role in his thought.[42]

---

[41] Thus Frege says: 'What is distinctive about my conception of logic is that I begin by giving pride of place to the content of the word "true", and then immediately go on to introduce a thought as that to which the question "Is it true?" is in principle applicable. So I do not begin with concepts and put them together to form a thought or judgment; I come by the parts of a thought by analyzing the thought.' This passage is from notes that he wrote about his thought for Ludwig Darmstaedter, and is published in *Nachgelassene Schriften*, v. ii. 273; I follow the translation in Frege, *Posthumous Writings*, 253.

[42] For elaboration of these ideas, see section I of Ricketts, 'Frege's 1906 Foray into Metalogic', on which my discussion in this paragraph draws.

These sorts of differences are, of course, most evident in the case of our knowledge of mathematics and logic, for these subjects are at the centre of Frege's concerns. For Russell, as we saw, our knowledge of these subjects must be based on acquaintance.[43] Philosophical analysis may be required to show you *which* abstract objects play a fundamental role—whether, for example, it is numbers or classes or propositional functions. But the fundamental abstract objects, whichever they turn out to be, are known by acquaintance. The objects are out there, and we are capable of standing in a direct cognitive relation to them. Russell's version of realism about abstract objects is thus backed up by his epistemology. Nothing similar can be said about Frege, and this has been taken to cast Frege's realism about abstract objects in doubt; those who take Russellian views as paradigmatic may indeed find Frege's realism less than robust. It would, however, be more accurate to say that in the context of different epistemological and metaphysical views, what realism comes to also differs.

As we have seen, the notion of a function cannot be primitive for Russell; functional expressions must be explained in other terms. It is to this explanation that I now turn. What Russell does is to define functional expressions in general in terms of expressions for what he calls 'propositional functions'. A propositional function is, very roughly, the non-linguistic correlate of an open sentence, i.e. a sentence containing one or more variables.[44] In a footnote in the Introduction to the first edition of *Principia Mathematica*, Whitehead and Russell say explicitly: 'When the word "function" is used in the sequel, "propositional function" is always meant' (p. 39). And *30 of that work is devoted to showing how non-propositional functions—descriptive functions, as they are there called—can be introduced on the basis of propositional functions. Roughly the idea is this: we do not begin by presupposing, say, the two-place plus function; we begin with the three-place propositional function represented by 'ADD(x, y, z)'. (Where this is read as 'The sum of x and y is z', so that 'ADD(2, 3, 5)' is a true sentence, 'ADD(5, 3, 2)' a false one, and so on.)

---

[43] Russell changed his mind about this under the influence of Wittgenstein. Beginning with his Lectures, 'The Philosophy of Logical Atomism', given early in 1918, he speaks of the truths of logic as 'tautologies'; see the end of Lecture V. This tendency is more marked in the book he wrote in later that year, *Introduction to Mathematical Philosophy*, where the position is somewhat elaborated. In these works, however, the new idea sits very uneasily alongside the earlier position, so that it is hard not to think that Russell is simply using the Wittgensteinian form of words without really having thought it through, or even without really understanding it. It is the earlier position which I attribute to Russell here.

[44] I thus claim that Russell uses 'propositional function' to refer to abstract objects, rather than using it to refer to linguistic objects, or in such a way that it is unclear which sort of object he means to be referring to. This claim is controversial; for some defence of it, see the work cited in n.14, above, especially pp. 217 f.

The plus function, '$x + y$' is then introduced by definition:

$$x + y \text{ is defined as: the object } z \text{ such that ADD}(x, y, z)$$

This technique enables us to define an $n - 1$ place descriptive function on the basis of any n-place propositional function which satisfies the relevant uniqueness condition: that for any given selection of n objects in places corresponding to the arguments of the descriptive function there should be exactly one object which makes the propositional function true. (Each definition of this sort, one for each non-propositional function that we want, will of course employ a definite description; this, I suspect, does something to explain the importance that Russell attributes to definite descriptions.)

The method of defining functions (descriptive functions, in Russell's sense) from propositional functions is technically quite straightforward. (No function is defined unless the propositional function satisfies the appropriate uniqueness condition, but this is the desired result.) What is problematic is to see exactly why Russell is willing to accept propositional functions as primitive, while he is not willing to accept functions in general as primitive. Clearly he is not thinking of propositional functions simply as a special case of functions, as a species of the genus *function*: but why not? How do propositional functions, in his view, differ from descriptive functions?

Recall the reason that Russell cannot accept a functional expression, such as '$2 + 3$' at face value, as a complex referring expression. Doing so would give rise to a need for an account of the semantic role of such phrases which requires some distinction analogous to the Fregean distinction between *Sinn* and *Bedeutung*. The reason for this is that the phrase has a semantic complexity which is not to be found in the object which it picks out. Thus if there were no more to the semantics of the phrase than its picking out a certain object, we would have no way of taking account of that complexity. This would make it impossible to understand the role that the phrase plays in language (in inferences, in particular). But propositional functions are in the relevant way unlike functions in general. A phrase expressing a propositional function, '$x + y = z$', for example, gives rise to sentences, '$2 + 3 = 5$', for example. On Russell's view, a sentence is related to—expresses, picks out—a proposition.[45] And a proposition *does* possess the requisite complexity.

Saying of the expression '$2 + 3$' that it refers to the number five is far from an adequate account of its semantics for there is, so to speak, no complexity in the number five which corresponds to the complexity of the functional expression. There is no way to understand the complexity in terms of relations and relata, of

---

[45] Although I speak here of propositions, and objects as constituents of propositions, what I say holds good also, *mutatis mutandis*, of the view that Russell holds after he adopts the multiple relation theory of judgment, briefly discussed above.

parts and wholes. Saying of '2 + 3 = 5' that it expresses the proposition that two plus three equals five, however, is, from a Russellian point of view, quite a different matter. For propositions are complex in just the ways that are needed. In particular, a proposition which is the value of a propositional function applied to a given object as argument will *contain* that object. And the resulting proposition has the same form as the propositional function. (Indeed we might think of a propositional function as simply being the form of a number of propositions.) Two propositions which are the values of a single propositional function have something in common in virtue of that fact. And from the proposition we can figure out of which propositional functions it is a value, for the proposition has a kind of complexity which marks its relation to the propositional functions of which it is a value. The propositional function, we might say, is *recoverable* from the proposition. None of these points apply to functions in general.[46]

The facts indicated above show why propositional functions will, while functions in general will not, fit into Russell's metaphysics. A function takes an object as argument and yields as value an object which bears no obvious systematic relationship to the argument or to the function itself; in particular, the value may be simple and unanalysable. A propositional function, by contrast, takes an object as argument and yields as value an object of a special kind—a proposition—which *does* have such systematic relationships: it contains the argument, and has the same structure as the propositional function.[47] What is unexplained in the case of a function—that *that* object taken as argument should yield *this* object as value—is transparent in the case of propositional functions.

VII

The differences between Frege and Russell emphasized in the previous sections are relevant to the accounts that each gives of logic. One point is this. For Frege there is, from the outset, a fundamental difference in kind between functions and objects, with concepts defined as a special case of functions. The idea of a concept's applying, or not applying, to itself is, for him, intrinsically absurd. A consequence of this is that no analogue of Russell's paradox arises directly from his fundamental metaphysics. By the same token, however, the ontology of that metaphysics is too weak to carry out the reduction of arithmetic to logic.[48] For

---

[46] These matters are discussed in somewhat greater detail in Ch. 7, above.

[47] On a Fregean account, by contrast, a sentence has both a *Sinn* (the thought it expresses) and a *Bedeutung* (its truth-value). Frege argues for the distinction between *Sinn* and *Bedeutung* for sentences in 'Function and Concept'. It is striking, from our point of view, that this argument proceeds by taking for granted the notion of a function.

[48] In particular, nothing guarantees that every natural number has a successor distinct from it.

that purpose it is necessary to bolster the fundamental ontology with an additional assumption. It is for this reason that Frege's system of logic in the *Grundgesetze* includes the notorious Axiom V, which asserts (roughly) that for every concept there is a corresponding object. This axiom gives Frege's system of logic the power necessary to carry out the logistic reduction, but it also, notoriously, leads his system into contradiction.

For Russell's logic the situation is reversed. The power needed to carry out the reduction is intrinsic to the underlying metaphysics, and it is the paradox that has to be blocked in more or less *ad hoc* fashion. The part–whole metaphor supports the idea that, at the most fundamental level, there are no different kinds of entity. The idea of a propositional function's being applied to itself to yield a proposition is not one that is obviously ruled out by the basic metaphysics; Russell's paradox thus threatens that metaphysics itself. Paradox is avoided by the theory of types, which is uneasily superimposed on the underlying metaphysics. The theory of types is based on the idea that a propositional function *presupposes* the propositions which are its values.[49] Russell argues that it follows from this that a propositional function cannot be a constituent of any of its values. Since a proposition presupposes its constituents, if a propositional function were a constituent of one of its values we would have that proposition both presupposing and being presupposed by the propositional function; this he holds to be absurd. The crucial consequence of this is that we cannot apply a propositional function to itself and obtain a proposition. These ideas, however, rely upon a notion of presupposition which is unexplained and which seems, indeed, to be at odds with Russell's object-based metaphysics.[50]

Let us now turn to a rather different issue, still having to do with the logics of Frege and of Russell and with the difference between Fregean functions (and hence also concepts) and Russellian propositional functions. The latter, as we saw, are complex structured entities, whereas Fregean concepts are not. It is tempting to phrase this point about Fregean concepts by saying that concepts true of exactly the same objects are identical. This is misleading, because identity in Frege's view is a *first-level* concept: it applies only to objects, not to concepts. Frege does, however, say explicitly that co-extensiveness is the analogue for functions (including concepts) of the notion of identity.[51] Two predicates which apply to the same objects are thus, on Frege's account, like two names which pick out the same object; nothing in the logic will turn on the difference between such

---

[49] See Ch. 5, above.

[50] One might take this as a partial vindication of Frege's reaction to *Principia Mathematica*: he complains that he does not understand Russell's notation for propositional functions, and the (related) use of the word 'variable'. See his letter to Jourdain, undated draft of a letter sent on 28 January 1914, and the letter dated 28 January 1914, *Philosophical and Mathematical Correspondence*, 78–84.

[51] See 'Ausführungen über Sinn und Bedeutung', in *Posthumous Writings*, 122 (*Nachgelassene Schriften*, 132).

predicates. Frege's logic is thus, in one sense of that word, *extensional* from the outset:[52] his fundamental entities, concepts, have their identity-conditions (or rather the analogue of identity-conditions) given by the objects of which they hold. His Axiom V partially undoes the concept–object distinction, by asserting that for every concept there is a corresponding object, but it does not impose extensionality, for Frege's concepts are already extensional.[53]

For Russell, however, the situation is quite different. A Russellian proposition is a complex structured entity, in some ways (though not others) more akin to the Fregean *Sinn* of a sentence than to its *Bedeutung*. At the most fundamental level, Russell's logic is thus not extensional. Propositional functions, moreover, have the same sort of complexity as propositions: it makes sense to say of a propositional function that it contains a given object or (crucially) that it contains a variable with a given range. This fact about propositional functions, moreover, is not adventitious. On the contrary, this is what makes propositional functions acceptable to Russell, whereas functions *simpliciter* are not. This fact is also what makes it comprehensible that Russell's theory of types is what Ramsey called a *ramified* theory: one in which two propositional functions applicable to entities of the same type may themselves be of different types. When a propositional function contains a quantifier which itself ranges over propositional functions, then on Russell's account it presupposes all those propositional functions. Hence, by the doctrine that lies at the basis of Russell's theory of types, such a propositional function cannot itself be one of those within the range of the quantifier. Hence it must be of higher type.[54]

The mathematical work of *Principia Mathematica* is of course done in extensional terms—it is done in terms of classes, which for Russell, as for everyone else, are extensional entities (in the sense in which we are using that word). Symbols for classes, however, are in that work a mere *façon de parler*, introduced by a definition which enables us to eliminate them (though at the cost of great complexity and prolixity) from any context in which they can legitimately occur. The purpose of the definition is to give us the appearance of extensional entities with which to work, since the reduction to mathematics demands such entities. Russell's definition of classes should thus not be compared with Frege's Axiom V;

---

[52] In the strictest, and clearest, sense, it is perhaps only *contexts*, not entities or logics, which can be said to be extensional or non-extensional: a context is extensional when replacing an expression in that context with any co-referential expression results in a whole with the same truth-value, or the same reference, as the original. The usage I follow here, however, is a common and natural way of extending the terminology.

[53] For this reason, Frege's logic without Axiom V might be thought of as equivalent to what Ramsey described as *Simple Type Theory*; the latter, however, allows for unlimited ascent up the hierarchy of types, whereas it is by no means clear that Frege would have been willing to accept an analogous ascent up the hierarchy of objects, functions of objects, functions of functions of objects, and so on. (For this latter point I am indebted to Warren Goldfarb.)

[54] In this paragraph I am indebted to David Kaplan.

as a mere definition, it adds no genuine power to the system. (Power is added to the system by the Axiom of Reducibility, which guarantees that for every propositional function there is a co-extensive propositional function of lowest type; this propositional function may, in effect, be treated as the class corresponding to the given propositional function.)

This extensional superstructure, however, is imposed upon a system which in its foundations is intensional through and through: Russellian propositions are not identical when they have the same truth-value, and his propositional functions are not identical when they hold of the same objects. It is this feature of the underlying logic of *Principia Mathematica* which has led some (perhaps most notably Church) to try and exploit it as a logic of such intensional notions as 'believes that'. It would be a mistake, however, to think that these intensional elements arise from any interest on Russell's part in that kind of logic. They arise, rather, from just those fundamental features of his philosophy which we have emphasized in contrasting his view with that of Frege.[55]

[55] Besides the particular debts indicated in other notes, I am indebted to Cora Diamond and Thomas Ricketts for their comments on earlier drafts.

10

The Theory of Descriptions

Russell's theory of descriptions was first published in his 1905 essay, 'On Denoting', which is surely one of the two or three most famous articles in twentieth-century analytic philosophy. It has been described as 'a paradigm of philosophy',[1] and has been employed by many later analytic philosophers, such as Quine,[2] although disputed by others, perhaps most notably Strawson.[3] Writing in 1967, an astute commentator said: 'In the forty-five years preceding the publication of Strawson's "On Referring", Russell's theory was practically immune from criticism. There is not a similar phenomenon in contemporary analytic philosophy'.[4]

What is the theory which has excited such interest and acclaim? To put it briefly and more or less neutrally, it is a method of analyzing *definite descriptions*, also called *singular descriptions*, i.e., phrases, in English typically beginning with the word 'the', which pick out or purport to pick out a single ('definite') object—e.g., 'the man who broke the bank at Monte Carlo', or 'the first President of the USA'. Many philosophers who have accepted the theory of definite descriptions, including Russell himself, have also treated some or all proper names in similar fashion. They are taken to be disguised definite descriptions,[5] and then subjected to the same analysis as overt definite descriptions. Definite descriptions may be contrasted with indefinite descriptions, which do not purport to pick out any particular number of objects—e.g., 'any President of the USA'. Note that while the two phrases 'the even prime number' and 'any even prime number' in fact direct our attention to the same object—the number two—the first is a definite description, while the second is an indefinite description. Either definite or indefinite descriptions may in fact fail to describe any object or objects; as we have said, the difference is that definite descriptions *purport* to pick out a single object.[6]

---

[1] The phrase 'that paradigm of philosophy' was used by Ramsey to describe Russell's theory of descriptions, and endorsed by Moore. See Moore's essay 'Russell's Theory of Descriptions', 175–225.

[2] See for example *Word and Object*, sections 37–8.   [3] See especially 'On Referring'.

[4] Linsky, *Referring*, p. ix.

[5] In 'Knowledge by Acquaintance', in *Collected Papers*, vi. 148–61, and in *Mysticism and Logic*, 209–32, Russell says: 'Common words, even proper names, are usually really descriptions' (*Collected Papers*, vi. 152); in Lecture V of his lectures on the 'Philosophy of Logical Atomism' he says that the (apparent) name 'Romulus' 'is really a sort of truncated or telescoped description' (*Collected Papers*, viii. 213).

[6] What does it mean to speak of a phrase 'purporting' to pick out a single object? As Quine comments: 'Such talk of purport is only a picturesque way of alluding to distinctive grammatical roles that singular and general terms play in sentences. It is by grammatical role that general and singular terms are properly to be distinguished', (*Word and Object*, 96).

The theory of descriptions has appeared to some philosophers as a definite philosophical advance, a *result*, which is independent of disputed metaphysical assumptions, including Russell's. We need to pay some attention to the theory as it appears in this light. On the other hand, to understand the importance that it had for Russell we need to relate it to his more general views around 1905, and this is a more complicated matter. We also need to see, at least briefly, how the theory has been exploited or criticized by philosophers whose metaphysical assumptions are, in most cases, quite different from those of Russell. We shall therefore proceed as follows. The first section will state the method of analysis, as neutrally as possible, and will also briefly point out some of its putative advantages which do not depend on particular features of Russell's views in the early years of the twentieth century. The next five sections will be devoted to placing the theory in its Russellian context. We shall start, in Section II, by sketching the relevant parts of Russell's general views in the period leading up to 1905. Those views pose a problem for him, which will be the subject of Section III; in Section IV we shall see how he attempted to solve that problem in the period before he discovered the theory of descriptions. Then, in Section V, we shall discuss his reasons for adopting the theory of descriptions; the most important such reason, I shall claim, is that it enables him to give a more satisfactory solution to the problem discussed in sections III and IV. Section VI will discuss the general significance of the theory of descriptions in Russell's thought. Finally, in Section VII, we shall consider more or less recent reactions to the theory, especially criticisms of it.

I. OUTLINE OF THE THEORY

Modern logic—quantification theory with identity—provides the essential background to the idea of analysis that is in question when we speak of *analyzing* definite descriptions. It gives us both the method by which the analysis proceeds and part of the point of the enterprise. Analysis here is to provide a way of reading definite descriptions that enables them to be incorporated into a system of logic in a way that gives the correct account of their inferential powers.

Let us begin by seeing how this goes in the case of *indefinite* descriptions, for the treatment of definite descriptions is analogous, though in some ways more complicated. The application of quantification theory to sentences in English presupposes that a phrase of the form 'any F' (for example 'any prime number') is not to be treated as the name of one or more objects (very similar points apply to descriptive phrases of other forms, such as 'Some Fs', 'All Fs' or 'No Fs'). A sentence in which it occurs, a sentence of the form 'Any F is G' (for example 'any prime number is odd') is, rather, equated with:

  1) Take any object: if it is F then it is G.

This clumsy, though comprehensible, piece of English goes over into logical notation very smoothly, as:[7]

2) $(\forall x)(Fx \supset Gx)$

Now the machinery of first-order logic can be applied in familiar fashion. Note that one feature of this analysis is that there is no very obvious answer to the question: how is the phrase 'any prime number' itself treated? What we are given is a method of analyzing complete sentences in which that phrase occurs. It might be said that the analysis provides no obvious account of the functioning of the phrase in isolation—but then it is far from clear what sense it makes to speak of that phrase as having a function in isolation at all. The most obvious sort of account of a phrase in isolation is perhaps an account of what the phrase names. One is not likely to think that an indefinite description names something; according to the above analysis it certainly does not.[8]

The analysis of definite descriptions is analogous, but more complex. A sentence of the form 'The F is G' is treated as making three related claims:

  i)   that there is something which is F,
  ii) that nothing other than that thing is F, and
  iii) that that thing—the unique thing which is F—is also G.

(These claims are related because they are all talking about the same object, saying that *it* is F, that *it* is uniquely F, and that *it* is G.) More compactly, a sentence of that form is treated as saying:

3) there is one and only one object which is F, and it is G.

This can be put into logical notation as:

4) $(\exists x)[Fx \ \& \ (\forall y)(Fy \supset x=y) \ \& \ Gx]$.

So a sentence such as 'The even prime number is less than ten' becomes:

5) there is one and only one object which is an even prime number, and it is less than ten.

And this in turn goes into logical notation as:

6) $(\exists x)[x$ is an even prime $\& \ (\forall y)(y$ is an even prime $\supset x=y) \ \& \ x$ is less than ten]

---

[7]   I use the upside-down 'A', used before the variable in parentheses including both it and the variable, to represent the universal quantifier, which is sometimes represented simply by putting the variable by itself in parentheses ['(x)']. I use the horseshoe, '⊃', to represent the truth-functional conditional, and the backwards 'E' to represent the existential quantifier.

[8]   I leave out of account here the idea that a phrase such as 'any prime number' might be treated as naming a higher-order property, or anything of that sort. For the purposes of the analogy with definite descriptions, the important point is that it does not name an object of the ordinary sort—in this case, that it does not name a prime number, or all the prime numbers, or any combination of them.

The predicate which we put in for 'F' may itself be complex, as it is in this case and usually is where we have something that looks like a plausible definite description. So it may be broken down further, to give, in this example, this:

   7) $(\exists x)[x$ is a prime number & x is even & $(\forall y)(y$ is a prime number & y is even $\supset x=y)$ & x is less than ten]

When sentences involving definite descriptions are treated in this way, they fit smoothly into our system of logic, which can then handle them formally without any additional axioms or rules. Let us distinguish two aspects here. One is that definite descriptions have semantic structure and complexity. Unlike proper names, they are significant phrases which are made up of independently significant parts. (The name 'Aristotle' contains the letters 'i' and 's' in sequence, but it does not contain the English word 'is'; those letters are not in that context independently significant. Contrast the word 'even' in 'the even prime number'.) This complexity is exploited in the way we reason. It follows immediately from 'The even prime number is less than ten' that there is at least one prime number less than ten. If we were to treat the definite description simply as a name, without semantically significant structure, then this inference would be quite opaque. Obviously, the definite description does have semantically significant structure, and obviously it is this that makes the inference a good one. But how can we understand the semantic structure of the phrase so as to make the correctness of the inference transparent to ourselves? How does the inference exploit the structure of the definite description? Russell's analysis of definite descriptions answers these questions. By treating the sentence in Russellian fashion the inference becomes a simple application of ordinary first-order logic.

The second aspect is a little less straightforward. It is very easy to construct definite descriptions which do not in fact describe anything: 'the largest natural number' is an obvious example. If we simply treat definite descriptions as singular terms, we are then faced with a large class of such terms which are evidently meaningful, yet do not in fact refer to anything. The existence of such singular terms threatens standard logic. From '$(\forall x)$ Fx', 'Fa' follows by the usual rules of logic, whatever predicate we may put for 'F', and whatever singular term we may put for 'a'. Yet this inference fails if 'a' does not in fact refer to anything. One response is to reconstruct logic so that it takes the possibility of empty singular terms into account; the result is so-called 'free logic', logic adapted to the possibility that there may be singular terms which do not refer to anything.[9] There is, however, reason to avoid the complications of free logic, and to retain the simpler structure of classical first-order logic. The theory of descriptions, by eliminating definite descriptions from the category of singular terms, removes one obstacle to our doing so. There is, however, another possible obstacle. On most accounts

---

[9] See for example Lambert, 'The Nature of Free Logic', and references given there.

it is not only definite descriptions but also ordinary names—terms without significant semantic structure—which can fail to refer. If we wish to retain the advantage of ordinary logic, we can do so by eliminating names as primitive terms of the language; such names as we want can be introduced by definition in terms of definite descriptions: a given name is introduced as short for a given definite description.

The mention of empty names suggests a further problem, independent of logic, to which such names are sometimes thought to give rise. How, it is asked, can a name be meaningful if it does not in fact name anything? And if a name which fails to name is not meaningful, then how can we ever sensibly deny that something exists—as we seem to be able to do? How can a sentence such as 'Homer never existed' even be a candidate for discussion? Treating names as definite descriptions, and subjecting them to Russellian analysis, certainly avoids this problem. But this is not generally taken as a very powerful argument for Russellian analysis, because the problem is easily avoided by a wholly different method. We may claim, plausibly enough, that the sense or meaning of an ordinary name is quite distinct from its reference or denotation, i.e., the object it names. Sense or meaning, here, is what the name must have to be understood, and to be used in a significant way; its reference or denotation is the actual object, if any, that it names.[10] Once the distinction is made, there is, on many views, no obvious reason to think that a name which lacks reference must on that account lack sense. Yet this is not to deny that philosophers have more or less explicitly made the assumption that a meaningful name must name an object, and been led into various kinds of excess by this assumption.

This issue will be of great relevance to our discussion, for Russell sought to deny the distinction between sense and reference. Indeed it might be said that part of the significance of the theory of descriptions for him was precisely that it made such a denial plausible (or at least less implausible).

II. RUSSELLIAN BACKGROUND

In this section we shall discuss relevant aspects of Russell's thought in the period leading up to and including his discovery of the theory of descriptions; a central text for these purposes is his 1903 book *Principles of Mathematics*.

---

[10] Frege's distinction between the *Sinn* of a word and its *Bedeutung* is obviously an example of the sort of distinction that I have in mind here. See 'Über Sinn und Bedeutung'. But Frege's distinction is only an example: the vaguer and more general idea of distinguishing intension from extension, or connotation from denotation, long antedates his work. (Note that Frege's word for what falls on the side of reference or denotation—for the actual object which the name names—is *'Bedeutung'*. This is apt to be confusing, because that word is in most contexts naturally translated as 'meaning', yet that English word is naturally used for the other side of the distinction. The confusions which threaten here are, I think, quite superficial.)

Until some time in the late 1890s, Russell had been an adherent of Absolute Idealism.[11] At some point in 1898 or 1899 he followed G. E. Moore in rejecting that doctrine and argued against it with the fervour of a convert. We can work our way into the views he held in the first few years of this century by seeing how they are directed against Idealism.[12] A central thought of Idealism is that our knowledge and understanding of the world are mediated by conceptual structures.[13] There are then questions as to where these structures come from, and whether their role is compatible with our having knowledge of an objective world. If the concepts through which I understand the world are purely subjective or arbitrary, just imposed by me with no particular reason, then my knowledge of the world—or what I claim as knowledge—will likewise be subjective or arbitrary. So it is natural to seek to deny that our conceptual structures are subjective. The claim that my conceptual structures are *objective*, that they correspond to the way the world really is, however, is a difficult one to sustain. For if *all* our knowledge of the world is mediated, then the knowledge that such-and-such a conceptual structure is objectively correct must in turn be mediated. So it might look as if we need some other conceptual structure, by means of which we come to know that our first conceptual structure corresponds to the world. But then our attention needs to be focused on the second conceptual structure: how do we know that the use of those concepts gives us objective knowledge, rather than a subjective pretense to knowledge? Clearly a regress would threaten.

The Idealists, of course, did not accept the view that what passes for knowledge is simply subjective; neither did they embark on the regress that I have sketched. On the contrary, they evolved extremely subtle and sophisticated ways of reconciling the idea that we have knowledge of a world that is, in some sense, independent of us with what I have taken as a central thought of Idealism.[14] The details of these attempts, however, do not concern us here. What is relevant is that they are all vulnerable to the charge that they do not give an account of knowledge which makes it objective, in a sufficiently strong sense of that word.

---

[11] I have in mind primarily the work of Hegel and his followers, especially his British followers such as T. H. Green and F. H. Bradley. Russell, and a number of the Idealists, counted Kant as more or less a member of the Idealist camp. (From here on I shall speak of 'Idealism', always meaning *Absolute* Idealism.)

[12] For a far more detailed account, see the present author's *Russell, Idealism and the Emergence of Analytic Philosophy*.

[13]   The application of this to Kant is problematic. He distinguished the conceptual from the intuitional and argued that Space and Time are matters of intuition, not of concepts. He accordingly held that our knowledge of the world is mediated by *a priori* forms of intuition (Space and Time), as well as by *a priori* concepts. For some purposes this distinction is crucial, but not for ours. I mean to be using the expression 'conceptual structures' to include Kant's view about Space and Time, in spite of the violence that this does to Kantian usage.

[14] It is crucial to remember here that one philosopher's sophistication and subtlety is another philosopher's sophistry and illusion.

In other words, if one reads 'objective' and 'independent of us' very strongly, then it may seem as if none of the Idealists succeed in giving an account of knowledge which makes it out to be objective. This was the position of Moore and Russell, after they rejected Idealism. They claimed that it is a result of that view that we cannot have knowledge of the world as it really is. If some form of Idealism were true, they claimed, then we would at best know the world as it is modified by our conceptual structure, which is not the same thing as really knowing the world. In this way, they argued, all judgments are, on the Idealist account, inevitably distorted or falsified. And this result they found to be unacceptable.

To deny the unacceptable results of Idealism, Moore and Russell denied the central thought that we began with. They cut through the idea that our knowledge of the world is mediated by postulating a direct and unmediated knowledge of reality. Thus it is that Moore speaks of a 'direct cognitive relation' which the mind may have to things, both abstract and concrete (including, it would seem, to that very relation itself); in *Principia Ethica* he speaks freely, and not in any obvious way metaphorically, of our having a 'direct perception' of this or that matter.[15] In the Preface to the *Principles of Mathematics*, Russell says that 'the chief part of philosophical logic' is 'the endeavour to see clearly, and to make others see clearly, the entities concerned, in order that the mind may have that kind of acquaintance with them which it has with redness or the taste of a pineapple' (p. xv). As time went by, the notion of acquaintance occupied an increasingly prominent place in his thought. The importance of acquaintance is that it is a relation between the mind and what is outside the mind, a relation which is direct, immediate, and wholly presuppositionless.

One way in which this notion is important for Russell's thought is in his conception of a proposition—roughly, what is expressed by a declarative sentence. He takes propositions to be non-linguistic and non-mental, abstract entities existing independently of us. When we make a judgment or assertion we are, in his view, directly and immediately related to such an entity. Propositions themselves, on his account, are objects of acquaintance: understanding a proposition involves being acquainted with it. More to the present point, however, are Russell's views on the constituents of propositions. One might think that a proposition about Bill Clinton, say, would contain some element which represents that man—an idea or meaning which stands in some representational relation to him. Such is not Russell's view, however, at least for the propositions which he takes as paradigmatic.[16] For him this would mean that our thought was not really getting through to Clinton himself: while we wanted to think about *him*, we would instead be confined to the idea of him; our thought would never

---

[15] See *Principia Ethica*, e.g., p. 126. The notion of the good is of course one of the things of which we have this sort of direct perception, according to that book.

[16] We shall see in the next section why this qualification is needed.

really get through to the man himself.[17] It is, rather, Russell's view that in paradigmatic cases propositions actually *contain* the objects they are about (propositions, recall, are not mental entities on Russell's account). He would thus take the proposition about Clinton to have that man as one of its constituents. For Russell, then, a proposition (again, in paradigm cases) does not have a representational element. It does not contain a constituent which somehow *represents* the things it is about; rather, it contains those very things.—In what follows I shall sometimes call this nexus of views 'direct realism', including under this head both Russell's insistence on a direct and unmediated relation between the mind and the known object and the idea that propositions paradigmatically contain the entities they are about.

According to Russell's direct realism, when we understand a sentence about something we are directly acquainted both with the object we are talking about and with a proposition which contains it, or has it as a constituent. This holds, at least, in the sorts of cases that Russell takes as paradigmatic. We have seen that he rejects the view that in making a judgment we are most directly related to *ideas*, psychological entities in our own minds. It is not only the subjectivity of ideas to which he objects. It is also—and more importantly, for present purposes—their role as intermediaries between us and the things we are attempting to talk about. This shows up in his attitude towards Frege's distinction between the *Sinn* of an expression and its *Bedeutung*, between what the words say, their sense or meaning, and what they are about, their denotation or reference. I shall quote an extended passage from a letter of Russell's to Frege which makes this point.

The issue arose from a discussion of truth. In a letter dated November 13, 1904. Frege had said: 'Truth is not a component part of a thought, just as Mont Blanc with its snowfields is not itself a component part of the thought that Mont Blanc is more than 4,000 metres high.'[18] Russell's reply, dated December 12, ignored the issue about truth, which was the point of Frege's remark (and with which he agreed), and seized on the incidental illustration to articulate his objections to Frege's distinction between *Sinn* and *Bedeutung*:[19]

I believe that in spite of all its snowfields Mont Blanc itself is a component part of what is actually asserted in the *Satze* 'Mont Blanc is more than 4,000 metres high'. We do not assert the thought, for this is a private psychological matter: we assert the object of the

---

[17] Thus Russell, speaking of 'the theory that judgments consist of ideas' says: 'in this view ideas become a veil between us and outside things—we never really, in knowledge, attain to the things we are supposed to be judging about, but only to the ideas of those things.' 'Knowledge by Acquaintance', 155–6.

[18] *Nachgelassene Schriften*, ii. 245; I rely on the English translation in *Philosophical and Mathematical Correspondence*, 163.

[19] Russell wrote to Frege in German, using Fregean terminology, presumably in (what he took to be) Frege's sense. I leave the terms *Sinn, Bedeutung, Satz*, and their cognates untranslated, so as to avoid confusion between Frege's terminology and Russell's.

thought, and this is, to my mind, a certain complex (an *objectiver Satz*, one might say) in which Mont Blanc is itself a component part. *If we do not admit this, then we get the conclusion that we know nothing at all about Mont Blanc.* . . . In the case of a simple proper name like 'Socrates', I cannot distinguish between *Sinn* and *Bedeutung*; I see only the idea, which is psychological, and the object. Or better: I do not admit the *Sinn* at all, but only the idea and the *Bedeutung*.[20]

The sentence I have emphasized in this passage reveals and illustrates the motivation we have been discussing: only if the object we are talking about— Mont Blanc, in this case—is actually a component part of the proposition which we grasp can our thought actually get through to that object; only so can we have knowledge which is really about it. I take this sentence, that is to say, as indicating that the danger is not that all of our beliefs about Mont Blanc are false, but rather that none of our beliefs are really *about* it at all. It is in response to the threat of this kind of difficulty that Russell holds the nexus of views which I have labeled 'direct realism'.

One consequence of Russell's direct realism, at least as we have so far articulated it, is that Russell is led to accept that there are certain entities which, on any ordinary account, do not really exist. The issue here is one that was briefly raised in the first section of this essay: how to deal with empty names, i.e., names (or definite descriptions) which do not in fact name (or uniquely describe) anything. The name 'Vulcan' was at one point introduced to name a supposed tenth planet in our solar system. For one who is familiar with that usage, the sentence 'Vulcan is between Mars and the Sun' presumably makes sense; it is even more plausible to say that the sentence 'Vulcan does not exist' must make sense, since some people were (presumably) surprised to be told that Vulcan does not exist. If these sentences make sense, then according to Russell's account they express propositions. And what are the constituents of these propositions? In particular, what constituent of them corresponds to the word 'Vulcan'? Russell's direct realism seems to imply that those propositions must contain Vulcan—that the (alleged) planet must therefore have some kind of ontological status. Since the planet does not really exist, there must be some other ontological status for it to have; Russell calls this status *subsistence*. All entities subsist, or have Being, as Russell also puts it. Some of them, those which are in space and time, have the interesting additional property of *existence*. So the non-existent objects, the merely subsistent objects, include both abstract objects such as numbers and classes, which are of course not in space and time, and also alleged concrete objects such as Vulcan which might exist but which merely happen not to, so to speak. (I shall speak of these latter as non-existent *concreta*.)

[20] *Nachgelassene Schriften*, ii. 250–1; translation in *Philosophical and Mathematical Correspondence*, 169; emphasis added.

The fundamental line of thought here is what I shall call the Meinongian argument, after Alexius Meinong, who advanced a sophisticated theory on the basis of a version of the argument. Russell accepts the argument, and puts it like this:

Being is that which belongs to every conceivable term, to every possible object of thought . . . If *A* be any term that can be counted as one, it is plain that *A* is something, and therefore that *A* is. '*A* is not' must always be either false or meaningless. For if *A* were nothing, it could not be said to not be; '*A* is not' implies that there is a term *A* whose being is denied, and hence that *A* is. Thus unless '*A* is not' be an empty sound it must be false—whatever *A* be, it certainly is. Numbers, the Homeric gods, relations, chimeras and four-dimensional spaces all have being, for if they were not entities of a kind, we could make no propositions about them. (*Principles* section 427)

The crux of the argument is that if a sentence containing a name is to make sense, then the name must in fact succeed in naming something—something that, in some sense at least, *is*. We shall return to this argument at the end of Section IV; as we shall see there, the views of *Principles* do not in fact commit Russell to accepting it, though clearly he does so at least at some points in that book.

III. DIFFICULTIES OF DIRECT REALISM

As we have said more than once, the idea that a proposition contains the object or objects it is about functions as a paradigm for Russell. It is, that is to say, a view which he finds natural and often takes for granted (as in the passage quoted above, from his December 1904 letter to Frege). But it is not a view that he can really hold without restriction, for in its unrestricted version it faces considerable difficulties. He attempted to resolve or to avoid those difficulties in one way in the period from 1900 or 1901 until June 1905; this way of resolving them I shall call 'the theory of denoting concepts'. In June 1905 he came across the fundamental idea of the theory of descriptions, which gave him quite a different way of resolving the same difficulties.[21]

Let us set out the relevant problems facing the underlying picture. One class of difficulty concerns the scope of acquaintance. Here direct realism generates conclusions which might seem to be quite implausible but which Russell was, at the time of *Principles*, simply willing to accept. (He later came to change his mind, even before 'On Denoting'.) There are various cases. One concerns distant

---

[21] The first statement of the new view is in a manuscript entitled 'On Fundamentals', published for the first time in *Collected Papers*, iv. 360–413; the manuscript is dated '1905', and the words 'begun June 7' are on the first folio.

or no-longer existing concrete objects. It is undeniable, one might suppose, that I understand propositions about Socrates, say, but it may appear as quite implausible that I stand in some direct epistemological relation to him, for he no longer exists. It might similarly be thought to be implausible that I stand in a direct epistemic relation to abstract objects. (In this case Russell continues to accept that we do stand in such relations; the most obvious sense in which Russell in 1914, say, is *not* an empiricist is that he holds that we have direct knowledge of abstract entities. This is knowledge which is not based on any of the five senses; it is altogether *sui generis*, though analogous to knowledge given by sensory perception, as Russell thinks of it.) The case of non-existent *concreta*, objects which might exist, so to speak, but in fact do not, such as Pegasus or the present King of France, might be thought to be even more troubling. In *Principles*, however, Russell has no scruples at all about accepting that such entities subsist and that we can be acquainted with them. So he was, for a time, willing to accept all these sorts of apparently implausible consequences of his direct realism.

There is another sort of difficulty, however, which he never accepted. Suppose I say, for example, 'Every natural number is either odd or even'. The underlying picture of direct realism might suggest that I am expressing (and grasping) a proposition which contains all of the infinitely many natural numbers. Russell was agnostic about whether there in fact *are* any such infinitely complex propositions. But he denied that we can grasp propositions that have this sort of infinite complexity (see *Principles*, section 72). Even in the most extreme and unrestrained phase of his realism, the idea that we grasp infinitely complex propositions was too implausible for Russell to accept. So the issue of *generality* — how we can, for example, grasp a proposition about all the natural numbers—is one which does not fit neatly into his direct realism. The difficulty which this issue creates for direct realism forces upon Russell some modification of that doctrine.

It is worth emphasizing that the problem of giving an account of generality—of the variable, or of *any*, as he sometimes says—had central importance for Russell at this period. In the Preface to the *Principles of Mathematics* he speaks of his work on the philosophy of dynamics, and says: 'I was led to a re-examination of the principles of Geometry, thence to the philosophy of continuity and infinity, and thence, with a view to discovering the meaning of the word *any*, to Symbolic Logic' (p. xvii). Why does he give such importance to this issue? Obviously, any account of mathematics must explain the use of variables. In the case of Russell's account this need is especially clear, since it is precisely the *generality* of mathematics that he emphasizes. His philosophical purposes also give him another reason for being concerned with generality. *Principles* was part of an argument against Idealism. Russell set out to show, in opposition to the Idealists, as he understood them, that mathematics gives genuine knowledge, something absolutely and unrestrictedly true. An obstacle to this task was the difficulty of understanding the infinite, which some had taken as showing that mathematics is inconsistent; Russell held that an understanding of generality was one of the essential points in defeating this view. Thus he says:

> Almost all mathematical ideas present one great difficulty: the difficulty of infinity. This is usually regarded by philosophers as an antinomy . . . . From this received opinion I am compelled to dissent . . . . all apparent antinomies . . . are, in my opinion, reducible to the one difficulty of infinite number, yet this difficulty itself appears to be soluble by a correct philosophy of *any* . . . (*Principles*, section 179, p. 188)

The need to arrive at some understanding of generality thus operates at the most fundamental level of Russell's metaphysics; and it is this need which, in the first instance, forces upon him a modification of his direct realism.

IV. THE THEORY OF DENOTING CONCEPTS

An unqualified version of direct realism serves as a paradigm for Russell. He relies on it and presupposes it at many points, and makes statements which seem to imply this unqualified view. But it is always a modified or qualified version which he explicitly advocates. He takes it that the most direct way in which a proposition can be about an object is simply by containing it; but he recognizes that we must have some way of making sense of cases in which a proposition is about an entity or entities which it does *not* contain—we might speak of a proposition's being *indirectly* about an entity.

From 1900 or 1901 until June 1905 the modification to the underlying picture, the way of accommodating indirect aboutness, is the theory of denoting concepts. This doctrine simply accepts that direct realism does not hold in all cases; it allows a large class of exceptions to the general rule that the entity which a proposition is about is contained in the proposition. The general rule functions as a paradigm in Russell's thought, but certain cases are allowed to violate it. For certain kinds of phrases Russell accepts a distinction in some ways analogous to Frege's distinction between *Sinn* and *Bedeutung*. The analogue of the *Sinn* of an expression is what Russell calls the *denoting concept* which it expresses, or as he later comes to say, its meaning; the analogue of the *Bedeutung* is denotation of the expression, or object it denotes, if in fact it denotes anything. (Russell explicitly accepts that it is possible that a proposition contains a denoting concept which does not in fact denote anything; see the end of this section.)

Russell's primary motive for introducing the distinction between denoting concept and denoted object[s] is to resolve the problem of generality which we emphasized above. (As we shall see, however, his attempted explanation does not succeed.) For this purpose, the crucial application of the theory is to indefinite descriptions, such as 'any prime number' or, perhaps most important, to the wholly general phrase 'any object'. From the outset, however, he also applies it to definite descriptions such as 'the President of the USA in 1999'.[22]

The theory functions like this. Where a description, definite or indefinite, occurs in a sentence, that sentence is taken to express a proposition which contains not the corresponding object or objects but rather a concept which *denotes* that object or those objects; the proposition contains a denoting concept but is about—indirectly about—the denoted object or objects. In these cases there is what we might speak of as a *representational* element in the proposition. On the other hand, a paradigmatic subject-predicate proposition for Russell, one that does not contain a denoting concept, will, as we saw, contain the subject itself. It does not contain something which represents its subject. When we employ a description, however, we express a proposition which contains an element that does in this sense *represent* the subject; this element is of course the denoting concept corresponding to the description, for that denoting concept is not itself the subject of the proposition, not what the proposition is about.[23]

In the *Principles of Mathematics*, Russell devoted considerable time and ingenuity to attempts to work out the details of this theory. A few examples will give us the flavour, at least, of the sorts of questions that occupied him. In the propositions expressed by the sentences 'All men are mortal' and 'Every man is mortal', do we have the same object or objects denoted? And if the same objects are denoted, are they denoted in the same way, or in different ways? And what of 'Any man is mortal'? Russell in fact concludes that there are differences among these cases: the denoting concept *all men* denotes all the men taken together; *every man* denotes men taken severally, not collectively; *any man* denotes an arbitrary man (see especially section 60). Questions of this sort can be multiplied indefinitely, and there is bound to be an element of arbitrariness in the answers. With few evident constraints on the theory, except for the alleged deliverances of 'direct inspection', such questions threaten to become quite vacuous.

Our concern here, however, is not with the fine details of the theory of denoting concepts but with the basic structure of that view. In particular, the

---

[22] As we shall see shortly, before he rejected the theory of denoting concepts he came to see that it could be extended to phrases other than descriptions, whether definite or indefinite—in particular, to proper names.

[23] Of course there can be propositions which are about denoting concepts, but a proposition of that sort does not contain the denoting concept which it is about, but rather some other denoting concept which denotes that denoting concept. For every instance of denoting there thus seems to be an infinite series of denoting concepts, each member past the first denoting the previous member. (See *Russell, Idealism, and the Emergence of Analytic Philosophy*, ch. 6, especially pp. 248 ff.)

theory presupposes, as fundamental and unexplained, a relation between denoting concepts and the objects or combinations of objects which they denote. The effect of this relation is to allow that a proposition which *contains* one entity—a denoting concept—is *about* another entity or entities, the denoted object or objects. Thus, we have exactly that representational element which Russell's direct realism in general hoped to avoid. He has no account of how representation, in this sense, is possible. If we ask: how, in virtue of containing a denoting concept, is the proposition *about* an entity distinct from it?—then Russell has no answer: the relation of denoting is simply stipulated to have that effect.

The theory of denoting concepts affects the Meinongian argument, discussed at the end of Section II; in the context of our concern with the theory of descriptions, this is a crucial consequence of the theory. (I put the matter this way because there is no sign that consequence was Russell's motive for introducing the theory. It is only in retrospect that this appears as the crucial aspect.) An unqualified form of direct realism would commit Russell to accepting the Meinongian argument. He does not, however, hold direct realism in unqualified form, because he holds the theory of denoting concepts. That theory permits violations of direct realism; by so doing, it undermines the Meinongian argument. If we have a sentence containing the name or the definite description '*A*' then, as before, if the sentence is meaningful it must express a proposition. Given the theory of denoting concepts, however, this proposition need not contain the object *A* itself; it may, rather, contain a denoting concept which denotes *A* (or purports to do so). There being a proposition of that kind, however, does not require that there actually be such an object as *A* (or at least the requirement is by no means obvious). It now becomes possible for the sentence '*A* is not' to be both meaningful and true—i.e., to be meaningful even though there is no such thing as *A*. The difference is that now *A* need not be counted among the constituents of the proposition; instead of containing an object (*A*), the proposition is now said to contain a denoting concept which, as it happens, does not denote anything.

The theory of denoting concepts thus undercuts the force of the Meinongian argument. Clearly, Russell does not fully appreciate that fact in *Principles*, for otherwise he would not have endorsed the argument as we saw him do (see the end of Section II above). Yet even in that book he explicitly recognizes that a denoting concept may in fact fail to denote, because there is no such thing as the purported denotation: 'A concept may denote although it does not denote anything' (Section 73, p. 73). In the period between the completion of *Principles* and his discovery of the theory of descriptions, Russell came to a clearer realization of the fact that his theory of denoting concepts blocks the Meinongian argument.

He comes to see quite clearly that this makes it possible for there to be definite descriptions which describe nothing, and also names that name nothing. The crucial text in the regard is his essay, 'The Existential Import of Propositions'.[24] There he says quite explicitly:[25]

'The present king of England' is a denoting concept denoting an individual; 'The present king of France' is a similar complex concept denoting nothing. The phrase intends to point out an individual, but fails to do so: it does not point out an unreal individual but no individual at all. The same explanation applies to mythical personages, Apollo, Priam, etc. These words all have a meaning, which can be found by looking them up in a classical dictionary; but they have not a *denotation*; there is no individual, real or imaginary, which they point out.

Russell's attitude towards the Meinongian argument at the time of *Principles* and in the period between that book and his discovery of the theory of descriptions is thus complicated. In *Principles* he advances a form of the argument as his own. Yet even in that book he explicitly accepts ideas which fairly obviously undercut it. Why does he do this? From a Russellian point of view, at least, the Meinongian argument stands or falls with the unqualified form of direct realism. As I have emphasized, this is a view which Russell often tends to assume, even though he does not actually hold it; it fits his metaphysical prejudices better than what he takes to be the alternatives. Certainly he is, in the early years after his rejection of Idealism, prejudiced in favour of an extreme form of realism. For most philosophers the Meinongian argument is something whose conclusion they would wish to avoid, if they can see a way. For Russell when he wrote *Principles*, I suspect, the conclusion was something that he welcomed, so he too easily allowed himself to avoid recognizing that his theory of denoting concepts blocks the argument. Over the subsequent few years his attitude began to shift. Even before he discovered the theory of descriptions he came to realize that he was not in fact committed to accepting the Meinongian argument, and he also started to think that there are reasons not to accept that argument.[26]

---

[24] The question of timing is important here. The manuscript in which we see Russell first coming across the crucial idea of the theory of descriptions is dated 1905, and contains, on the first folio, the note 'Begun 7 June'. The essay 'On the Existential Import of Propositions' was *published* in July 1905, and Russell's correspondence about it dates from April and May of that year. (For these points, see *Collected Papers*, iv. 359, 480–1.) These facts, as well as internal evidence, make it clear that the essay was written while Russell still held the theory of denoting concepts.

[25] The passage quoted is at p. 399 of *Mind* for 1905, and p. 487 of *Collected Papers*, iv.

[26] Early in 1903 Russell studied Meinong's work closely, and wrote a long article on the subject. The article is generally very laudatory, and accepts Meinong's ontological views, which are similar to those which Russell held in *Principles*. Russell does, however, begin to find problems with those views. It is thus a reasonable speculation that it was his thinking through these issues in connection with Meinong which led to a shift in his own ontological views.

V. THE THEORY OF DESCRIPTIONS IN RUSSELLIAN CONTEXT

We now have in place the background we need to understand the change that took place when Russell abandoned the theory of denoting concepts, and adopted the theory of descriptions. One important point here is negative. It is—or at least was until quite recently—very widely believed that Russell adopted the theory of descriptions in order not to have to accept the present King of France, the golden mountain, and other nonexistent *concreta*; more generally, it was widely believed that he adopted the theory in order to avoid the conclusion of the Meinongian argument. This idea is, indeed, asserted by Russell himself, although writing over fifty years later. In *My Philosophical Development* he says:

> [Meinong] argued, if you say that the golden mountain does not exist, it is obvious that there is something that you are saying does not exist—namely the golden mountain; therefore the golden mountain must subsist in some shadowy Platonic realm of being, for otherwise your statement that the golden mountain does not exist would have no meaning. I confess that, until I hit upon the theory of descriptions, his argument seemed to me convincing. (p. 84)

This statement seems quite mistaken, for reasons that we emphasized at the end of the previous section. The view that Russell held in the years before he adopted the theory of descriptions also enabled him to avoid golden mountains in shadowy Platonic realms; his 'Existential Import of Propositions' shows that he was aware of this fact. That a theory has this result may, by mid-1905, have become for him a criterion of adequacy, but it is a criterion that is equally met by the theory of denoting concepts. It cannot, therefore, be Russell's reason, or even one among a number of reasons he had, for discarding that theory and adopting the theory of descriptions.

We cannot then suppose that Russell adopted the theory of descriptions in order to avoid the Meinongian argument—in spite of his own later statements. What other reasons can we attribute to him? Let us distinguish four.

First, as we saw in section I, the theory of descriptions gives us an analysis of definite descriptions—and of names, if we treat them as disguised definite descriptions—which is well integrated with the needs of logic. Obviously correct inferences involving definite descriptions become a matter of ordinary logic, as antecedently understood. Failure of reference is treated without resort to truth-value gaps, which would complicate logic. No doubt these matters carried considerable weight with Russell, but I shall not discuss them further here.

Second, the theory of denoting concepts is subject to considerable internal difficulties. Some of these are simply about what denotes what—the sorts of questions indicated in Section III, above. Others concern threatened incoherences in the very idea of such a theory. In 'On Denoting', Russell argues for the theory of descriptions by using difficulties of this sort as reasons to reject the theory of denoting concepts.[27] This passage of 'On Denoting' is notoriously difficult, and commentators have not arrived at any agreed understanding of it. We can gain some inkling of the difficulties faced by the theory of denoting concepts by seeing that a proposition which is *about* a given denoting concept cannot contain that denoting concept, for then, of course, it would be about its denotation. There are no propositions which are about denoting concepts in what for Russell remains the paradigmatic way, i.e., directly about them, by containing them. A proposition which is about a denoting concept must be indirectly about it, by containing another denoting concept which denotes it. A consequence of this is that there must be an infinite hierarchy of denoting concepts, each one after the first denoting the previous member of the hierarchy. To investigate the details of the difficulties that Russell finds in that theory would occupy more space than we have to spare.[28]

Third, the theory of denoting concepts was simply not successful on Russell's own terms. Although he exploited it, more or less successfully, for various other purposes, it does not in fact succeed in performing the task for which he primarily introduced it. This task, as we saw, was to explain generality. The idea here was that one could explain the proposition expressed by 'All prime numbers are odd' by saying that it contains the denoting concept, *all prime numbers* (or possibly that it should be understood as containing an unrestricted variable; in that case we explain the variable by means of the denoting concept *any term*, and we take the proposition as a whole to say of any term that if it is a prime number then it is odd). Given the mechanism of denoting, this explanation seems to work well for examples of this kind. As Russell himself came to see in *Principles*, however, the same sort of explanation cannot be extended to more complex cases, at least not without auxiliary assumptions which he was not prepared to make. In particular, suppose we have a sentence containing two or more variables (unrestricted variables, let's say). In that case we can hardly explain each variable by means of the denoting concept *any term*, for the distinctness of the variables is crucial. Yet, from within the theory of denoting concepts, no other means of explanation readily suggests itself. (See *Principles*, chs VII and VIII, and especially section 93, pp. 93–4, for these difficulties.)

---

[27] Russell's ostensible target here is Frege's distinction between the *Sinn* of an expression (its sense, more or less equivalent to its meaning, in Russell's sense) and its *Bedeutung* (the object to which it refers, more or less equivalent to its denotation in Russell's sense). His arguments, however, apply more clearly to his own distinction between denoting concept and denoted object than they do to its Fregean analogue.

[28] For an attempt to come to terms with these arguments of 'On Denoting' in detail see Pakaluk, 'The Interpretation of Russell's "Gray's *Elegy*" Argument', 37–65. See also Noonan, 'The "Gray's *Elegy*" Argument—and Others' and Kremer, 'The Argument of "On Denoting" '.

Fourth, and I believe most fundamentally, is the fact that the theory of denoting concepts was an anomaly from the outset. It flatly contradicted the direct realism which issued from Russell's most general philosophical views; it simply stipulated a class of exceptions to direct realism, with no explanation of how exceptions are possible. I shall enlarge upon this point shortly.

There are important connections among these various reasons. First, the fact that the theory of denoting concepts cannot give a satisfactory explanation of generality makes it possible for Russell to adopt the theory of descriptions without loss. This latter theory begins by assuming generality as a primitive and unexplained idea. It does not attempt an explanation of generality, nor does it contain the materials from which an explanation of that sort might be constructed. If the theory of denoting concepts did in fact explain generality, then giving up that theory would be a considerable loss. As it does not, however, Russell is free to abandon the theory of denoting concepts as soon as he sees another way of dealing with the problems other than generality which had led him to that theory in the first place. Second, it is the general background of Russell's direct realism which lies behind the detailed arguments which Russell gives, in 'On Denoting', against the theory of denoting concepts. Only in the context of Russell's views in general can we hope to arrive at a satisfactory understanding of those arguments, which should therefore not be thought of as operating independently of those more general considerations. It is to those considerations (and hence to the fourth of the above reasons) that we now turn.

As a first step here we can say: the theory of descriptions avoids the representational element which plays the central role in the theory of denoting concepts. (Here and in what follows I ignore the complications arising from the fact that Russell now assumes generality as a primitive notion. It might be said that this fact means that he does not, after all, eliminate the representational element, but merely reduces it all to that one case.) At first sight, the claim that the theory of descriptions eliminates representation may seem odd, even paradoxical, for the theory of descriptions does not seem to eliminate what we called 'indirect aboutness'. When subject to the new method of analysis, the sentence 'The President of the USA in 1999 is a Democrat' is still about Bill Clinton, and the proposition which it expresses still does not contain that man, so the sentence is still indirectly about him. And one might think that indirect aboutness invariably demands a representational element. But this is not so (unless, again, one takes the variable as such an element). The difference is that as analyzed by the theory of descriptions, the sentence is directly about its constituents, and is indirectly about Bill Clinton in virtue of being directly about those constituents. Most obviously: the sentence is directly about the property, *being President of the USA in 1999* (no doubt this property is complex, and must be subject to further analysis; but let us ignore that point). And it says of this property that one and only one thing satisfies it or falls under it (and that thing is a Democrat). That is how it gets to be (indirectly) about Bill Clinton: by being (directly) about a property which he and only he satisfies.

Contrast this with the way that sentence looks when analyzed according to the theory of denoting concepts. On that analysis the sentence is not directly about anything. It is not in any sense *about* the denoting concept *the President of the USA in 1999*. Rather it contains that concept without being about it. This is why the role of the denoting concept is a representational one: its only role is to point to another object, which the proposition is indirectly about.

This fact—that the proposition contains an entity which it is in no sense about—is, it seems to me, quite contrary to the spirit of Russell's direct realism. The 'pointing to' involved in the theory of denoting concepts, moreover, relies on the mysterious and *ad hoc* relation of denoting. In virtue of containing *this* entity (a denoting concept) the proposition is about *that* entity, with no story about how this is possible beyond the bare statement that the one entity denotes the other, i.e., stands towards it in a relation which just does have the desired effect. When the sentence is analyzed according to the theory of descriptions, by contrast, the crucial relation is that of an object's satisfying or falling under a property, and this is not in the same way mysterious or *ad hoc*.

In eliminating the representational element of the theory of denoting concepts, the theory of descriptions thus restores Russell's direct realism—it enables him to avoid a large class of exceptions to that paradigm. This is not to say that the triumph of direct realism is complete in Russell's view after the theory of descriptions. That theory, after all, begins by taking for granted the notion of generality, the very issue which first prompted him to make an exception to his paradigm by invoking the theory of denoting concepts. Generality continues not to fit the paradigm; Russell simply gives up the attempt to explain it. On the other hand, the theory of denoting concepts, as we briefly saw, also does not actually succeed in explaining generality either, so Russell certainly has every reason to prefer the theory of descriptions.

VI. THE SIGNIFICANCE OF THE THEORY IN RUSSELL'S PHILOSOPHY

What is the significance of the theory of descriptions for Russell's philosophy more generally? One major point here is summed up in the slogan: definite descriptions are incomplete symbols. What Russell means by an incomplete symbol is, he says, 'a symbol which is not supposed to have any meaning in isolation, but is only defined in certain contexts' (*Principia*, i. 66). Why should we think that, according to the theory of descriptions, a definite description has no meaning in isolation? Russell's fundamental idea of meaning is referential: a symbol has a meaning if it stands for something, and the thing for which it stands *is* its meaning. There is a certain sense in which a definite description may stand for something—'The President of the USA in 1999' we may say, stands for a certain man. But according to the theory of descriptions, a definite description does not function referentially. In a proposition expressed by a sentence using a definite description, that is to say, there is no entity for which the definite description stands. The proposition expressed by 'The President of the USA in 1999' does not contain Bill Clinton. Nor does it contain a denoting concept which denotes him. There is no entity in that proposition for which the definite description stands. That is what Russell means by saying that definite descriptions have no meaning in isolation. Sentences in which definite descriptions occur, however, often succeed in expressing propositions: the sentences as wholes *are* meaningful. This is what Russell means by saying that definite descriptions, like other incomplete symbols, are 'defined in certain contexts'. An incomplete symbol makes a systematic contribution to a sentence in which it occurs, only it does not do so by indicating an entity which is contained in the proposition which the sentence expresses.

The idea of an incomplete symbol made an immense difference to Russell's thought. Before 'On Denoting' he had generally taken the unit of analysis to be subsentential. A referring term, or a predicate, is analyzed to see exactly what entity it stands for. A paradigm here is the analysis of numbers in terms of classes: we understand a number-word by seeing that it should be taken as standing for a certain class. Another way of putting the same point is to say that analysis will, at least in general, leave unaltered the overall form of the sentence being analyzed. The constituents of the proposition may not be those suggested by the parts of the sentence, but each part of the sentence will generally stand for some constituent in the proposition, and the constituents will generally be arranged in the sort of way suggested by the arrangement of the parts of the sentence. Thus in *Principles of Mathematics* he says:

> The correctness of our philosophical analysis of a proposition may . . . be usefully checked by the exercise of assigning the meaning of each word in the sentence expressing the proposition. On the whole, grammar seems to me to bring us much nearer to a correct logic than the current opinions of philosophers . . . (p. 42, section 46)

After 'On Denoting', Russell's idea of analysis is quite different. He comes to assume that analysis of a sentence will generally reveal that it expresses a proposition of a quite different logical form. The unit of analysis becomes the sentence, and Russell's attention is focused on the logical forms of propositions. The analysis of sentences containing definite descriptions is a paradigm here: the sentence has subject-predicate form, but analysis in accordance with the theory of descriptions reveals that it expresses a proposition which is an existential quantification.

A consequence of Russell's new view is that he comes to take it for granted that our ordinary language is generally misleading.[29] In sharp contrast to his view in *Principles*, he holds that our sentences generally have forms quite different from the real forms of the propositions which they express. A primary task of philosophy thus becomes that of getting past the misleading surface structure of language to the underlying structure. Here we have a crucial contribution to an important theme in twentieth-century analytic philosophy quite generally: the idea that language is systematically misleading, in philosophically significant ways. We also have one of the points of origin for the more specific idea of a contrast between the surface structure of language and its deep structure, or between grammatical form and underlying logical form. Along with this, however, Russell is also forced to pay more attention to language (in the sense of surface structure) and symbolism. In *Principles* language, in this sense, was never at the centre of his attention; he treated it as a more or less transparent medium through which we can perceive the underlying reality which is our concern. Now, however, he has to be more self-conscious about symbolism, if only to avoid being misled by it. In a course of lectures given early in 1918, Russell said:

There is a great deal of importance to philosophy in the theory of symbolism, a good deal more than at one time I thought. I think the importance is almost entirely negative, i.e., the importance lies in the fact that unless you are fairly self-conscious about symbols . . . you will find yourself attributing to the thing properties which only belong to the symbol. (p. 166)

This shift of attention towards language—towards the actual words spoken or written—was to be of the greatest importance both for Russell's own thought and for that of philosophers who came after him.

A further aspect of the importance of the idea of an incomplete symbol in Russell's thought is simply that it goes along with the notion of contextual definition—that is, that in order to define a symbol it is sufficient to define the contribution that it makes to all the sentences in which it may occur. This was an idea that Russell exploited increasingly over the ensuring ten years, perhaps most notably with his definition of classes in terms of propositional functions.

---

[29] Thus Wittgenstein in the *Tractatus* says that it is Russell's service to have shown that the apparent form of the sentence need not be its real form: 'Russells Verdienst ist es, gezeight zu haben, dass die scheinbare logische Form des Satzes nicht seine wirkliche sein muss'. *Tractatus Logico-Philsophicus*, 4.0031.

According to this definition, a subject-predicate sentence whose subject is a class-symbol is to be understood as an existential quantification, asserting the existence of a propositional function satisfying certain conditions.

Russell's idea of an incomplete symbol is clearly new with 'On Denoting'. According to the theory of denoting concepts definite descriptions *do* stand for constituents of propositions, namely denoting concepts; hence they are not incomplete symbols. In the case of other Russellian ideas which are also associated with the theory of descriptions, however, the contrast is less clear-cut. I have in mind here Russell's views having to do with names, acquaintance, and the elimination of non-existent *concreta*. These views could have been developed in the context of the theory of denoting concepts and to a limited extent were. But it was the theory of descriptions which provided the context within which the views were developed in detail. To some extent we may have here coincidences of timing: Russell's views on a number of related topics began to shift, or at least to become sharper, at around the same time that he developed the theory of descriptions or perhaps a little earlier. This may not entirely be a matter of coincidence, however. Russell's theory of denoting concepts was, as we have emphasized, in rather open conflict with his fundamental metaphysical tenets. Under these circumstances, one might expect him to shrink from taking steps which would require heavy use of that theory. The theory of descriptions (except for the worry about generality) was, by contrast, right in line with his basic views, and it is not surprising that he was ready to exploit it to the full.

Let us begin with the question of non-existent *concreta*—whether there *is*, in some sense, such a thing as the planet Vulcan or the present King of France. As we saw, the theory of denoting concepts in fact gives Russell the means to avoid accepting that there are any such things. He can say that whenever we appear to have a proposition containing a non-existent *concretum*, what we really have is a proposition containing a denoting concept which lacks a denotation. Russell, as we saw, came to appreciate this possibility before 'On Denoting' but, whether by coincidence of timing or not, he does not fully exploit it. Once the theory of descriptions is in place, by contrast, he has no hesitation in exploiting that theory to rid his ontology of non-existent *concreta*. What appears to be a definite description of such an object is, of course, analyzed to show that the proposition does not contain the alleged object, but only properties which are claimed to be uniquely satisfied. More strikingly, *names* which appear to name such objects must be treated in the same fashion. They are, on this view, not genuine proper names at all, but rather disguised definite descriptions. Understanding a sentence in which a (non-genuine) name of this sort appears does not involve simply fastening the name to an object with which one is acquainted. It involves, rather, having in mind (being acquainted with) a property (possibly quite complex), and asserting that it is uniquely satisfied.

How widely is this tactic to be applied? Obviously, it is to be applied whenever we have a sentence which appears or purports to be about a concrete object which in fact does not exist. What of sentences which appear to be about concrete objects which, as far as the speaker knows, may or may not exist? Russell seems to think that the analysis of a proposition should be available to one who understands it. But clearly he does not think that merely by analyzing propositions one can tell whether some supposed object in fact exists. So the general rule is: if there is a proposition apparently about a certain concrete object, but the existence of that object is at all open to doubt, then the proposition is to be analyzed in accordance with the theory of descriptions, i.e., as not really containing the object after all. So the presence of a name in a sentence does not indicate the presence of the named object in the corresponding proposition unless we have a guarantee that the object really exists. (Without such a guarantee the name is thus not, by Russell's standards, a genuine proper name at all.)

What could give us such a guarantee? From within Russell's thought, the answer is easy: our being *acquainted* with an object of course guarantees that it is real (and hence, if it is a concrete object, that it exists). In a proposition which I can understand, all the constituents must be entities with which I am acquainted. At the end of 'On Denoting' Russell claims that this principle—sometimes known as the Principle of Acquaintance—is a *result* of the theory of descriptions.[30] Superficially this claim is quite misleading. In one sense the Principle of Acquaintance is by no means new in Russell's thought with the theory of descriptions; it is implicit, at least, in *Principles*, and I think Russell would have accepted it at any time from 1900 onwards. But in a deeper sense there is something new. Russell's denial of non-existent *concreta* goes along with a difference in the role that acquaintance plays in his thought. (This new role, and the denial of non-existent *concreta*, perhaps could have been worked out in terms of the theory of denoting concepts, but in fact were not.)

In *Principles* Russell took a very lax attitude towards acquaintance: if the exigencies of his theorizing required that we be acquainted with objects of a certain kind, then he was willing to assert that we are in fact acquainted with objects of that kind. The notion of acquaintance, we might say, functioned to deflect epistemological worries but did not impose any constraints on Russell's thought. This changes from 1905 on; over the following decade the constraints imposed by the notion of acquaintance come to dominate his views. The denial of non-existent *concreta* is the first step in this process. We are not acquainted with the (alleged) planet Vulcan. By the argument which we indicated above, it seems that we cannot be acquainted with the (actual) planet Mars either, since we have no absolute epistemological guarantee of its existence. But then it is clearly an

---

[30] The principle is reiterated in 'Knowledge by Acquaintance', without the claim that it follows from the theory of descriptions; see *Collected Papers*, vi. 154.

open question: with what (concrete) objects are we acquainted? Once Russell's attention is focused on this question he draws narrower and narrower limits to the scope of our acquaintance with concrete objects. (In the case of abstract objects, however, it is notable that Russell continues to think that acquaintance has a very wide scope; here, it seems, the notion continues to impose no independent constraints.)

Russell's thought after 1905 (at least up to and including his lectures on the 'Philosophy of Logical Atomism', given in the first few months of 1918) thus makes heavy use of the theory of descriptions. He no longer took at face value most—or, as time went by almost all—words which appear to refer to concrete objects, the most familiar words there are. Instead of being thought of as names of the relevant objects, such words were treated as definite descriptions, and analyzed accordingly. He invoked the notion of a *sense-datum* in order to have appropriate objects for us to be acquainted with. When I look at and touch a familiar table, say, what I am actually acquainted with is not the table itself but certain immediate deliverances of the senses—a certain coloured shape and a certain sensation of hardness, perhaps. A sentence which is, as we ordinarily say, about the table, in fact expresses a proposition which does not contain the table itself but rather contains immediate deliverances of the senses—sense-data— and uses them to give a definite description of the table. Here we have a vivid illustration of the point made in connection with incomplete symbols: most sentences that we utter, perhaps in the end just about all of them, express propositions whose real constituents, and real structure, are quite different from what is suggested by the superficial structure of the sentence uttered. Language is systematically misleading.

VII. OBJECTIONS TO THE THEORY

The concern of this essay, as of this volume, is with Russell; to this point we have dealt primarily with Russell's reasons for adopting the theory of descriptions and with the significance of that theory in his thought. In this final section, however, we shall shift focus and consider objections made to Russell's theory since 1950.[31] The discussion will, necessarily, be very brief; the aim is merely to give

---

[31] We should also point out that by no means all references to Russell's theory in the second half of the twentieth-century have been unfavourable. On the contrary, a number of authors adhere to the theory, and put it to their own uses. Perhaps most notable is Quine; see the references in n. 2, above. Not surprisingly, various authors have put the theory to various philosophical uses. See the present author's 'Analysis and Analytic Philosophy'.

Russell's theory as an analysis of definite descriptions (though not of names) is the subject of a sustained defense in Neale, *Descriptions*. I have to some extent drawn on that work in part i) of the present section, and on Mark Sainsbury's 'Philosophical Logic' in both parts i) and ii).

some idea of the best-known objections to Russell's theory. These objections can be divided into two sorts: those that concern the analysis of definite descriptions and those that concern the idea that some or all proper names can be treated as if they were definite descriptions. It will be convenient to discuss these separately.

(i) Objections to the theory as an analysis of definite descriptions

One objection of this sort is put forward by Strawson, who argued that Russell's theory is mistaken or misleading about what we ordinarily mean by sentences of the form 'The F is G'. Such a sentence, Strawson claims, does not *assert* that there is one and only thing which is F, rather it *presupposes* that fact. If someone said that 'The King of France is wise', then we would not say that he had said something false (as we should, on Russell's view), nor, of course, would we say that he had said something true. Rather, we 'would be inclined, with some hesitation' to say that 'the question of whether his statement was true or false simply *did not arise*' (*Logico-Linguistic Papers*, 12).

It is hard to assess this objection. One fundamental point at stake is how we are to think of the relation between ordinary language and the notation of modern logic, and on this point we have a true missing of minds. The advantages of the sort of method of analysis that Russell adopts, it might be said, are precisely that they make explicit what is otherwise merely presupposed—that is, they replace presupposition with assertion. But this is the very thing to which Strawson objects. We can think of the advantages of the theory of descriptions as arising from the fact that it shows us how we can smoothly incorporate the idiom of definite descriptions into logic, with corresponding gains in clarity. Standard modern logic, the logic inherited from Frege and Russell, leaves no room for the category of the merely presupposed, as opposed to the asserted. Strawson rejects the theory of descriptions on the grounds that it does not do justice to the nuances of ordinary usage. Advocates of the theory, such as Quine, may insist upon the benefits of the theory in facilitating inference and may claim that Strawson's concern with ordinary usage is not to the point.[32] This may seem to leave matters at a complete impasse, but there is more that can be said on each side.

The Strawsonian side might emphasize that there are systems of logic which take some account of the idea of presupposition.[33] This fact holds out the prospect

---

[32] Besides the section of *Word and Object* referred to in n. 2, see also Quine's review of Strawson's *Introduction to Logical Theory* in Quine's *Ways of Paradox*, 137–57. Reacting to what he takes to be Strawson's general attitude, Quine says there: 'even the humdrum spinning out of elementary logical principles in modern logic brings insights, concerning the general relation of premise to conclusion in actual science and common sense, which are denied to men who scruple to disturb a particle of natural language in its full philological correctness,' (*Ways of Paradox*, 149).

[33] See, for example, van Frassen, 'Singular Terms, Truth-Value Gaps, and Free Logic', and 'Presupposition, Implication, and Self-Reference'.

of the best of both worlds: enabling us to have the advantages of representing our ordinary discourse in logical terms without giving up on the idea of presupposition which is, presumably, part of that discourse. It may be doubted, however, whether any system of logic will really do what the Strawsonian wants. It may be doubted, that is to say, whether it is possible to do full justice to the nuance and subtlety of ordinary discourse while also imposing on that discourse the sort of clarity of form that would enable us to subject it to the mathematical treatment of modern (Russellian and post-Russellian) logic.

On the Russellian or Quinean side, it may be possible to undermine the idea that ordinary discourse is really committed to the notion of presupposition. Strawson bases his claim upon the fact that we do not actually say, of a sentence containing a definite description which we know to be empty, that it is *false*; we tend to use more complicated terms of criticism. For all that, it might be said, such sentences *are* false. The reason we do not call them false, according to this suggestion, is not that they are not false, or even that we do not hold them to be false. It is, rather, that calling them false is liable to be misleading, by suggesting that they are false in the most straightforward way (by there being a unique F which is not G). Our reluctance simply to say of such a sentence that it is false is, on this account, to be explained in terms of our wish to avoid misleading our audience—a reluctance which therefore does not suggest that the sentence is in fact anything other than false. This line of thought gets some encouragement and theoretical backing from ideas of Paul Grice's.[34] Grice emphasizes that the thought conveyed in a sentence is often not, or not only, what the sentence literally says. Thus, to adapt his famous (though by now anachronistic) example. Suppose I am asked to give my opinion of a student of mine who is being considered for a position teaching philosophy, and I say: 'He has beautiful handwriting, and is always punctual'. If that is all that I say, then the reader of my letter will quite rightly infer that I have a poor opinion of the student's ability. Yet that is certainly not what my letter literally says, as is shown by the fact that I could without contradiction add a paragraph saying how able the student is, what a good philosopher, and how well read. Similarly, it might be said, our reluctance to say of a sentence such as 'The King of France is bald' that it is false, and nothing else, arises from the fact that we could reasonably expect our audience to infer, from our saying that, that there is a King of France (or at least that we think there is); we wish to prevent that inference. So our reluctance to *say* that the sentence is false, even when all the facts are before us, may be compatible with the sentence's in fact being false.

Another kind of criticism of the theory of descriptions arises from the fact that our definite descriptions are very often radically incomplete. Strawson gives as

---

[34] See especially his 'Logic and Conversation', *in Studies in the Ways of Words*.

an example the sentence: 'The table is covered with books' (*Logico-Linguistic Papers*, 14). Certainly there are contexts in which this sentence seems to express something true; yet there are, of course a large number of tables in the world, not only one. The response to this sort of case is that much of what we say is dependent upon the context in which we say it, and not only when we are using definite descriptions. (Russell was largely concerned with the context-independent propositions of mathematics, and so perhaps gave this point less weight than it should carry.) On the way to a party with a group of friends I may say 'No one knows the street number'; once safely at the party I may say 'There's no more wine'. In each case, the remark may be perfectly appropriate, yet each is obviously false unless one supposes some tacit restriction—no one *in my group of friends* knows the street number; there is no more wine *at the party*. In the case of the table, if the remark is a sensible one then most likely we are in a room containing only one table, or one table in the room is more noticeable than any other. Yet perhaps there are cases where the room contains two tables, equally noticeable but for the fact that one of them is covered with books. In such a case 'the table' is perhaps being used to mean 'that table'. Perhaps this usage can be dismissed as incorrect; if we accept it as correct, then we have here a limited class of exceptions to the theory of descriptions.

Another category of criticism of the theory of descriptions is associated with Keith Donnellan.[35] Suppose we are at a party, and I see a man, looking slightly inebriated, drinking a clear liquid from a martini glass. (Suppose further, if you like, that there are open bottles of gin and vermouth on the table beside him, and that everyone else in the room is, quite evidently, drinking red wine.) I know that he is a famous philosopher, and say to you: 'The man drinking the martini is a famous philosopher'. In fact, however, his glass contains water.

Building on this kind of example, Donnellan distinguishes two kinds of uses of definite descriptions: the *attributive* use, which is as the theory of descriptions claims, and the *referential* use, in which a definite description is used simply to refer to some person or thing, without regard for whether the descriptive predicate in fact holds uniquely, or holds at all, of the object being referred to. On Donnellan's account, the example of the previous paragraph is a referential use. I use the phrase to refer to the inebriated-looking man with the martini glass and go on to say something about him; since he in fact is a famous philosopher, my utterance is true. As interpreted by the theory of descriptions, by contrast, the utterance is false (since there is no man—within the relevant context—drinking a martini).

Donnellan appeals to the alleged fact that, in the above sort of example, the utterance clearly is a true one. But a number of philosophers who have discussed

---

[35] See his 'Reference and Definite Descriptions', from which the following example is adapted.

this sort of case dispute this claim. They appeal to the same Gricean distinction which we invoked above. Clearly, one of the things I mean when I make my remark, is that that man, the one we can both see, is a famous philosopher. Perhaps, in context, it is clear that this is the thing I mostly mean to convey. Yet this fact is compatible with the idea that what I literally say is something else, something in accord with the way the sentence reads according to the theory of descriptions. Further plausibility accrues to this idea from the thought that what I say at the party has both something right about it and something wrong. The Russellian line, as supplemented by Grice, seems able to do justice to this: what I literally say is false, but what I clearly mean to convey is correct. Donnellan's line, however, seems harder pressed to explain why there is anything at all wrong with what I say.

Both Donnellan and his opponents here agree that there is such a thing as what I literally say in such a case. Perhaps it is fitting to close this section on a note of partial scepticism about this assumption. If we are to fit our language into the scheme of logic (of any logic), then we have to find a definite claim made by any given utterance. To think that Russell's theory gives us as good a way of doing this as any is compatible with acknowledging that any such schematization will distort our ordinary thought and language, if only because in casual contexts we are not as definite as logic requires.

(ii) Objections to the theory as a way of treating ordinary proper names

Our concern here is with objections not to Russell's analysis of definite descriptions but rather to the idea that it can be extended to ordinary proper names, via the claim that names are 'disguised definite descriptions'. All the objections that I shall mention are to be found in Kripke's *Naming and Necessity*.[36]

One objection here concerns the behaviour of proper names and definite descriptions in counterfactual or modal contexts. Suppose I say, for example,

1) Alexander Fleming might have died in childhood

I am inviting my audience to imagine circumstances which (fortunately) did not actually occur. To whom, in those circumstances, does the name 'Alexander Fleming' refer? To Alexander Fleming, the same person to whom it refers in fact, in the actual circumstances. But consider the description, 'the inventor of penicillin', which is perhaps the most plausible description to use if we think of the name as a disguised definite description. To whom does that description refer in the imagined circumstances? *Not* to Alexander Fleming, for in those circumstances he would not have been the inventor of penicillin. Kripke puts the point

---

[36] Kripke, *Naming and Necessity*.

by saying that proper names are 'rigid designators', meaning that they designate the same thing in all possible circumstances; whereas a definite description is not, for it may designate various distinct objects in various counterfactual situations.[37] (Hence, he of course concludes, proper names cannot be satisfactorily analyzed as definite descriptions.)

Kripke claims that this distinction can make a difference. Contrast 1) with:

2) The inventor of penicillin might have died in childhood

1) seems to be straightforwardly true (at least as straightforwardly as claims about what might have been are). 2), however, is less clear. If it is making the claim that penicillin might have been discovered by a child genius who then died young we may be inclined to dismiss it as false; discovering penicillin in fact took more scientific sophistication, and more time, than any child could have had. Clearly, however, this is not the only or even the most natural way in which to construe 2). Perhaps because we tend to interpret what we are told charitably, we would be more likely to construe it as saying that the person who in fact (that is, in the actual circumstances, not in the counterfactual circumstances we are being asked to imagine) discovered penicillin might have died in childhood. This ambiguity can be captured by Russell's analysis. On the first reading, less plausible both as a reading and as a truth, we have:

3) It might have been the case that: $(\exists x)$ [x discovered penicillin & $(\forall y)$(y discovered penicillin $\supset$ y = x) & x died in childhood]

On the second, more plausible, reading we have:

4) $(\exists x)$ [x discovered penicillin & $(\forall y)$(y discovered penicillin $\supset$ y = x) & it might have been the case that: x died in childhood][38]

The difference is one of *scope*; in 3) the modal operator ('might have') has larger scope than the definite description; in 4) it is the other way around.

Note that 4) achieves the same effect as 1). This has led some to claim that there is nothing more to the distinction between rigid and non-rigid designators than that the former must always be read with largest scope.[39] On that view, Kripke's argument has little force against the view that names are disguised definite descriptions; it merely shows that they are disguised definite descriptions which

---

[37] In this explanation of the notion of a rigid designator I have attempted to avoid the technical, and philosophically disputed, interpretations of modality which are usually invoked in such explanations.
[38] This sentence involves quantifying in to the intensional context created by the phrase, 'it might have been the case that', i.e., a quantifier outside the scope of that phrase binds a variable within its scope. The difficulties involved in such cases have been forcefully argued by Quine. See especially his 'Quantifiers and Propositional Attitudes', reprinted as essay 17 of his *Ways of Paradox*, and 'Intensions Revisited', reprinted as essay 13 of his *Theories and Things*. It should be noted that Quine has little sympathy with the sorts of considerations that seem to give rise to a need for rigid designators, or for definite descriptions to be read in a way that involves quantifying in to intensional contexts.
[39] See for example Dummett, *Frege: Philosophy of Language*, especially pp. 113 f.

must be read with largest scope. Kripke denies that his distinction amounts to no more than a distinction in scope, and he adduces various arguments to this effect. One is that the distinction applies when we have a simple sentence—one lacking modal operators, and to which no scope distinctions apply—which is evaluated for truth or falsehood in counterfactual circumstances. (You say: Alexander Fleming was a great scientist. I reply: Yes, but that would not have been true if he had died in childhood.)

Another ground on which Kripke objects to using Russell's theory to analyze names is that people often use names although they have in mind nothing like an identifying description of the thing or person they are talking about. Kripke's example is the physicist, Feynman. Non-specialists are unlikely to be able to produce a definite description of him. Nevertheless, Kripke says: 'The man in the street . . . may . . . still use the name "Feynman". When asked he will say: well he's a physicist or something. He may not think that this picks out anyone uniquely. I still think he uses "Feynman" as a name for Feynman' (p. 81). It is, however, unclear that Kripke's man in the street really does lack identifying knowledge of Feynman, because he knows enough to use his name. The description: 'famous physicist called "Feynman" ' presumably applies uniquely to Feynman. Russell, indeed, seems to have anticipated this point. When we talk of Julius Caesar, he says: 'We have in mind some *description* of Julius Caesar . . . perhaps, merely "the man whose name was *Julius Caesar*" '.[40] Kripke objects to this idea on the grounds of circularity, but it not clear that his objections are conclusive. If they are not, then one might use Russell's theory to get a picture not unlike that which Kripke himself suggests: some people have identifying descriptions of (say) Feynman which are independent of uses of his name; others (most of us) do not, but refer to him as the person called 'Feynman', where what we mean is the person so-called by members of the first group.

The last objection I shall consider arises in a different way. Most people who have an identifying description of Gödel which is *not* dependent upon his being called 'Gödel' probably identify him as the person who proved the incompleteness of any formalization of arithmetic, or the person who proved the completeness of first-order logic. But, Kripke asks, what if the man called 'Kurt Gödel', who held a position at the Institute for Advanced Study in Princeton, did not in fact prove those results? What if he stole them from someone else, who died 'under mysterious circumstances' (p. 84)? Nevertheless, Kripke maintains, our ordinary uses of the name 'Gödel' would refer to the man who lived in Princeton, not the one who died in Vienna in the nineteen-thirties. Again, the example is compelling; again, however, it is not entirely clear that it shows as much as

---

[40] *Problems*, 91–2 (= *Problems*, 2nd edn., 59). cf. a similar passage in 'Knowledge by Acquaintance', 155.

Kripke claims. For one thing, it may be that 'the man who was called "Gödel" ' is a crucial part of the identifying description of Gödel for all of us who did not actually know that famous logician. For another, the non-expert would perhaps make no very clear distinction between identifying Gödel as 'the man who proved such-and-such' and identifying him as 'the man who is widely thought to have proved such-and-such'. The experts to whom the second description implicitly defers would presumably have other ways of referring to Gödel, which would survive any discoveries about the true provenance of the theorems attributed to him.[41]

---

[41] For their comments on an earlier draft, I am indebted to Nicholas Griffin and to Thomas Ricketts.

ABBREVIATIONS

Russell

Collected Papers, i	*The Collected Papers of Bertrand Russell,* i: *Cambridge Essays, 1888–99*, ed. Kenneth Blackwell et al.
Collected Papers, iii	*The Collected Papers of Bertrand Russell*, iii: *Towards the 'Principles of Mathematics', 1900–02*
Collected Papers, iv	*The Collected Papers of Bertrand Russell,* iv: *Foundations of Logic, 1903–5*, ed. Alistair Urquhart, with the assistance of Albert Lewis
Collected Papers, vi	*The Collected Papers of Bertrand Russell*, vi: Logical and Philosophical Papers: 1909–13, ed. John G. Slater
Collected Papers, vii	*The Collected Papers of Bertrand Russell*, vii: *Theory of Knowledge: The 1913 Manuscript*, ed. Elizabeth Ramsden Eames, in collaboration with Kenneth Blackwell
Collected Papers, viii	*The Collected Papers of Bertrand Russell*, viii: *The Philosophy of Logical Atomism and Other Essays, 1914–19*, ed. John G. Slater
Foundations of Geometry	*An Essay on the Foundations of Geometry*
IMP	*Introduction to Mathematical Philosophy*
'Knowledge by Acquaintance'	'Knowledge by Acquaintance and Knowledge by Description'
Leibniz	*A Critical Exposition of the Philosophy of Leibniz*
'Mathematical Logic'	'Mathematical Logic as Based on the Theory of Types'
'Meinong'	'Meinong's Theory of Complexes and Assumptions'
OKEW	*Our Knowledge of the External World as a Field for Scientific Method in Philosophy*
Principles	*Principles of Mathematics*
Problems	*Problems of Philosophy*

Whitehead and Russell

Principia	*Principia Mathematica*

BIBLIOGRAPHY

Ayer, A. J., *Bertrand Russell* (London: Fontana, 1972).

Baker, G. P., and Hacker, P. M. S., *Frege: Logical Excavations* (Oxford: Basil Blackwell, 1984).

Berlin, Isaiah, *The Magus of the North* (New York: Farrar, Straus and Giroux, 1993).

Biletzki, Anat, and Matar Anat (eds.), *The Story of Analytic Philosophy* (London: Routledge, 1998).

Black, Max, *A Companion to Wittgenstein's 'Tractatus'* (Ithaca, NY: Cornell University Press, 1964).

—— 'Russell's Philosophy of Language', in Schilpp (ed.), *The Philosophy of Bertrand Russell*, 227–55.

Bradley, F. H., *Appearance and Reality*, 2nd edn. (Oxford: Clarendon Press, 1968; 1st edn. 1893).

—— *Principles of Logic*, 2nd edn. (London: Oxford University Press, 1999; 1st pub. London: Kegan Paul and Trench, 1883).

Bynum, T. W. (ed.), *Conceptual Notation and Related Articles* (Oxford: Oxford University Press, 1972).

Carnap, Rudolf, *Logische Syntax der Sprache* (Vienna: Julius Springer Verlag, 1934); trans. Amethe Smeaton as *Logical Syntax of Language* (London: Kegan Paul, Trench, Trubner & Co., 1937).

—— *Meaning and Necessity* (Chicago: University of Chicago Press, 1947, enlarged edn. 1956).

Carroll, Lewis, 'What the Tortoise Said to Achilles', *Mind*, 4 (1895), 278–80.

Cavell, Stanley, *Must We Mean What We Say?* (New York: Scribner, 1969).

Church, Alonzo, *Introduction to Mathematical Logic* (Princeton: Princeton University Press, 1956).

—— 'Russell's Theory of Identity of Propositions', *Philosophia Naturalis*, 21 (1984), 513–21.

Clark, Ronald, W., *The Life of Bertrand Russell* (New York: Alfred A. Knopf, 1976).

Davidson, D., *Inquiries into Truth and Interpretation* (Oxford: Oxford University Press, 1984).

Donnellan, K., 'Reference and Definite Descriptions', *Philosophical Review*, 77 (1966), 203–15.

Dreben, B., and van Heijenoort, J., 'Introductory Note', in Gödel, *Collected Works*, i. 44–59.

Dummett, Michael, *Frege, Philosophy of Language* (London: Duckworth, 1973).

—— *Truth and Other Enigmas* (Cambridge, Mass.: Harvard University Press, 1978).

—— *Frege and Other Philosophers* (Oxford: Oxford University Press, 1991).

—— *Origins of Analytical Philosophy* (Cambridge, Mass.: Harvard University Press, 1993).

Dummett, Michael, 'Frege's "Kernsätze sur Logik" ', *Inquiry*, 24 (1981), 439–54; repr. as ch. 4 of Dummett's *Frege and Other Philosophers*.

Fogelin, R. J., *Wittgenstein* (London: Routledge & Kegan Paul, 1976).

Frassen, Bas, C. van, 'Singular Terms, Truth-Value Gaps, and Free Logic', in Karel Lambert (ed.), *Philosophical Applications of Free Logic* (Oxford: Oxford University Press, 1991).

—— 'Presupposition, Implication, and Self-Reference', in Karel Lambert (ed.), *Philosophical Applications of Free Logic* (Oxford: Oxford University Press, 1991).

Frege, Gottlob, *Begriffsschrift* (Halle: Verlag von Louis Nebert, 1879); trans. as *Conceptual Notation*, in Bynum (ed.), *Conceptual Notation and Related Articles*.

—— *Die Grundlagen der Arithmetik* (Breslau: Verlag von Wilhelm Koebner, 1884); trans. J. L. Austin as *The Foundations of Arithmetic*.

—— '*Funktion und Begriff*' (Jena: Herman Pohle, 1891); trans. Peter Geach as 'Function and Concept', in Frege, *Collected Papers*, 137–56.

—— *Grundgesetze der Arithmetik* (Jena: Verlag von Hermann Pohle, vol. i 1893, vol. ii 1903); partial trans. by M. Furth as *The Basic Laws of Arithmetic* (Berkeley and Los Angeles: University of California Press, 1967).

—— *The Foundations of Arithmetic* (Oxford: Blackwells, 1950; 2nd edn. 1953).

—— *Collected Papers on Mathematics, Logic, and Philosophy*, trans. Max Black et al., ed. Brian McGuinness (Oxford: Basil Blackwell, 1984).

—— *Nachgelassene Schriften und Wissenschaftliche Briefwechsel*, vol. i, ed. Hans Hermes et al. (Hamburg: Felix Meiner Verlag, 1969); trans. as *Posthumous Writings*.

—— *Nachgelassene Schriften und Wissenschaftliche Briefwechsel*, vol. ii, ed. G. Gabriel et al. (Hamburg: Felix Meiner Verlag, 1976); trans. as *Philosophical and Mathematical Correspondence*.

—— *Posthumous Writings* (Oxford: Basil Blackwell, 1979).

—— *Philosophical and Mathematical Correspondence* (Chicago: University of Chicago Press, 1980).

—— 'Über den Zweck der Begriffsschrift', *Sitzungsberichte der Jenaischen Geselleschaft für Medicin und Naturwissenschaft*, 16 (1882–3), 1–10; trans. T. W. Bynum as 'On the Aim of the "Conceptual Notation" ', in Bynum (ed.), *Conceptual Notation and Related Articles*.

—— 'Über Sinn und Bedeutung', *Zeitschrift für Philosophie und philosophische Kritik*, 100 (1892), 25–50; trans. Max Black as 'On Sense and Meaning', in Frege, *Collected Papers*, 157–77.

—— 'Über Begriff und Gegenstand', *Vierteljahrsschrift für wissenschaftliche Philosophie*, 16 (1892), 192–205; trans. Peter Geach as 'On Concept and Object', in Frege, *Collected Papers*, 182–94.

—— 'Der Gedanke', *Beiträge zur Philosophie des deutschen Idealismus*, 1 (1918–19), 58–77; trans. Peter Geach and R. H. Stoothoff as 'Thoughts', in Frege, *Collected Papers*, 351–72.

Friedman, Michael, 'Kant's Theory of Geometry', *Philosophical Review*, 94 (1985), 455–506.

—— 'Logical Truth and Analyticity in Carnap's *Logical Syntax of Language*', in W. Aspray and P. Kitcher (eds.), *Essays in the History and Philosophy of*

Mathematics (Minneapolis: University of Minnesota Press, 1987); repr. in Friedman, *Reconsidering Logical Positivism* (Cambridge: Cambridge University Press, 1999), 165–76.

Gödel, Kurt, *Collected Works*, vol. i, ed. Solomon Feferman et al. (Oxford: Oxford University Press, 1986).

—— 'Russell's Mathematical Logic', in Schilpp (ed.), *The Philosophy of Bertrand Russell*, 125–53, repr. Gödel, *Collected Works*, vol. ii, ed. Solomon Feferman et al. (Oxford: Oxford University Press, 1990), 119–41.

Goldfarb, Warren, 'Logic in the Twenties: The Nature of the Quantifier', *Journal of Symbolic Logic*, 44/3 (Sept. 1979), 351–68.

—— 'Russell's Reasons for Ramification', in C. Wade Savage and C. Anthony Anderson (eds.), *Rereading Russell: Essays in Bertrand Russell's Metaphysics and Epistemology* (Minneapolis: University of Minnesota Press, 1989), 24–40.

Grattan-Guinness, I. (ed.), *Dear Russell, Dear Jourdain* (New York: Columbia University Press, 1977).

—— 'The Russell Archives: New Light on Russell's Logicism', *Annals of Science*, 31 (1974), 387–406.

Grayling, A. C. (ed.), *Philosophy: A Guide through the Subject* (Oxford: Oxford University Press, 1995).

Green, Thomas Hill, *Prolegomena to Ethics*, ed. A. C. Bradley (Oxford: Clarendon Press, 1883).

—— *The Works of Thomas Hill Green*, 3 vols., 3rd edn. (London: Longmans, Green & Co., 1894).

Grice, H. P., *Studies in the Ways of Words* (Cambridge, Mass.: Harvard University Press, 1989).

Guttenplan, S. (ed.), *Mind and Language* (Oxford: Oxford University Press, 1975).

Hart, W. D., 'Clarity' in David Bell and Neil Cooper (eds.), *The Analytic Tradition* (Oxford: Basil Blackwell, 1990), 197–222.

Hegel, G. W. F., *Wissenschaft der Logik* (Nurenberg, 1812–16), trans. A. V. Miller as *Hegel's Science of Logic* (London: George Allen & Unwin, 1969).

—— *Vorlesungen über die Geschichte der Philosophie*, vol. iii (Frankfurt am Main: Suhrkamp Verlag, 1971); trans. E. S. Haldane and Frances H. Simon as *Lectures on the History of Philosophy*, vol. iii (London: Routledge & Kegan Paul, 1955).

Heijenoort, J. van (ed.), *From Frege to Gödel: A Source Book in Mathematical Logic, 1879–1931* (Cambridge, Mass.: Harvard University Press, 1967).

Hume, David, *Treatise of Human Nature*, ed. T. M. Grose and T. H. Green, 4 vols. (London: Longmans, 1874–5).

Hylton, Peter, *Russell, Idealism, and the Emergence of Analytic Philosophy* (Oxford: Oxford University Press, 1990).

—— 'Analysis and Analytic Philosophy', in Anat Biletzki and Anat Matar (eds.), *The Story of Analytic Philosophy*, 37–55.

Jager, R., *The Development of Bertrand Russell's Philosophy* (London: George Allen & Unwin, 1972).

Kant, Immanuel, *Critique of Pure Reason*, trans. Norman Kemp Smith (London: Macmillan, 1968; 1st edn. 1929).

Kremer, Michael, 'The Argument of "On Denoting" ', *Philosophical Review*, 103/2, (Apr. 1994).

Kripke, S. A., *Naming and Necessity* (Cambridge, Mass.: Harvard University Press, 1980). The text is based on lectures given in 1970; a slightly different version was published under the same title in *Semantics of Natural Language*, ed. D. Davidson and G. Harman (Dordrecht: D. Reidel, 1972).

Kuhn, Thomas, S., *The Structure of Scientific Revolutions* (Chicago: Chicago University Press, 1962; enlarged edn. 1970).

—— *The Essential Tension* (Chicago: Chicago University Press, 1977).

Lambert, Karel, 'The Nature of Free Logic', in Karel Lambert (ed.), *Philosophical Applications of Free Logic* (Oxford: Oxford University Press, 1991).

Leibniz, Gottfried Wilhelm, *Philosophical Papers and Letters*, ed. L. E. Loemker (Chicago: Chicago University Press, 1956).

Linsky, Leonard, *Referring* (New York: Humanities Press, 1967), p. ix.

Mackie, John, *Problems from Locke* (Oxford: Oxford University Press, 1976).

McTaggart, John M. E., *Studies in Hegelian Dialectic*, 2nd edn. (Cambridge: Cambridge University Press, 1921).

Moore, G. E., 'The Nature of Judgement', *Mind* (1898), 176–93.

—— *Principia Ethica* (Cambridge: Cambridge University Press, 1903).

—— *Some Main Problems of Philosophy* (London: George Allen & Unwin, 1953).

—— 'Russell's Theory of Descriptions', in Schilpp (ed.), *The Philosophy of Bertrand Russell*.

—— 'The Metaphysical Basis of Ethics', two versions of same title, both unpublished dissertations (1897 and 1898), currently in the library of Trinity College, Cambridge.

Neale, Stephen, *Descriptions* (Cambridge, Mass.: MIT Press, 1990).

Noonan, Harold, 'The "Gray's Elegy" Argument—and Others', in R. Monk and A. Palmer (eds.), *Bertrand Russell and the Origins of Analytical Philosophy* (Bristol: Thoemmes Press, 1996).

Pakaluk, Michael, 'The Interpretation of Russell's "Gray's *Elegy*" Argument', in A. D. Irvine and G. A. Wedeking (eds.), *Russell and Analytic Philosophy* (Toronto: University of Toronto Press, 1993), 37–65.

Parsons, Charles, *Mathematics in Philosophy* (Ithaca, NY: Cornell University Press, 1983).

—— 'Infinity and Kant's Conception of "The Possibility of Experience" ', repr. in *Mathematics in Philosophy*, 95–109.

—— 'Kant's Philosophy of Arithmetic', repr. in *Mathematics in Philosophy*, 110–49.

Pears, D. F., 'The Relation between Wittgenstein's Picture Theory of Propositions and Russell's Theories of Judgment', *Philosophical Review*, 86 (1977), 176–93.

Poincaré, Henri, 'La Logique de i'Infini', *Revue de métaphysique et de morale*, 17 (1909), 461–82.

Quine, W. V., *From a Logical Point of View* (Cambridge, Mass.: Harvard University Press, 1953).

—— *Word and Object* (Cambridge, Mass.: MIT Press, 1960).

—— *Set Theory and its Logic* (Cambridge, Mass: Harvard University Press, 1963; rev. edn. 1969).

—— *Ways of Paradox* (New York: Random House, 1966; 2nd edn, enlarged, Cambridge, Mass.: Harvard University Press, 1976).

—— *Philosophy of Logic* (Englewood Cliffs, NJ: Prentice-Hall Inc., 1970).

—— *Theories and Things* (Cambridge, Mass.: Harvard University Press, 1981).

—— 'Mr Strawson on Logical Theory', *Mind*, NS 62 (1953), 433–51; repr. in Quine, *Ways of Paradox*.

—— 'Carnap and Logical Truth', in *The Philosophy of Rudolf Carnap*, ed. P. A. Schilpp (LaSalle, Ill.: Open Court, 1963), 385–406; repr. in Quine, *Ways of Paradox*.

—— 'Russell's Ontological Development', in Schoenman (ed.), *Bertrand Russell, Philosopher of the Century*, 304–14.

—— Introduction to Russell's 'Mathematical Logic as Based on the Theory of Types', in Jean van Heijenoort (ed.), *From Frege to Gödel*, 150–2.

—— 'The Nature of Natural Knowledge', in Guttenplan (ed.), *Mind and Language*.

—— 'Intensions Revisited', in *Theories and Things*, 113–23.

Ramsey, Frank, P., *The Foundations of Mathematics*, ed. R. B. Braithwaite (London: Routledge & Kegan Paul, 1931).

—— 'The Foundations of Mathematics', *Proceedings of the London Mathematical Society*, series 2, 25/5 (1925), 338–84, repr. as ch. 1 of *The Foundations of Mathematics*.

Ricketts, Thomas, G., 'Objectivity and Objecthood: Frege's Metaphysics of Judgment', in L. Haaparanta (ed.), *Frege Synthesized* (Dordrecht: Reidel, 1986), 65–95.

—— 'Generality, Meaning and Sense', *Pacific Philosophical Quarterly*, 67 (1986), 172–95.

—— 'Truth and Propositional Unity in Early Russell', in Juliet Floyd and Sanford Shieh (eds.), *Future Pasts: The Analytic Tradition in Twentieth-Century Philosophy* (Oxford: Oxford University Press, 2001).

—— 'Frege's 1906 Foray into Metalogic', *Philosophical Topics* 25 (1997), 169–87.

Russell, Bertrand, *An Essay on the Foundations of Geometry* (Cambridge: Cambridge University Press, 1897).

—— *A Critical Exposition of the Philosophy of Leibniz* (Cambridge: Cambridge University Press, 1900; 2nd edn. London: George Allen & Unwin, 1937).

—— *Principles of Mathematics* (Cambridge: Cambridge University Press, 1903; 2nd edn. London: George Allen & Unwin, 1937).

—— *Philosophical Essays* (London: Longmans, Green & Co., 1910; 2nd edn. London: George Allen & Unwin, 1966).

—— *The Problems of Philosophy* (London: Williams & Norgate, 1912; 2nd edn. Oxford: Oxford University Press, 1946).

—— *Our Knowledge of the External World as a Field for Scientific Method in Philosophy*, 2nd edn. (London: George Allen & Unwin, 1926).

—— *Mysticism and Logic* (New York: Longmans, Green & Co., 1918).

—— *Introduction to Mathematical Philosophy* (London: George Allen & Unwin, 1919).

—— *The Analysis of Mind* (London: George Allen & Unwin, 1921).

—— *The Analysis of Matter* (London: Routledge, Kegan Paul, Trench, Trubner & Co., 1927).

—— *My Philosophical Development* (London: George Allen & Unwin, 1959).

—— *Autobiography*, 3 vols. (London: George Allen & Unwin, 1967–9).

—— *Logic and Knowledge*, ed. R. Marsh (London: George Allen & Unwin, 1956).

Russell, Bertrand, *Essays in Analysis*, ed. D. Lackey (New York: Braziller, 1973).

—— *The Collected Papers of Bertrand Russell*, i: *Cambridge Essays, 1888–99*, ed. Kenneth Blackwell et al. (London: George Allen & Unwin, 1983).

—— *The Collected Papers of Bertrand Russell*, iii: *Towards the 'Principles of Mathematics' 1900–02*, ed. Gregory H. Moore (London: Routledge, 1993).

—— *The Collected Papers of Bertrand Russell*, iv: *Foundations of Logic, 1903–5*, ed. Alistair Urquhart, with the assistance of Albert Lewis (London: Routledge, 1994).

—— *The Collected Papers of Bertrand Russell*, vi: *Logical and Philosophical Papers: 1909–13*, ed. John G. Slater (London: George Allen & Unwin, 1992).

—— *The Collected Papers of Bertrand Russell*, vii: *Theory of Knowledge: The 1913 Manuscript*, ed. Elizabeth Ramsden Eames, in collaboration with Kenneth Blackwell (London: George Allen & Unwin, 1984).

—— *The Collected Papers of Bertrand Russell*, viii: *The Philosophy of Logical Atomism and Other Essays, 1914–19*, ed. John G. Slater (London: George Allen & Unwin, 1986).

—— 'The Logic of Relations', in *Logic and Knowledge*, ed. Marsh, 3–38; repr. in, *Collected Papers*, iii. 314–49. This is a translation of 'Sur la logique des relations', *Rivista di mathematica*, 7 (1900–1), 115–48; the translation is by R. C. Marsh, with corrections by Russell.

—— 'Meinong's Theory of Complexes and Assumptions', *Mind*, NS 13 (1904), 204–19, 336–54, and 509–24; repr. in *Essays in Analysis*, ed. Lackey, 21–76 and in *Collected Papers*, iv. 432–74.

—— Letter to G. Frege, 12 Dec. 1904, in *Philosophical and Mathematical Correspondence*, trans. Hans Kaall, ed. Gottfried Gabriel et al. (Oxford: Basil Blackwell, 1980), 166–70. Originally in G. Frege, *Wissenschaftlicher Briefwechsel*, ed. G. Gabriel et al. (Hamburg: Meiner, 1976), 250–1.

—— 'The Existential Import of Propositions', *Mind*, NS 14 (1905), 398–401; repr. in *Essays in Analysis*, ed. Lackey, 98–102 and in *Collected Papers*, iv. 486–90.

—— 'On Some Difficulties in the Theory of Transfinite Numbers and Order Types', *Proceedings of the London Mathematical Society*, series 2, 4 (1906), 29–53; repr. in *Essays in Analysis*, ed. Lackey.

—— 'On the Substitutional Theory of Classes and Relations', read to the London Mathematical Society in Apr. 1906 but withdrawn from publication; first published in *Essays in Analysis*, ed. Lackey.

—— 'On "Insolubilia" and their Solution by Symbolic Logic', *Revue de métaphysique et de morale*, 14 (1906), 627–50 under the title 'Les Paradoxes de la logique'; English version, from Russell's original, first published in *Essays in Analysis*, ed. Lackey.

—— 'The Nature of Truth', *Proceedings of the Aristotelian Society*, NS 7 (1906–7), 28–49. The first two sections of this essay were reprinted under the title 'The Monistic Theory of Truth' in Russell, *Philosophical Essays*.

—— 'The Regressive Method of Discovering the Premises of Mathematics', read to the Cambridge Mathematical Club in Mar. 1907, first published in *Essays in Analysis*, ed. Lackey.

—— 'Mathematical Logic as Based on the Theory of Types', *American Journal of Mathematics*, 30 (1908), 222–62; repr. in *Logic and Knowledge*, ed. Marsh.

—— 'Transatlantic Truth', *Albany Review*, 2/10 (1908), 393–410; repr. under the title 'James's Conception of Truth' in Russell, *Philosophical Essays*.

—— 'On the Nature of Truth and Falsehood', published for the first time in Russell's *Philosophical Essays*; repr. in Russell's *Mysticism and Logic* and in *Russell's Collected Papers*, vi.

—— 'Knowledge by Acquaintance and Knowledge by Description', *Proceedings of the Aristotelian Society*, NS 11 (1910–11), 108–28; repr. in Russell, *Mysticism and Logic* and in *Collected Papers*, vi. 148–61.

—— Letter to G. E. Moore, 25 Oct. 1905, unpub.

Sainsbury, R. M., *Russell* (London: Routledge & Kegan Paul, 1979).

—— 'Philosophical Logic', in Grayling, (ed.), *Philosophy: A Guide through the Subject*.

Schilpp, P. A. (ed.), *The Philosophy of G. E. Moore* (Evanston, Ill.: Northwestern University Press, 1942).

—— (ed.), *The Philosophy of Bertrand Russell* (Evanston, Ill.: The Library of the Living Philosophers, 1946).

—— (ed.), *The Philosophy of Rudolf Carnap* (LaSalle, Ill.: Open Court, 1963).

Schoenman, R. (ed.), *Bertrand Russell, Philosopher of the Century* (London: George Allen & Unwin, 1967).

Sluga, H. D., *Gottlob Frege* (London: Routledge & Kegan Paul, 1980).

Strawson, P. F., *Individuals* (London: Methuen, 1959).

—— *Introduction to Logical Theory* (London: Methuen, 1952).

—— *Logico-Linguistic Papers* (London: Methuen, 1971), 1–27.

—— 'On Referring', *Mind*, NS 59 (1950), 320–44, repr. in Strawson, *Logico-Linguistic Papers*.

—— 'Logic as Calculus and Logic as Language', *Synthese*, 17 (1967), 324–30.

Whitehead, Alfred North, *Process and Reality* (London: Macmillan, 1929).

—— and Russell, Bertrand, *Principia Mathematica*, 3 vols. (Cambridge: Cambridge University Press, 1910–13; 2nd edn. 1925–7).

Wittgenstein, Ludwig, *Notebooks 1914–16* (Oxford: Basil Blackwell, 1961).

—— *Tractatus Logico-Philosophicus*, with a translation by C. K. Ogden (London: Routledge & Kegan Paul Ltd., 1922; corrected edn. 1933).

—— *Letters to Russell, Keynes and Moore* (Oxford: Basil Blackwell, 1974).

INDEX